www.EZmethods.com

EZ SOLUTIONS

TEST PREP SERIES

MATH REVIEW

WORD PROBLEMS

EZ SIMPLIFIED SOLUTIONS – THE BREAKTHROUGH IN TEST PREP!

LEADERS IN TEST PREP SOLUTIONS – WE MAKE IT EZ FOR YOU!

AUTHOR: PUNIT RAJA SURYACHANDRA

EZ Solutions
P O Box 10755
Silver Spring, MD 20914
USA

EZ SOLUTIONS
P.O. Box 10755
Silver Spring, MD 20914
USA

Conceived, conceptualized, written, and edited by:
Punit Raja SuryaChandra, EZ Solutions

PRINTED AND MANUFACTURED IN THE UNITED STATES OF AMERICA

TABLE OF CONTENTS

PREFACE 5
- About EZ Solutions 5
- About Our Author 6
- About EZ Books 7
- About This Book 14

PART 0.0: INTRODUCTION TO WORD PROBLEMS: 15
0.1: Basics About Word Problems: 15
0.2: Systematic Method for Solving Word Problems: 18
0.3: Word Problem Translation Table: 22
0.4: Basic Examples of Word Problems: 23
0.5: Different Levels of Word Problems: 27

PART 1.0: ARITHMETIC WORD PROBLEMS: 31
1.1: Basic Arithmetic Operations: 32
1.2: Advanced Arithmetic Word Problems: 34
1.3: Part-Whole Arithmetic Word Problems: 36
1.4: Multiple Operations Arithmetic Word Problems: 37
Practice Exercise – Questions and Answers With Explanations: Arithmetic Word Problems: 38

PART 2.0: ALGEBRAIC WORD PROBLEMS: 49
2.1: Equation Based Word Problems: 50
2.2: Inequality Based Word Problems: 51
Practice Exercise – Questions and Answers With Explanations: Algebraic Word Problems: 52

PART 3.0: NUMERAL PROBLEMS: 61
3.1: Number Problems: 62
3.2: Consecutive Integers: 63
3.3: Non-Consecutive Integers: 65
3.4: Coin Problems: 66
Practice Exercise – Questions and Answers With Explanations: Numeral Word Problems: 67

PART 4.0: LITERAL EXPRESSIONS: 77
4.1: Communicating with Letters: 78
Practice Exercise – Questions and Answers With Explanations: Literal Expressions: 79

PART 5.0: AGE & WEIGHT PROBLEMS: 83
5.1: Age Related Word Problems: 84
5.2: Weight Related Word Problems: 86
Practice Exercise – Questions and Answers With Explanations: Age/Weight Problems: 88

PART 6.0: WORK PROBLEMS: 95
6.1: Work Problems Involving Simple Rates: 96
6.2: Work Problems Involving Multiple Workers: 98
Practice Exercise – Questions and Answers With Explanations: Work Problems: 103

PART 7.0: MOTION PROBLEMS: 111

7.1: Basics About Motion Problems: 112
7.2: Different Types of Motion Problems: 115
Practice Exercise – Questions and Answers With Explanations: Motion Problems: 123

PART 8.0: MIXTURE PROBLEMS: 131
8.1: Cost per Unit of Mixture: 132
8.2: Simple Mixtures: 133
8.3: Mixture of Weaker & Stronger Solution: 134
8.4: Dilution/Concentration of Mixture: 135
Practice Exercise – Questions and Answers With Explanations: Mixture Problems: 136

PART 9.0: MEASUREMENTS: 139
9.1: Unit of Measure: 140
9.2: Time Measures: 148
9.3: Currency Exchange: 150
9.4: Temperature Measures: 151
9.5: Calibrated Scales: 152
Practice Exercise – Questions and Answers With Explanations: Measurement Conversions: 153

EZ BOOK STORE: ORDERS & SALES: 159

EZ BOOK LIST: 160

PREFACE

HIGHLIGHTS:
- About EZ Solutions
- About Our Author
- About EZ Books
- About This Book

▪ABOUT EZ SOLUTIONS

EZ Solutions – *the breakthrough in test-preparation*!

EZ Solutions is an organization formed to provide **simplified solutions** for test-preparation and tutoring. Although EZ Solutions is a fairly new name in the publishing industry, it has quickly become a respected publisher of test-prep books, study guides, study aids, handbooks, and other reference works. EZ publications and educational materials are highly respected, and they continue to receive an unprecedented amount of praise from professionals, instructors, librarians, parents, and students.

OBJECTIVE: Our ultimate objective is to help you **achieve academic and scholastic excellence**. We possess the right blend and matrix of skills and expertise that are required to not only do justice to our programs and publications, but also to handle them most effectively and efficiently. We are confident that our state-of-the-art programs/publications will give you a completely **new dimension** by enhancing your skill set and improving your overall performance.

MISSION: Our mission is to foster continuous knowledge to develop and enhance each student's skills through innovative and methodical programs/publications coupled with our add-on services – leading to a **better career and life** for our students.

OUR PHILOSOPHY: We subscribe to the traditional philosophy that everyone is equally capable of learning and that the natural, though sometimes unfulfilled and unexplored impetus of people is towards growth and development. We know that the human brain is undoubtedly a very powerful and efficient problem-solving tool, and every individual is much more capable than they realize. We strive to implement this philosophy throughout our books by helping our students explore their **potential** so that they can **perform at their optimum level**.

OUR COMMITMENT TOWARDS YOUR SATISFACTION: Reinventing, Redesigning, and Redefining Success: We are committed to providing **total customer satisfaction** that exceeds your expectations! Your satisfaction is extremely important to us, and your approval is one of the most important indicators that we have done our job correctly.

Long-Term Alliance: We, at EZ, look forward to forming a **long-term alliance** with all our readers who buy our book(s), for the days, months, and years to come. Moreover, our commitment to client service is one of our most important and distinguished characteristics. We also encourage our readers to contact us for any further assistance, feedback, suggestions, or inquiries.

EZ Solutions publishing series include books for the following major standardized tests:
- GMAT
- SAT
- PSAT
- ASVAB
- PRAXIS Series
- GRE
- ACT
- CLEP
- TOEFL
- Other (national and state) Standardized Tests

EZ Solutions aims to provide good quality study aides in a wide variety of disciplines to the following:
- Students who have not yet completed high school
- High School students preparing to enter college
- College students preparing to enter graduate or post-graduate school
- Anyone else who is simply looking to improve their skills

Students from every walk of life, of any background, at any level, in any field, with any ambition, can find what they are looking for among EZ Solutions' publications.

FOREIGN STUDENTS: All of our books are designed, keeping in mind the unique needs of students from North and South America, U.K., Europe, Middle East, Far East, and Asia. Foreign students from countries around the world seeking to obtain education in the United States will find the assistance they need in EZ Solutions' publications.

CONTACT US: Feel free to contact us, and one of our friendly specialists will be more than happy to assist you with your queries, or feel free to browse through our website for lots of useful information.
E-Mail: info@EZmethods.com
Phone: (301) 622-9597
Mail: EZ Solutions, P.O. Box 10755, Silver Spring, MD 20914, USA
Website: www.EZmethods.com

FEEDBACK: The staff of EZ Solutions hopes that you find our books helpful and easy to use. If you have any specific suggestions, comments, or feedback, please email us at: feedback@EZmethods.com

BUSINESS DEVELOPMENT: If you are interested in exploring business development opportunities, including forming a partnership alliance with us, kindly email us at: partners@EZmethods.com.

PRODUCT REGISTRATION: In order to get the most up-to-date information about this and our other books, you must register your purchase with EZ solutions by emailing us at: products@EZmethods.com, or by visiting our website www.EZmethods.com.

ERRORS AND INACCURACIES: We are not responsible for any typographical errors or inaccuracies contained in this publication. The information, prices, and discounts given in this book are subject to change without prior notice. To report any kind of errors or inaccuracies in this publication, kindly email us at: errors@EZmethods.com.

▪ABOUT OUR AUTHOR

The name of the man behind EZ publication series is **Punit Raja SuryaChandra**, who is also the founder of our company. He holds a Bachelors in Business and an MBA. It took him many years to write and publish these unique books. He researched every single book available in the market for test-preparation, and actually realized there is not even one book that is truly complete with all the content and concepts. This was the single most important reason that prompted him to write these books, and hence our **EZ prep guidebooks were born**. He has made every effort to make these books as comprehensive and as complete as possible. His expertise and experience are as diverse as the subjects that are represented in our books. He has the breadth and depth of experience required to write books of this magnitude and intensity. Without his unparalleled and unmatched skills and determination, none of this would have been possible.

In developing these books, his primary goal has been to give everyone the same advantages as the students we tutor privately or students who take our classes. Our tutoring and classroom solutions are only available to a limited number of students; however, with these books, any student in any corner of the world can benefit the same level of service at a fraction of the cost. Therefore, you should take this book as your personal EZ tutor or instructor, because that's precisely how it has been designed.

ACKNOWLEDGEMENTS:
Our author would like to extend his vote of appreciation and gratitude to all his family members for their unconditional and continuous support, to all his close friends for their trust and confidence in him, and to all his colleagues for their helpful consultation and generous advice.

Our EZ books have benefited from dedicated efforts and labors of our author and other members of the editorial staff. Here at EZ, we all wish you the best as you get comfortable, and settle down with your EZ tutor to start working on preparing for your test. In pursuing an educational dream, you have a wonderful and an exciting opportunity ahead of you. All of us at EZ Solutions wish you the very best!

-ABOUT EZ BOOKS

THE EZ NAME:

All our books have been written in a very easy to read manner, and in a very easy to understand fashion, so that students of any background, of any aptitude, of any capacity, of any skill-set, of any level, can benefit from them. These books are not specifically written for the **dummies** or for the **geniuses**; instead, they are written for students who fit into any category of intellectual acumen. This is how we acquired the name **"EZ Solutions"** for our publications – and as the name itself suggests, **we make everything EZ for you**!

THE EZ TUTOR:

Like any good tutor, EZ Tutor will work with you **individually and privately**, providing you with all the tools needed to improve your testing skills. It will assist you in recognizing your weaknesses, and enlighten you on how to improve upon them while transforming them into strengths. Of course, it will also point out your strengths as well, so that you can make them even stronger. By employing innovative techniques, EZ tutor will **stimulate, activate, and accelerate your learning process**. Soon after you start working with your EZ tutor, you will see **remarkable and noticeable improvement** in your performance by utilizing your newly acquired learning skills.

Whenever, Wherever, and However: EZ tutor also has the **flexibility** to work with you whenever you like – day or night, wherever you like – indoors or outdoors, and however you like – for as long or as short. While working with your EZ tutor, you can work at your own pace, you can go as fast or as slow as you like, repeat sections as many times as you need, and skip over sections you already know well. Your EZ tutor will also give you explanations, not just correct answers, and it will be **infinitely patient and adaptable**. Hence, our EZ Tutor will make you a more intelligent and smarter test-taker, and will help you maximize your score!

ADD-ON OPTIONS: *Turn your EZ Virtual Tutor into a Real Tutor!*

EZ TUTORING OVER THE PHONE:

Along with buying the entire series of our modules, students can also add on services like email/online support and/or telephone support. In fact, you can get the best preparation for your test by blending our professional 1-on-1 tutoring with our state-of-the-art books. The most important feature of our add-on features is our individualized and personalized approach that works toward building your self-confidence, and enhancing your ability to learn and perform better. This will also invigorate your motivational, organizational, as well as your learning skills. Our phone specialists are highly qualified, experienced, innovative, and well trained. You can do all this in the exclusivity and comfort of your home. Students can get in touch with one of our specialists anytime they need help – we'll be there for you, whenever you need us! We offer several packages with different levels, features, and customizations for tutoring over the phone to suit your individualized needs. Contact us for more details.

EZ 1-ON-1 TEST-TAKING & ADMISSION CONSULTATION:

We understand that standardized tests and school/college admissions can sometimes become very stressful. Our 1-on-1 Test-Taking & Admission Consulting Program can dramatically reduce your stress and anxiety. One of our consultants can personally guide you through the entire process, starting from familiarizing you with a test to getting you successfully admitted into a school/college of your choice. Again, you can do all this in the exclusivity and comfort of your home. We offer several packages with different levels, features, and customizations for test-taking and admission consultation over the phone to suit your individualized needs. Contact us for more details.

The following are some of the features of our EZ 1-on-1 Test-Taking & Admission Consulting Program:
- Familiarize you with a particular test
- Equip you with test-taking skills for each section of your test
- Reduce test-taking anxiety, stress, nervousness, and test-fever with personal counseling
- Draft and edit your essays
- Re-design your resume
- Prepare you for a telephone or personal interview
- Select the right school/college & help with admission application procedures
- Presentation Skills – how to present and market yourself

EZ UNIQUE FEATURES:
Your EZ Tutor offers you the following unique features that will highlight important information, and will let you find them quickly as and when you need to review them.

EZ STRATEGIES: It provides you with many powerful, effective, proven, and time tested strategies for various concepts, and shows you exactly how to use them to attack different question types. Many of these test-taking strategies cannot be found in any other books!

EZ SHORTCUTS: It gives you many time-saving shortcuts you can apply to save yourself some very valuable testing-time while solving a question on your actual test.

EZ TACTICS: It shows you several important tactics to use so that you can solve problems in the smartest way.

EZ DEFINITIONS: It defines all the key definitions in an easy to understand manner so that you get a clear description and concise understanding of all the key terms.

EZ RULES: It presents all the important rules in an orderly manner so that you can learn the basic rules of all the concepts.

EZ STEPS: It walks you through hundreds of concepts, showing you how to tackle every question type in an organized user-friendly step-by-step easy-to-understand methodology that adapts to your understanding and needs so that you get the best procedural knowledge.

EZ MULTIPLE/ALTERNATE METHODS: It gives you a choice of multiple methods of answering the same question so that you can choose the method that seems easiest to you.

EZ SUMMARIES: It lists a complete summary of all the important concepts in an ordered and organized manner so that you will never have to hunt for them.

EZ FACTS: It provides you with numerous key facts about various principles so that you know all the facts-and-figures of the material you are reviewing.

EZ HINTS: It supplies you with innumerable hints and clues so that you can use them to become a smarter and wiser test-taker.

EZ TIPS: It also presents you with many tips and pointers that will prevent you from making any careless mistakes or falling into traps.

EZ NOTES: It reminds you to make notes of some important points that will come handy while answering a question.

EZ WARNINGS/CAUTIONS: It warns you of some obvious mistakes that will prevent you from making them while answering a question.

EZ EXCEPTIONS: It makes you aware of the exceptions and exclusions that apply to any particular rule.

EZ REFERENCES: It gives you references of related materials that you may want to refer to in other parts of the same or different modules, while learning a specific concept.

EZ SPOTS: It lists buzzwords and phrases that will help you easily spot some specific question types.

EZ PROBLEM SET-UP: It converts even some of the most complex problems into an easy to understand mathematical statement so that you understand accurately how to interpret the problems.

EZ PROBLEM EXPLANATIONS: It provides easy to understand explanations within square brackets for each step of the problem so that you know exactly what you need to do in each step.

EZ SOLVED EXAMPLES: It also throws several realistic solved examples with easy to understand detailed explanations for each and every question type explained so that you can understand and learn how to apply the concepts.

EZ PRACTICE EXERCISES: Last but not the least; it also includes intensive realistic practice exercises with easy to understand detailed explanations for each and every question type explained so that you can put to practice what you learned in an actual test question – solved examples will help you understand the concepts & practice will make you perfect!

GUESS WHAT!! No other book offers you so much. Your EZ tutor strives to provide you with the **best possible training** for your test, and **best value for your time and money**; and it is infinitely committed to providing you with **state-of-the-art** material.

Advantages: Amazing results in the first few days of the program!

Disadvantages: Only if you don't make use of our programs and publications!

THE EZ ADVANTAGE:

EZ TEST-PREP PROGRAM BROKEN INTO MODULES:
Instead of having a **big fat ugly scary all-in-one gigantic book**, we have broken our entire test-prep program into **small easy-to-use modules**.
- **Exclusivity:** Each module is exclusively dedicated to covering one major content area in extensive depth and breadth, allowing you to master each topic by getting an in-depth review.
- **More Content:** You will find many more topics and many more pages per topic than what you can find in all other books combined.
- **Tailored and Customized:** Separated modules offer test-takers of all levels with a more tailored and customized approach towards building specific foundational and advanced skills, and successfully preparing for the test.

EZ TO READ, CARRY, AND MANAGE:
EZ Modules are convenient – they are **easier to read, carry, and manage**.
- **EZ to Read:** EZ Modules are easier to read with text in spacious pages with a bigger font size than those other books with overcrowded pages with a small print.
- **EZ to Carry:** EZ Modules are easier to carry and hold than those other big fat bulky gigantic books.
- **EZ to Manage:** EZ Modules are overall easier to manage than those other all-in-one books.

BUY ONE MODULE OR THE ENTIRE SERIES:
The individually separated modules give you the flexibility to buy only those modules that cover the areas you think you need to work on; nevertheless, we strongly suggest you buy our entire series of modules. In fact, the most efficient and effective way to get the most out of our publications is to use our entire set of modules in conjunction with each other, and not just a few. Each module can be independently bought and studied; however, the modules are somehow connected with and complement the other modules. Therefore, if you are serious about getting a good score on your test, we sincerely recommend you purchase our entire series of modules. Contact us to order, or go to www.EZmethods.com, or check your local bookstore (look at the EZ Book Store on the last page for more information).

NO NEED TO REFER TO ANY OTHER BOOK:
Almost all other test-prep books contain a small disclaimer in some corner. They themselves spell it out very loud and clear, and admit that their book is only a brief review of some important topics; hence, it should not be considered to be an overall review of all the concepts. Most other test-preparation guides only include information for you to get familiar with the kind of topics that may appear on the test, and they suggest that you refer to additional textbooks, or consult other reference books if you want more detailed information and to get an in-depth knowledge of all the concepts. These books are not designed to be a one-stop book to learn everything you must know; instead, they are more like a

summary of some important points. Moreover, they assume that you already know everything, or at least most of the concepts.

However, if you are using our EZ modules to prepare for your test, it's the opposite case, you don't need to refer or consult any other book or text or any other source for assistance. On the contrary, we, in fact, discourage you from referring to any other book, just because there is absolutely no reason to. Our EZ modules contain everything that you need to know in order to do well on your test. We haven't left anything out, and we don't assume anything. Even if you don't know anything, you will find everything in our modules from topics that are frequently tested to topics that are rarely tested, and everything in between. The only topics that you won't find in our books are the topics that will probably never appear on your test!

Frequently Tested: Included in our review – topics that are repeatedly tested on your test, on a regularly basis
Occasionally Tested: Included in our review – topics that are sometimes tested on your test, every now and then
Rarely Tested: Included in our review – topics that are seldom tested on your test, very infrequently
Never Tested: Not included in our review – since these topics are never tested on your test, we don't even mention them anywhere in our review

The bottom line is, if something can be on your test, you'll find it in our modules; and if something is not going to be on your test, it's not going to be in our modules. Each and every math concept that even has the slightest possibility to be on the test can be found in our modules.

THE OFFICIAL REAL PRACTICE TESTS:
Although we don't suggest you refer to any other book, the only time we recommend using other books is for practicing previously administered tests to exercise your skills. The best resources for actual practice tests are the official guides published by the test makers that have several actual previously administered tests. One can *replicate* these tests as closely as one can, but no one other than the test administrators can *duplicate* them, and have the ability to reproduce or publish them. Therefore, to get the maximum effect of our approach, you must practice the actual tests from the official guide. You can also take a free online practice test by going to their website. EZ's practice tests are also based upon the most recently administered tests, and include every type of question that can be expected on the actual exam.

HOW OUR BOOKS CAN HELP YOU:
Our books are designed to help you identify your strengths and the areas which you need to work on. If you study all our modules, you will be fully equipped with all the tools needed to take your test head-on. Moreover, you'll also have the satisfaction that you did all you possibly could do to prepare yourself for the test, and you didn't leave any stone unturned. The amount of content covered in our books is far more than what you would learn by studying all the other test-prep books that are out there, put together, or by even taking an online or an actual prep course, and of course, spending thousands of dollars in the process. This will give you an idea of how material we have covered in our books.

STRUCTURE OF OUR MODULES:
All our modules are *structured in a highly organized and systematic manner*. The review is divided into different modules. Each module is divided into units. Each unit is further subdivided into chapters. Each chapter covers various topics, and in each specific topic, you are given all that you need to solve questions on that topic in detail – explaining key concepts, rules, and other EZ unique features. Also included in some topics are test-taking strategies specific to the topics discussed. Following each topic are solved sample examples with comprehensive explanations, which are exclusively based on that topic, and utilizing the concepts covered in that topic and section. Finally, there are practice exercises with thorough explanations containing real test-like questions for each topic and section, which are very similar to actual test questions. All units, chapters, and topics are chronologically numbered for easy reference.

Moreover, the modules, units, chapters, and topics are all arranged in sequence so that later modules, units, chapters, and topics assume familiarity with the material covered in earlier modules, units, chapters, and topics. Therefore, the best way to review is to work through from the beginning to the end.

SERIES > MODULES > UNITS > CHAPTERS > TOPICS > SUB-TOPICS > SOLVED EXAMPLES > PRACTICE EXERCISES

THE EZ DIFFERENCE:

DIFFERENCE BETWEEN EZ SOLUTIONS' PUBLICATIONS AND OTHER BOOKS:

Most of the other test-prep books suggest that your exam only tests your ability to take the test, and it does not test any actual content knowledge. In other words, they claim that your test is all about knowing the test-taking strategies, and it has very little to do with the actual knowledge of content; others claim that your test is all about knowing a few most commonly tested topics. While we have great respect for these books and the people who write or publish them, all these books have one thing in common: they all want to give their readers a quick shortcut to success. They actually want their readers to believe that just by learning a few strategies and memorizing some key formulas, they'll be able to ace their test. We are not sure if it's the fault of the people who write these books or the people who use them; but someone is definitely trying to fool someone – either those test-prep books for making the readers believe it, or the readers for actually believing it (no pun intended).

With a test as vast as this, it's simply not possible to cover the entire content in just a few pages. We all wish; however, in life, there really aren't any shortcuts to success, and your test is no exception to this rule. Nothing comes easy in life, and that is also precisely the case with your test. You have to do it the hard way by working your way through. Unfortunately, there is no magic potion, which we can give you to succeed in math! Therefore, if you want to do well on your test – be mentally, physically, and psychologically prepared to do some hard work. In this case, efforts and results are directly proportional, that is, greater the efforts you make, better your results are going to be.

While most test-preparation books present materials that stand very little resemblance to the actual tests, EZ's publication series present tests that accurately depict the official tests in both, degree of difficulty and types of questions.

Our EZ books are like no other books you have ever seen or even heard of. We have a completely different concept, and our books are structured using a totally different model. We have *re-defined the way test-prep books should be*.

STRATEGIES SEPARATED FROM CONTENT:

What we have done in our modules is, *separated the actual content-knowledge from the test-taking strategies*. We truly believe that a test-prep program should be more than just a *cheat-sheet of tricks, tips, and traps*. The test you are preparing for is not a simple game that you can master by learning these quick tactics. What you really need to do well on your test is a program that builds true understanding and knowledge of the content.

PERFECT EQUILIBRIUM BETWEEN STRATEGIES AND CONTENT:

In our modules, we've tried our best to present a *truly unique equilibrium* between two competing and challenging skills: test-taking strategies and comprehensive content-knowledge. We have *blended* the two most important ingredients that are essential for your success on your test. We have *enhanced* the old traditional approach to some of the most advanced forms of test-taking strategies. To top all this, we have *refined* our solved examples with detailed explanations to give you hands-on experience to real test-like questions before you take your actual test.

Other Books: Most of the other test-prep books primarily concentrate on teaching their readers how to *guess* and *use the process of elimination,* and they get so obsessed with the tactics that in the process they completely ignore the actual content. Majority of the content of these books consists of pages of guessing techniques.

EZ Books: With our EZ Content-Knowledge Modules, you'll find *100% pure content* that has a highly organized and structured approach to all the content areas, which actually teaches you the content you need to know to do well on your test. Therefore, if you are looking to learn more than just guessing by process of elimination, and if you are serious about developing your skills and confidence level for your exam, then our highly organized and structured test-prep modules is the solution. By studying our books, you'll learn a systematic approach to any question that you may see on your test, and acquire the tools that will help you get there.

EZ Solutions' publications are packed with important information, sophisticated strategies, useful tips, and extensive practice that the experts know will help you do your best on your test.

You should use whichever concept, fact, or tip from that section that you think is appropriate to answer the question correctly in the least possible time. If you've mastered the material in our review modules and strategy modules, you should be able to answer almost all (99.99%) of the questions.

LEARN BACKWARDS AND MOVE FORWARD: Smart students are the ones who make an honest attempt to learn what they read, and also learn from their mistakes, but at the same time, who moves ahead. Therefore, you should learn backwards, that is, learn from your past experiences, and move forward, that is, keep moving ahead without looking back!

ONE CONCEPT, EZ MULTIPLE METHODS:
Our books often give you a *choice of multiple methods* of answering the same question – you can pick the method that seems easiest to you. Our goal is not to *prescribe* any *hard-and-fast* method for taking the test, but instead, to give you the *flexibility and tools you can use to approach your test with confidence and optimism*.

STRATEGIES OR CONTENT?

In order to do well on your test, it is absolutely essential that you have a pretty good grasp of all the concepts laid out in our review modules. Our review modules contain everything you need to know, or must know to crack your test. They cover everything from basic arithmetic to logical reasoning, and everything in between. Nonetheless, that's not enough. You should be able to use these concepts in ways that may not be so familiar or well known to you. This is where our EZ Strategies kick in.

CONTENT VERSUS STRATEGIES:

There is a *succinct* difference between knowing the math content and knowing the math strategies.

Hypothetically speaking, let's assume there is a student named Alex, who learns only the test-taking strategies; and there is another student named Andria, who learns only the math-content. Now when the test time comes, Andria who learns only the math-content is extremely likely to do a lot better than Alex, who learns only the test-taking strategies.

The truth is that someone who has the knowledge of all the math content, but doesn't know anything about the strategies, will almost always do better on the test than someone who knows all the strategies but doesn't know the content properly.

Now let's assume there is another student named Alexandria, who learns both, the test-taking strategies and the math-content. Yes, now we are talking! This student, Alexandria, who knows both the strategies and the content, is guaranteed to do a lot better than Alex, who only knows the strategies, or Andria who only knows the content.

This brings us to our conclusion on this topic: don't just study the strategies, or just the content; you need to know both simultaneously – the strategies and the content, in order to do well on your test. How quickly and accurately you can answer the math questions will depend on your knowledge of the content and the strategies, and that will have an overall effect on your success on the test.

Hence, the equation to succeed on your test is: **Strategies + Content = Success!**

We are confident that if you study our books on test-taking strategies along with our books on content-knowledge, you'll have everything you possibly need to know in order to do well on your test, in fact, to ace your test, and come out with flying colors!

The good thing is that you made the smart decision to buy this book, or if you are reading this online, or in a bookstore, or in a library, you are going to buy one soon!

CONTENT-KNOWLEDGE REVIEW MODULES:

THOROUGH IN-DEPTH REVIEW:
Most other test-prep books briefly touch upon some of the concepts sporadically. On the other hand, our books start from the basics, but unlike other books, they do not end there – **we go deep inside, beyond just touching up the surface** – all the way from fundamental skills to some of the most advanced content that many other prep books choose to ignore. **Each concept is first explained in detail, and then analyzed for most effective understanding** – each and every concept is covered, and we haven't left any stone unturned. Overall, our program is more challenging – you simply get the **best-of-the-best**, and you get more of everything!

COMPREHENSIVE REVIEW:
Our Content-Knowledge Review Modules provide the **most comprehensive and complete review** of all the concepts, which you need to know to excel in your test. Each module is devoted to one of the main subject areas so that you can focus on the most relevant material. The ideal way to review our modules is to go through each topic thoroughly, understand all the solved examples, and work out all of the practice exercises. You must review each topic, understand every solved example, and work out all of the practice exercises. If you don't have enough time, just glimpse through a section. If you feel comfortable with it, move on to something else that may potentially give you more trouble. If you feel uncomfortable with it, review that topic more thoroughly.

Moreover, if you carefully work through our review, you will probably find some topics that you already know, but you may also find some topics that you need to review more closely. You should have a good sense of areas with which you are most comfortable, and in which areas you feel you have a deficiency. Work on any weaknesses you believe you have in those areas. This should help you organize your review more efficiently. Try to give yourself plenty of time and make sure to review the skills and master the concepts that you are required and expected to know to do well on your test. Of course, the more time you invest preparing for your test and more familiar you are with these fundamental principles, the better you will do on your test.

There is a lot of content reviewed in our modules. Although the amount of material presented in our books may appear to be overwhelming, it's the most complete review to get prepared for your test. To some of you, this may seem like a great deal of information to assimilate; however, when you start reviewing, you'll probably realize that you are already comfortable with many concepts discussed in our review modules. We also suggest that you spread your use of our modules over several weeks, and study different modules at your own pace. Even if you are sure you know the basic concepts, our review will help to warm you up so that you can go into your test with crisp and sharp skills. Hence, we strongly suggest that you at least touch up on each concept. However, depending on your strengths and weaknesses, you may be able to move quickly through some areas, and focus more on the others that seem to be troublesome to you. You should develop a plan of attack for your review of the wide range of content. Work on your weaknesses, and be ready to take advantage of your strengths.

Finally, our main objective in the content review modules is to refresh your knowledge of key concepts on the test and we attempt to keep things as concrete and concise as possible.

PRACTICE MODULES:

BASIC WORKBOOK:
Our math practice basic workbook contains a variety of questions on each and every topic that is covered in our review modules. The best way is to first learn all the concepts from our review modules and then apply your skills to test your knowledge on the actual test-like questions in our basic workbook.

ADVANCED WORKBOOK:
Our math practice advanced workbook also contains a variety of questions on each and every topic that is covered in our review modules. Once you become comfortable with the questions in our basic workbook, you should try your hands on our advanced workbook so that you can gain more experience with some of the most difficult questions. For students who are aiming for a very high score, practicing from our advanced workbook is very important. For students who are aiming for a mediocre score, practicing from our advanced workbook is not so important.

▪ ABOUT THIS BOOK

In order to excel on your test, it's important that you master each component of your test. That's why we have broken the entire test into different sections and each book focuses only on only one component. It's important to learn the art of tackling the questions you'll see on the test; nevertheless, it's equally important to get a strong hold of the mathematical fundamentals and principles. Apparently it's not enough to only know the test taking strategies, you also need to have a solid knowledge of the math content, and know how to solve the problems mathematically. This book is exclusively dedicated to the **Word Problems** that apply to the math section of your test.

WHAT'S COVERED IN THIS BOOK:

In this book, you will learn everything related to **Word Problems** content that can be used on different types of questions throughout the math section. Mastering the content of this book will not only improve your performance on the math section, but will also make you a smarter and wiser test-taker. In this book, you'll learn all the strategies and the content related to word problems, so that you can solve the word problems quickly, correctly, and more efficiently. In fact, being able to solve word problems is one of the most important factors to succeed on the math section.

WHAT'S NOT COVERED IN THIS BOOK:

This book does not cover any content other than Word Problems – to learn about other content areas, you must refer to the other books in the series.

PRE-REQUISITES FOR THIS BOOK:

The pre-requisite for this book is your thorough familiarity with arithmetic and algebraic principles and concepts. Hence, when you go through this book, you are already expected to know the content covered in some of the other books in the series.

RELATED MODULES FOR THIS BOOK: You will get the best out of this book if you use it in conjunction with some of the other related books in the series that are listed below.

List of related modules for this book:
- EZ Solutions – Test Prep Series – Math Strategies
- EZ Solutions – Test Prep Series – Math Review – Arithmetic
- EZ Solutions – Test Prep Series – Math Review – Algebra
- EZ Solutions – Test Prep Series – Math Review – Applications
- EZ Solutions – Test Prep Series – Math Review – Geometry
- EZ Solutions – Test Prep Series – Math Review – Word Problems
- EZ Solutions – Test Prep Series – Math Review – Logic & Stats
- EZ Solutions – Test Prep Series – Math Practice – Basic Workbook
- EZ Solutions – Test Prep Series – Math Practice – Advanced Workbook

Note: Look at the back of the book for a complete list of EZ books

PART 0.0: INTRODUCTION TO WORD PROBLEMS:

HIGHLIGHTS:
0.1 Basics About Word Problems
0.2 Systematic Method for Solving Word Problems
0.3 Word Problem Translation Table
0.4 Basic Examples of Word Problems
0.5 Different Levels of Word Problems

0.1: BASICS ABOUT WORD PROBLEMS:

Not all math problems are given in terms of numbers, variables, and mathematical symbols. Some math problems are presented in terms of words, and are classified as **"word problems"**. In fact, word problems account for the majority of the math problems on standardized tests. They essentially require you to apply mathematical skills to everyday situations. Since word problems can often be thorny, we're going to discuss them exclusively in this book.

This section intends to give you an overall review of all the fundamentals of word problems and the principles used to solve these problems. You will learn how to deal with different types of word problems and illustrate some of the techniques or concepts used in solving such problems.

TOPICS TESTED IN WORD PROBLEMS:
Word problems test the same concepts covered in arithmetic, algebra, and geometry, but they do so in a slightly different manner. Word problems are presented in ordinary language, and they often involve some very ordinary situations, such as, rate, discount, mixture, etc., things that we encounter frequently in our daily lives.

A word problem can be based on almost any math topic. You have already encountered word problems in some of our other books, such as, percents, ratios & proportions, logical reasoning, averages, geometry word problems, etc. Many common word problems are those involving percents and ratios; in fact, the majority of percent and ratio problems are presented in the form of word problems. Incidentally, many of the math topics that we commonly come across in the real world, such as, percents, ratios, averages, rates of work, etc., are often presented as word problems.

Although we have already covered word problems in our other books, there are some topics that are exclusively explained in this book, such as, work problems, motion problems, age problems, weight problems, mixture problems, etc.

Word problems can be either real-life problems or abstract problems. While solving word problems mathematically, becoming proficient at working with formulas of all kinds is essential to your success. However, to solve the word problems, the first step is to be able to translate the problems into mathematical terms.

DIFFERENCE BETWEEN WORD PROBLEMS AND ARITHMETIC/ALGEBRAIC PROBLEMS:
Word problems generally have a bad reputation, as most people dislike them, and they are usually considered to be very difficult by many students; however, on the contrary, this should not be the case. Word Problems are in fact just like any arithmetic or algebraic problem, the only difference is that the same problems are expressed in terms of words instead of numbers and variables. Therefore, first, you have to convert the word problems into straightforward problems, for which you have to go through the trouble of translating the problems before you can start solving them. The flip side is that once you translate the problem, it is generally easy to solve it, sometimes even easier than most other non-word problems. The concepts and techniques involved are rather simple. Some of the word-problems can be solved with just arithmetic, but most of them require the use of algebra.

The Extra Step: As you may have noticed, it's the extra step of translation from English to Math that makes word problems a little bit more difficult than other problems. However, once you have passed this step, you have done the hard part, and then, it's just a matter of solving them. If your arithmetic/algebraic concepts are clear, then you shouldn't have any difficulty in solving the word problems correctly.

Translation from English to Algebra:

Word problems require translating the verbal description of a mathematical fact or relationship into mathematical terms. Hence, to solve word problems, you must be able to translate English into algebra. The best way to solve word problems mathematically is to treat them as a foreign language, and try to translate *"word for word"* from English into arithmetic and algebra, just as you would from English into French or Spanish or any other foreign language.

Direct Translations of Words or Phrases into Numbers, Variables, and Symbols: The best approach to solve word problems, especially those involving variables or unknowns, is to translate or convert words and phrases into numbers, variables, and mathematical operations, determine the relationship between them, and then write that relationship in the form of an algebraic equation in a way that makes sense and satisfies the guidelines specified in the problem. While translating into algebra, we use letters or variables, such as, x, y, z, a, b, n, etc., to represent the unknown quantities that we are trying to figure out, and we need to connect those quantities by using arithmetic symbols, such as, (+), (−), (×), (÷), etc.

A word problem is an exercise in translation: The most important part of solving a word problem is to understand exactly what's being asked and how to set up the problem correctly by translating it. The translation process can sometimes become a little complicated or confusing, or can at least cause some level of difficulty for a few students. Once the translation process is completed, that is, once the word problem is set up in the form of numbers, variables, and mathematical operations, solving it is usually simple. Simply solve it like any other arithmetic or algebraic problem, using the techniques we have already reviewed and discussed in this and other modules. In fact, the actual math in word problems tends to be quite easy; the translation process is often the hard part. Translating from words to symbols and from symbols to words is an important skill, one that is inevitable to posses while answering word problems.

Translate As You Read: As you read a word problem, translate the words into mathematical expressions and equations. In doing so, isolate the key words and phrases that relate to a particular mathematical process. Hence, as you read a word problem, look out for the key words, and systematically translate word and phrases into algebraic expressions, and English sentences into algebraic sentences, i.e., into equations. Always take one step at a time, reading each sentence carefully and translating the information into equations or other useful mathematical expressions. By the time you finish reading the problem, you should have already translated the whole word problem into mathematical expressions and/or equations. Your ability to translate word problems from "*prose*" to "*math*" is the single most important skill that you need to develop to master the word problems.

Linguistic Tricks:
Word Problems are often phrased in a manner as if the person who wrote them doesn't know how to speak English or is trying to say something in a code language. This is done intentionally because they think that the best way to trap you or test your math skills is by using verbal tricks. A good way to beat this hideous trap is by paraphrasing the words in a form that is simpler to deal with. Remember, while using translation and manipulation in word problems, you will often reveal some very simple information that has been deliberately camouflaged by the test writers with the sole purpose of making the problem look more complex than it actually is.

Forming Equations is a Two Step Method:
First Write the Relationship, Then Translate into Equation: If you are not sure how to construct the equation directly from the word problem, make it a two-step method. First, rephrase the relationship between the known and the unknown values in your own words, and then translate that relationship into mathematical terms.

Mistranslation:
Always read the word problem carefully, and double-check to ensure that you have translated it correctly and accurately without changing its context or meaning.
For instance, beware of the order in which you translate terms. For example, consider the following common mistake: $5x$ less than $7y$ equals 9. This translates as $7y − 5x = 9$, not $5x − 7y = 9$.
Moreover, be cautious of the order in which you place the numbers with word problems involving subtraction and division because the order of these operations is irreversible.
For instance, $(7 − 5)$ is not the same as $(5 − 7)$, and $(5 ÷ 7)$ is not the same as $(7 ÷ 5)$. For more in-depth information on arithmetic, refer to our module on arithmetic.

Parallel Thinking:

The primary skill required to form word problems is to take a boring story and conceptualize it mathematically. If you have trouble with word problems, it's probably because you're unable to reveal the math that is involved in the story. What you need to do is keep practicing until you can see a word problem and visualize the math you are reading. When you read the word problem, your mind needs to work parallel, mathematically. Once you are able to acquire this skill, you will have mastered the most difficult part of word problems.

For instance, if you get a problem that tells you, "John has ten dollars less than twice as much as Tom," your mind should be thinking, "Let's use J for how much John has, and T for how much Tom has. Twice as much as Tom means $2T$, and ten dollars less means -10, so $J = 2T - 10$."

UNDERSTANDING BEFORE TRANSLATING:

Before completely diving into a word problem, read through the entire question and the answer choices to gain a general understanding of the given situation and conditions. One way to get an overall sense of a problem is to first read the whole problem, without pausing for details. Some of you follow this rule intuitively without even realizing it. If you are not one of those, you need to work on this skill until it becomes almost like a spontaneous reflex action. This process normally shouldn't take more than a few seconds.

SOLVING WORD PROBLEMS IS MORE THAN SIMPLE MATH:

Figuring out some of the word problems takes more than just knowing a bunch of math formulas. You have to think about what math skills and tools you need to apply to the questions in order to reason your way through to the correct answers.

DRAW FIGURES FOR WORD PROBLEMS:

Drawing figures is essential in geometry problems; however, drawings should not be limited to only geometry questions. There are many non-geometry word problems on which drawing figures would help. It will help you **"connect the dots"** and make some sort of **"plan-of-action"**. A good figure requires no artistic abilities. Usually, a rough figure with a few line segments is all you need. Add or modify information to your figure as you find out.

REMAIN FOCUSED, DON'T LOSE TRACK:

To solve word problems efficiently, it helps to make sure you know exactly what is being asked. So always remain focused and keep track of what you know and what precisely you need to know. Don't try to find anything that is not asked in the question or won't assist you in finding what is being asked in the question. In all word problems, remember to circle what you're looking for. Don't answer the wrong question or find something that you don't need!

ONE STATEMENT CAN RESULT IN MULTIPLE EQUATIONS:

In word problems, one statement can mean or imply multiple relationships, and that can result in multiple variations of equations.

For instance, if John is exactly 5 years older than Tom, we can express this relationship by the following equivalent equations: (J represents John's age and T represents Tom's age)

(A) John is exactly 5 years older than Tom $\Rightarrow J = T + 5$
(B) Tom is exactly 5 years younger than John $\Rightarrow T = J - 5$.
(C) The difference of John's and Tom's age is 5 $\Rightarrow J - T = 5$

VALIDITY OF STATEMENTS IN WORD PROBLEMS:

Unconditional: Some Statements are Always True: In word problems, some statements can be taken as true and valid under all conditions and circumstances.

For instance, if John is exactly 5 years older than Tom $\Rightarrow$ then, at any point in time, 20 year ago, or 50 years from now – he will always be 5 years older than Tom, and we can express this relationship by the equation: $J = T + 5$.

Conditional: Some Statements are Not Always True: In word problems, some statements cannot be taken as true and valid under all conditions and circumstances.

For instance, John will be exactly 5 years old when Tom turns 17 $\Rightarrow$ then, John will be exactly 5 years old "**only**" when Tom turns 17, not at any other point in time, not 20 year ago, or 50 years from now – we can express this relationship by a conditional statement: $J = 5$ when $T = 17$.

0.2: SYSTEMATIC METHOD FOR SOLVING WORD PROBLEMS:

Some word problems can sometimes be quite complicated; however, the solution merely involves understanding the given scenario, translating the given information in terms of words, and applying our systematic technique given in this section.

The easiest way to solve world problems is to carefully study the following EZ Step-by-Step Method.

EZ STEP-BY-STEP METHOD: Apply the following step(s) to solve any type of Word Problem:

STEP 1: Read the question, and determine what all information is *"given"* ⇒ these are the given, and they are known as the *"known quantities"*.

STEP 2: Read the question and interpret what's being asked or, what needs to be solved, or what information you need to know to answer the question ⇒ these are the quantities you are seeking, and they are known as the *"unknown quantities"*.

STEP 3: Name the Unknown Quantities by selecting *variables*, such as, x, y, z, etc.

STEP 4: Determine the relationships between the *knowns* and the *unknowns*, that is, the variables and the other given quantities in the problem, and connect them using *arithmetic symbols*, such as, (+), (−), (×), (÷), etc. and write them as *algebraic expressions*.

STEP 5: In most cases, these known and unknown quantities can be expressed in terms of the original variable. If not, a separate variable may have to be used to represent a quantity.

STEP 6: Using these *variables* and the relationships between the *known* and *unknown quantities* ⇒ form *algebraic equations* by applying the appropriate mathematical formulas.

STEP 7: Once all the algebraic equations that represent the problem have been formed, solve the resulting equations to find the value of the unknown(s), and plug that value in other relationships or equations that involve this variable in order to find any other unknown quantities, if there are any.

Note: Not all these steps are necessary on all word problems; apply only the ones that are required.

EZ REFERENCE: For more in-depth knowledge about solving equations, refer to our Algebra Module.

EZ CHECK: Once you solve the problem, double-check to make sure you answered the question asked, and that your answer makes sense. You can do so by first checking if you formed the correct equations, and then plugging in the values of the variables in the equations to see if the equations hold true; and finally plugging in the answer in the question to see if it makes sense. If it does, then your answer is correct; if not, check back, you obviously made a mistake. While checking a word problem, it's recommended to substitute your answer into your equations; however, since the equations that you formed can be wrong, it would be a good idea to check your answer also with the original words in the problem.

HOW TO ASSIGN & NAME VARIABLES:
Be careful while assigning variables in a word problem. While translating statements, you must first decide which quantity the variable will represent, sometimes this is obvious, and other times there can be more than one possibility. You often have a choice as to what quantity you will let the variable represent. You don't necessarily have to let the variable represent what you're looking for or what the question is asking for; instead, you should choose whatever will make it easier to solve the problem.

Try to use only one variable: If possible, use only one variable to represent the unknown quantity. If there are more than one unknown quantities, you should often be able to use the relationships given in the problem to write an expression for the other unknowns in term of the same variable you used for the first unknown. In cases, where you are not able to do so, you will have to introduce another variable, but you should avoid doing so unless it's inevitable.

Naming Variables: If there is more than one variable in the problem, it is important to keep track of what each variable represents. It is often helpful to use variables that suggest what quantity the variable actually represents. So name the variables in a way that makes it easy for you to remember what they actually stand for.

For instance, if you have to deal with the equation such as, Profit = Revenue – Expenses, use the variable P for Profit, R for Revenue, and E for Expenses. So the equation now becomes $P = R - E$, which is much more user-friendly and informative than a more generic equation like $x = y - z$.

In general, try to use the first letter of the word to name the unknown quantity. For instance, to name John's age, use J, and to name Monika's age, use M. This way you will know what each variable means.

Make Notes: It's easy to lose track of what each variable represents, so make sure to make a note of what each variable represents before working out the problem.

EZ NOTE: Variables can be letters such as, "x, y, J, M, etc.," which represent the unknown quantities. Each time the same variable is used within the same expression, it represents the same quantity.

USE CHARTS/GRIDS TO ORGANIZE VARIABLES:

When a word problem involves several variables with multiple relationships, the best way to approach the problem is by making a chart/grid to organize the information. Some of the most complicated word problems can be very effectively solved using a chart. Note that the chart doesn't repeat the values of the variables. The basic purpose of creating a chart is to assign variables that can be used to write equations.

For Example: In a family of three, the father weighs 6 times as much as the child, and the mother weighs ¾ as much as the father does. If the total weight of all three of them is 230 pounds, how much does the mother weigh?

Unknowns: ⇒ Weight of Father
⇒ Weight of Mother
⇒ Weight of Child

Find?   ⇒ Weight of Mother

As you can see in this problem, there are three unknowns and we have to find the value of one of them. We also know the following:
⇒ Weight of Child + Weight of Father + Weight of Mother = Total Weight of the Family

Let's try to assign the variable "x" for one of the above three unknowns. Now, the question is whether we should assign x to the weight of the father, mother, or child. Although we are asked to find the weight of the mother, it may not always be the best choice to assign to x.

Let's analyze all three scenarios and see which one turns out to be the easiest:

1st. Scenario: Let x represent the weight of the child:
If we let x represent the weight of the child, then $6x$ will be the weight of the father, and $\frac{3}{4}$ of $6x$ will be the weight of the mother.

Now, our equation would be: $x + 6x + \frac{3}{4}(6x) = 230$

⇒ This is clearly the BEST choice.

2nd. Scenario: Let x represent the weight of the father:
If we let x represent the weight of the father, then $\frac{1}{6}x$ will be the weight of the child, and $\frac{3}{4}x$ will be the weight of the mother.

Now, our equation would be: $x + \frac{1}{6}x + \frac{3}{4}x = 230$

⇒ This is the second best choice.

3rd. Scenario: Let x represent the weight of the mother:

If we let x represent the weight of the mother, then $\frac{4}{3}x$ will be the weight of the

father, and $\frac{1}{6}$ of $\frac{4}{3}x$ will be the weight of the child.

Now, our equation would be: $x + \frac{4}{3}x + \frac{1}{6} \cdot \frac{4}{3}x = 230$

$\Rightarrow$ This is clearly the WORST choice.

Note: This example is solved later in the section on Weight Problems.

HOW WORDS CAN COMPLICATE EASY PROBLEMS:
If you notice in the following two pairs of examples, once we translate the words into arithmetic expression or algebraic expression, 1a & 1b and 2a & 2b are exactly identical. The only difference is that the first ones in each pair (1a & 2a) are regular algebra problems, and the second ones (2a & 2b) are expressed in terms of word problems. After going through the following two examples, you will then realize how words can sometimes transform a very easy arithmetic or algebra problem into a very complicated or difficult word problem. The good news is that if you use our techniques and English to algebra translation table we have given in this section, it really isn't that hard.

Example #1a: $x + 5 = 2(x - 7)$

Example #1b: In five years, John will be twice as old as he was 7 years ago. How old is John now?

Solution: Let John's age now = x
Then, John's age 7 years ago = $x - 7$
And, John's age 5 years from now = $x + 5$
Since, in five years, John will be twice as old as he was 7 years ago, therefore:
$\Rightarrow x + 5 = 2(x - 7)$
$\Rightarrow x + 5 = 2x - 14$
$\Rightarrow x = 19$
Therefore, John's age now = 19

Example #2a: What is 5% of 5% of 50,000?

Example #2b: In a college raffle, 5% of the tickets printed can be redeemed for prizes, and 5% of those tickets have values in excess of $500. If the college prints 50,000 tickets, how many of them can be redeemed for more than $500.

Solution: Let x be the number of tickets worth more than $500, then,
$\Rightarrow x = $ 5% of 5% of 50,000 = $0.05 \times 0.05 \times 50{,}000 = 125$

Most word problems are sometimes complicated but are usually not very difficult to crack. After going through this section, you will no longer be afraid of word problems. If you still face a problem understanding or solving word problems, we would suggest you go through this section a few more times. If you still have a hard time or get stuck with word problems, don't worry, try to make use of our "EZ Alternate Strategies" given in our module "Math Strategies". For instance, you can try using back-solving strategy by plugging-in the answer choices. If the answer choices are not given, you can still use "trial and error" method by making up your own logical answer choices and then back-solving.

ALTERNATE METHODS TO WORD PROBLEMS:
Often times, word problem can be solved by using just arithmetic, other times, algebra needs to be applied; however, sometime, word problems can be solved either by using just arithmetic or by applying algebra.

For Example: Three brothers divided a prize as follows: the oldest received $\frac{1}{5}$ of it, the middle one received $\frac{1}{2}$ of it,

and the youngest received the remaining $150. What was the value of the prize?

Solution: **Method #1:** By Setting-Up an Equation:

If the value of prize = x, then:

$\Rightarrow \dfrac{1}{5}x + \dfrac{1}{2}x + 150 = x$ [Convert the words into an equation]

$\Rightarrow (10)\dfrac{1}{5}x + (10)\dfrac{1}{2}x + (10)150 = (10)x$ [Multiply all terms in the equation by the LCM, which is 10]

$\Rightarrow 2x + 5x + 1{,}500 = 10x$ [Apply distributive property]

$\Rightarrow 7x + 1{,}500 = 10x$ [Combine like-terms]

$\Rightarrow 3x = 1{,}500$ [Subtract $7x$ from both sides]

$\Rightarrow x = 500$ [Divide both sides by 3]

$\Rightarrow$ Therefore, the total value of the prize was $500

Method #2: By Using the Concept of Fractions:
Let the value of total prize = x.
Now, we know that the oldest and the middle brother together got:

$\Rightarrow \dfrac{1}{5} + \dfrac{1}{2} = \dfrac{2}{10} + \dfrac{5}{10} = \dfrac{7}{10}$

Since the total prize must be 1, the youngest brother received:

$\Rightarrow 1 - \dfrac{7}{10} = \dfrac{10}{10} - \dfrac{7}{10} = \dfrac{3}{10}$

EZ Problem Set-Up $\Rightarrow$ Since the youngest brother received $150 in his share of prize, which implies: 3/10th of what is 150:

$\Rightarrow \dfrac{3}{10}x = 150$

$\Rightarrow x = 150 \times \dfrac{10}{3}$

$\Rightarrow x = 500$

0.3: WORD PROBLEM TRANSLATION TABLE:

DICTIONARY: FROM ENGLISH WORDS TO MATHEMATICAL MEANINGS AND OPERATIONS:

The following translation table presents some of the most common key words and phrases used in the word problems, and their corresponding mathematical translation, conversion, or interpretation.

"ENGLISH KEY WORDS"	"MATHEMATICAL MEANING"	"OPERATION"
equals, is, was, will be, had, has, will have, is equal to, is the same as, the result is, add up to, costs, weighs	"Equals"	(=)
plus, total, more than, sum, and, exceeds, added to, increase, increased by, received, got, older than, farther than, greater than, sum of, combined with	"Addition"	(+)
minus, fewer, less, less than, difference, difference between, decreased, decreased by, diminished by, subtracted from, reduced by, fewer, younger than, gave, lost, have left	"Subtraction"	(−)
times, of, product, multiplied by, twice, double, triple, half	"Multiplication"	(×)
quotient, divisor, dividend, divided by, per, for, ratio of, out of, parts, each	"Division"	(÷)
more than, greater than	Inequality: "Greater Than"	(>)
at least, greater than or equal to	Inequality: "Greater Than or Equal To"	(≥)
fewer than, less than	Inequality: "Less Than"	(<)
at most, less than or equal to	Inequality: "Less Than or Equal To"	(≤)
what, how many, how much, a number, etc.	"Unknown Quantity" (Any variable/letter)	n, x, y, z, a, b

0.4: BASIC EXAMPLES OF WORD PROBLEMS:

Most of the basic word problems only involve numbers and they are quite easy to solve; however, some of them can be quite tricky. The word problems become even more complicated and challenging when variables are used instead of numbers. Moreover, use of multiple variables makes them some of the most difficult math problems.

The following are examples of a few basic word problem statements that are translated into mathematical expressions or equations, which can be used to solve them indicating when to use each of the basic operations: addition, subtraction, multiplication, division, etc., using the translation table. Translating these statements into algebraic expressions and equations will assist you in solving word problems.

WORD PROBLEM STATEMENTS   **MATHEMATICAL TRANSLATION**

(A) ADDITIONS:

DIFFERENT WAYS OF EXPRESSING ADDITION PROBLEMS:

For example $(m + n)$ or $(9 + 7)$ can be expressed in the following different ways:

$(m + n)$	$(9 + 7)$
$\Rightarrow$ the addition of m and n	$\Rightarrow$ the addition of 9 and 7
$\Rightarrow$ m plus n	$\Rightarrow$ 9 plus 7
$\Rightarrow$ the sum of m and n	$\Rightarrow$ the sum of 9 and 7
$\Rightarrow$ the total of m and n	$\Rightarrow$ the total of 9 and 7
$\Rightarrow$ m added to n	$\Rightarrow$ 9 added to 7
$\Rightarrow$ m more than n	$\Rightarrow$ 9 more than 7
$\Rightarrow$ m greater than n	$\Rightarrow$ 9 greater than 7
$\Rightarrow$ m increased by n	$\Rightarrow$ 9 increased by 7
$\Rightarrow$ give m to n	$\Rightarrow$ give 9 to 7

Some of the following situations require you to apply addition:

(i) You are given the value of individual quantities and you want to find their total:
- "The sum of 5 and some other number is 12" $\Rightarrow 5 + n = 12$
- "The sum of some number and 5 is 12" $\Rightarrow n + 5 = 12$
- "The addition of two integers is 12" $\Rightarrow x + y = 12$
- "The sum of two integers is 12" $\Rightarrow x + y = 12$
- "Total cost of an item is \$10 plus \$1.25 in taxes" $\Rightarrow \$10 + \$1.25 = \$11.25$
- "If there are 10 boys and 5 girls, then the total number of students is 15" $\Rightarrow 10 + 5 = 15$

(ii) You are given the value of an original quantity and the value of increase, and you want to find the new value:
- "A number n increased by 5 is 12" $\Rightarrow n + 5 = 12$
- "5 more than a number n is 12" $\Rightarrow n + 5 = 12$
- "A number that is n more than 5 is 12" $\Rightarrow 5 + n = 12$
- "The sum of two integers is 25" $\Rightarrow x + y = 25$
- "A number more than another number is 12" $\Rightarrow x + y = 12$
- "Price of an item increased from \$7 by \$5" $\Rightarrow \$7 + \$5 = \$12$
- "John has 5 more dollars than Tom" $\Rightarrow J = T + 5$
- "John is 5 dollars richer than Tom" $\Rightarrow J = T + 5$
- "John is 5 years older than Tom" $\Rightarrow J = T + 5$
- "John weighs 5 pounds more than Tom" $\Rightarrow J = T + 5$
- "John ran 5 miles farther than Tom" $\Rightarrow J = T + 5$
- "John bought one apple and two bananas for \$5" $\Rightarrow A + 2B = 5$

(B) SUBTRACTIONS:

DIFFERENT WAYS OF EXPRESSING SUBTRACTION PROBLEMS:

For example $(m - n)$ or $(9 - 7)$ can be expressed in the following different ways:

$(m - n)$	$(9 - 7)$
$\Rightarrow$ the subtraction of n from m	$\Rightarrow$ the subtraction of 7 from 9
$\Rightarrow$ m minus n	$\Rightarrow$ 9 minus 7
$\Rightarrow$ the difference of m and n	$\Rightarrow$ the difference of 9 and 7
$\Rightarrow$ subtract n from m	$\Rightarrow$ subtract 7 from 9
$\Rightarrow$ n fewer than m	$\Rightarrow$ 7 fewer than 9
$\Rightarrow$ n less than m	$\Rightarrow$ 7 less than 9
$\Rightarrow$ m decreased by n	$\Rightarrow$ 9 decreased by 7
$\Rightarrow$ m less n	$\Rightarrow$ 9 less 7
$\Rightarrow$ from m take n	$\Rightarrow$ from 9 take 7

Some of the following situations require you to apply subtraction:

(i) You are given the value of two quantities, and you want to know how much more or less one quantity is than the other, that amount is called the difference. So in other words you want to find the difference between two quantities. Note: In word problems, difference usually means absolute difference; i.e., larger value – smaller value.
You are given the total and the value of one part of the total, and you want to find the value of the other part (i.e., the remaining):

- "The difference between some number and 5 is 12" $\Rightarrow n - 5 = 12$
- "The difference between 5 and some other number is 12" $\Rightarrow 5 - n = 12$
- "The difference between two integers is 12" $\Rightarrow x - y = 12$
- "The subtraction of one number from the other is 12" $\Rightarrow x - y = 12$
- "Total cost of an item is \$10 minus \$1.25 in rebates" $\Rightarrow \$10 - \$1.25 = \$8.75$
- "If there are 15 total students and 10 of them are boys, then the number of girls is 5" $\Rightarrow 15 - 10 = 5$

(ii) You are given the value of an original quantity and the value of decrease, and you want to find the new value:
- "A number n decreased by 5 is 12" $\Rightarrow n - 5 = 12$
- "5 less than a number n is 12 $\Rightarrow n - 5 = 12$
- "A number that is n less than 5 is 12" $\Rightarrow 5 - n = 12$
- "A number less another number is 12" $\Rightarrow x - y = 12$
- "Price of an item decreased from \$7 by \$5" $\Rightarrow \$7 - \$5 = \$2$
- "John has 5 less dollars than Tom" $\Rightarrow J = T - 5$
- "John is 5 dollars poorer than Tom" $\Rightarrow J = T - 5$
- "John is 5 years younger than Tom" $\Rightarrow J = T - 5$
- "John weighs 5 pounds less than Tom" $\Rightarrow J = T - 5$
- "John ran 5 miles less than Tom" $\Rightarrow J = T - 5$

(iii) To compare how much one item is smaller or bigger than the other:
- "How much larger than a is b?" $\Rightarrow b - a = ?$
- "How much smaller than b is a?" $\Rightarrow b - a = ?$
- "How much larger than 5 is 7?" $\Rightarrow 7 - 5 = 2$
- "How much smaller than 7 is 5?" $\Rightarrow 7 - 5 = 2$

(C) MULTIPLICATIONS:

DIFFERENT WAYS OF EXPRESSING MULTIPLICATION PROBLEMS:
For example $(a \times b = n)$ or $(10 \times 2 = 20)$ can be expressed in the following different ways:

$(a \times b = n)$	$(10 \times 2 = 20)$
$\Rightarrow$ n is the product of a and b	$\Rightarrow$ 20 is the product of 10 and 2
$\Rightarrow$ a is a factor of n	$\Rightarrow$ 10 is a factor of 20
$\Rightarrow$ b is a factor of n	$\Rightarrow$ 2 is a factor of 20
$\Rightarrow$ n is a multiple of a	$\Rightarrow$ 20 is a multiple of 10
$\Rightarrow$ n is a multiple of b	$\Rightarrow$ 20 is a multiple of 2

Some of the following situations require you to apply multiplication:

(i)   You are given the value of one item and you want to find the total value of many of these same items.

- "5 multiplied by n is 10" $\Rightarrow 5 \times n = 10$
- "A number n multiplied by 5 is 10" $\Rightarrow n \times 5 = 10$
- "The product of 5 and a number is 10" $\Rightarrow 5n = 10$
- "If one item costs \$5, then 10 of the same item cost \$50" $\Rightarrow \$5 \times 10 = \$50$
- "5 times the quantity $(2x + 5)$" $\Rightarrow 5(2x + 5)$
- "John has five times as many dollars as Tom has" $\Rightarrow J = 5T$
- "John has ¼ of what Tom has" $\Rightarrow J = ¼T$

(ii) You are given the value of one item when many items are contained in the whole group and you want to find the total value of all the items that belong to the group.

- "If there are 10 students in one group and there are 5 such groups, then there are a total of 50 students." $\Rightarrow 10 \times 5 = 50$

(D) DIVISIONS:

DIFFERENT WAYS OF EXPRESSING DIVISION PROBLEMS:
For example $(n \div a = b)$ or $(10 \div 2 = 5)$ can be expressed in the following different ways:

$(n \div a = b)$ $(10 \div 2 = 5)$
$\Rightarrow n$ divided by a is b $\Rightarrow$ 10 divided by 2 is 5
$\Rightarrow b$ is the quotient of n and a $\Rightarrow$ 5 is the quotient of 10 and 2
$\Rightarrow a$ divided into n is b $\Rightarrow$ 2 divided into 10 is 5

Some of the following situations require you to apply division:

(i)   You are given the total value of many of the same items, and you want to find the value of one item.
    Note: Division is the inverse of multiplication

- "5 divided by n is 10" $\Rightarrow 5 \div n = 10$
- "5 divided into a number n is 10" $\Rightarrow n \div 5 = 10$
- "The quotient of 5 and a number is 10" $\Rightarrow 5 \div n = 10$
- "If the cost of 10 of the same items is \$50, then the cost of 1 item is \$5" $\Rightarrow \$50 \div 10 = \$5$
- "John travels at the rate of 50 miles per 2 hours" $\Rightarrow R = 50$ miles $\div 2$ hours $= 25$ mph

(ii) You are given the value of one item and the total value of all the items belonging to a group, and you want to find how many items are contained in the whole group.

- "If a total of 50 students are divided into groups of 10 students, then there are 5 such groups." $\Rightarrow 50 \div 10 = 5$
- "John makes half as much as Tom makes" $\Rightarrow J = \dfrac{1}{2}T$

(E) EQUALITY: Some of the following situations require you to apply equal sign:
- "The number of days John worked is the number of days Tom worked" $\Rightarrow J = T$
- "John's salary is the same as Tom's salary" $\Rightarrow J = T$

(F) INEQUALITY: Some of the following situations require you to apply inequalities:
- "John's salary is always greater than five dollars" $\Rightarrow J > 5$
- "John's salary is always less than five dollars" $\Rightarrow J < 5$
- "John's salary is at least five dollars" $\Rightarrow J \geq 5$
- "John's salary is at most five dollars" $\Rightarrow J \leq 5$

(G) ABSOLUTE VALUE: Some of the following situations require you to apply absolute value:
- "The difference between Tom's height and John's height is 12 cm" $\Rightarrow |J - T| = 12$
- "The difference between Tom's height and John's height is less than 12 cm" $\Rightarrow |J - T| < 12$

(H) AVERAGES: Some of the following situations require you to apply averages:

- "The average score of three students is 85" $\Rightarrow \dfrac{a+b+c}{3} = 85$

- "John can buy two erasers and five markers for nine dollars" $\Rightarrow \$9 = 2E + 5M$

(I) RATIOS: Some of the following situations require you to apply ratios or rates:

- "John has 5 dollars for every 2 dollars Tom has" $\Rightarrow \dfrac{J}{T} = \dfrac{5}{2}$

- "For every \$5 in increase of gasoline prices, the oil prices increases by \$2" $\Rightarrow \dfrac{G}{O} = \dfrac{5}{2}$

- "7 out of every ten voted for the proposition" $\Rightarrow \dfrac{7}{10}$

- "50 miles per 2 hours" $\Rightarrow \dfrac{miles}{hours} = \dfrac{50}{2} = 25$ miles/hour

(J) PERCENTS: Some of the following situations require you to apply percents:
- "The discount is 25% off the original price" $\Rightarrow D = 0.25P$
- "John makes 25% of what Tom makes" $\Rightarrow J = 0.25T$
- "25% of John's salary goes towards rent" $\Rightarrow R = 0.25S$
- "John makes 25% more than what Tom makes" $\Rightarrow J = 1.25T$

(K) MULTIPLE OPERATIONS: Some of the following situations require you to apply multiple operations:
- "Twice a number increased by 5" $\Rightarrow 2n + 5$
- "Five times the difference of 7 and a number" $\Rightarrow 5(7 - n)$

- "5 less than the quotient of a number and 2" $\Rightarrow \dfrac{n}{2} - 5$

- "One number is five less than twice the other" $\Rightarrow x = 2y - 5$
- "John has five fewer marbles than twice the number Tom has" $\Rightarrow J = 2T - 5$
Caution: Don't make the mistake of writing it as $J = 5 - 2T$
(both are different $\Rightarrow 2T - 5 \neq 5 - 2T$)
- "The product of 2 and a number exceeds that number by 5" $\Rightarrow 2n = n + 5$
- "Five times the first integer less two times the other integer is 12" $\Rightarrow 5x - 2y = 12$
- "n is 5 less than 25% of m" $\Rightarrow n = 0.25m - 5$
- "The sum of square and square root of a number" $\Rightarrow n^2 + \sqrt{n}$
- The sum of a, b, and c is twice the sum of a minus b and a minus c $\Rightarrow a + b + c = 2[(a - b) + (a - c)]$
- The sum of x and 9 decreased by the sum of y and 7 is the same as

  dividing y decreased by z by 7 decreased by y $\Rightarrow (x + 9) - (y + 7) = \dfrac{y - z}{7 - y}$

0.5: DIFFERENT LEVELS OF WORD PROBLEMS:

Word Problems can be divided into different levels depending upon their level of difficulty. Most problems in this book are arranged in the order of topic, and within each topic, the problems are arranged in the order of difficulty. It is important to recognize the level of difficulty of a problem before tackling it. Following are the different levels of difficulty.

BASIC-LEVEL WORD PROBLEMS

There are some basic word problems that don't involve any algebra. Such problems may not require you to write down an algebraic equation or expression. These types of problems test your ability to correctly apply arithmetic operations in a problem-solving situation. To solve such problems, you need to identify what quantities are being given, what is being asked for, which arithmetic operations must be applied to the given quantities, and how those arithmetic operations must be carried out in order to get the correct answer.

Following is an example of basic-level word problem:

For Example: Jack saves $7 every day. If 11 days ago he had $546, how many dollars will he have 11 days from now?

Solution:
Amount of money Jack saves in 11 days	$\Rightarrow 11 \times \$7 = \$77$
Amount of money Jack had 11 days ago	$\Rightarrow \$546$
Amount of money Jack has now	$\Rightarrow \$546 + \$77 = \$623$
Amount of money Jack will have 11 day from now	$\Rightarrow \$623 + \$77 = \$700$

MEDIUM-LEVEL WORD PROBLEMS:

There are some medium or intermediate level word problems that are not as easy as the basic word problems and are not as complex as the advanced level word problems. Such problems may require you to write down a simple algebraic equation or expression. These types of problems test your ability to correctly apply arithmetic and algebraic operations in a problem-solving situation. To solve the problem, you need to identify what quantities are being given, what is being asked for, which arithmetic or algebraic operations must be applied to the given quantities, and how those arithmetic and algebraic operations must be carried out in order to get the answer.

Following is an example of medium-level word problem:

For Example: If Monika weighs six-fifth as much as Susan, Nancy weighs one-half as much as Monika and the total weight of Monika, Susan, and Nancy is 588 pounds, how much does Nancy weigh?

Solution:

Let, Susan's Weight $\Rightarrow x$

Then, Monika's Weight $\Rightarrow \dfrac{6}{5}x$

And, Nancy's Weight $\Rightarrow \dfrac{1}{2} \bullet \dfrac{6}{5}x = \dfrac{3}{5}x$

Total Weight $\Rightarrow 588$

EZ Problem Set-Up $\Rightarrow$ Weight of Susan + Weight of Monika + Weight of Nancy = Total Weight

$\Rightarrow x + \dfrac{6}{5}x + \dfrac{3}{5}x = 588$ [Set up the equation]

$\Rightarrow (5)x + (5)\dfrac{6}{5}x + (5)\dfrac{3}{5}x = (5)588$ [Multiply both sides by 5 to eliminate fractions]

$\Rightarrow 5x + 6x + 3x = 2,940$ [Apply distributive property]

$\Rightarrow 14x = 2,940$ [Combine like-terms]

$\Rightarrow x = 210$ [Divide both sides by 14]

Therefore: Susan's Weight $\Rightarrow x = 210$ pounds

Monika's Weight $\Rightarrow \dfrac{6}{5}x = \dfrac{6}{5} \times 210 = 252$ pounds

Nancy's Weight $\Rightarrow \frac{1}{2}\left(\dfrac{6}{5}x\right) = \frac{1}{2} \times 252 = 126$ pounds

ADVANCED-LEVEL OR COMPLEX WORD PROBLEMS:

Advanced or complex word problems usually involve forming multiple equations that are generally quite easy to solve; however, some of them can be quite tricky. These types of complex word problems may become even more complicated and challenging when you fall into the wrong track.

Complex problems are nothing more than an advanced form of simple word problems. Some seemingly difficult or complex word problems are just a series of easy problems. In other words, they are a bunch of simple word problems put together in one problem, and that's what makes them more complex. Moreover, use of multiple unknowns makes them some of the most difficult word problems. You may even be asked to find numerical values for various unknown quantities; however, the word problems will always give you enough information to set up a sufficient number of equations to solve for those quantities.

The ideal way to solve the complex word problems is by breaking them into simple word problems and converting them into equations individually. Once all the equations are formed, simply try to connect those individual equations with each other and solve for what's being asked in the problem; although, you may have to do a little bit of manipulation in the process. You should start from a point that is given in the problem or is at least easily solvable, and then make it into a chain process, that is, one value will help you get another value, and that will help you get another value until you reach the solution to the problem.

If you are unable to see which operations to use or what equations to form, imagine that the variables are numbers and see if that gives you any indication. Also, check your answer by using back-solving technique, that is, plug-in your answer into the problem to see if it makes sense. Moreover, most word problems can be solved in more than one way. So there are multiple ways of solving the same word problem, pick the one that seems easiest to you.

Following is an example of advanced-level word problem:

For Example: Turbine X and Turbine Y, both generates electricity. It takes Turbine X 10 hours longer to generate 1,650 mega watts of electricity than it take Turbine Y. Turbine Y generates 10 percent more electricity per hour than Turbine X. How many mega watts of electricity per hour does Turbine X generate?

Solution: Let the amount of time taken by Turbine Y to produce 1650 mega watts of electricity be $\Rightarrow x$ hours

Then, the amount of electricity generated by Turbine Y in 1 hour $\Rightarrow \dfrac{1650}{x}$

Now, the amount of time taken by Turbine X to produce 1650 mega watts of electricity $\Rightarrow x + 10$ hours

Then, the amount of electricity generated by Turbine X in 1 hour $\Rightarrow \dfrac{1650}{x+10}$

EZ Set-Up $\Rightarrow$ Turbine Y generates 10 percent more electricity per hour than Turbine X:

$\Rightarrow \dfrac{1650}{x} = 110\%\left(\dfrac{1650}{x+10}\right)$ [Set up the equation]

$\Rightarrow \dfrac{1650}{x} = \dfrac{110}{100}\left(\dfrac{1650}{x+10}\right)$ [Convert the percent into a fraction]

$\Rightarrow \dfrac{1650}{x} = \dfrac{11}{10}\left(\dfrac{1650}{x+10}\right)$ [Reduce the fraction to its lowest terms]

$\Rightarrow \left(\dfrac{10}{11}\right)\dfrac{1650}{x} = \dfrac{11}{10}\left(\dfrac{1650}{x+10}\right)\left(\dfrac{10}{11}\right)$ [Multiply both sides by 10/11]

$\Rightarrow \dfrac{16500}{11x} = \dfrac{1650}{x+10}$ [Apply distributive property]

$\Rightarrow 16500(x + 10) = 1650(11x)$ [Cross-multiply]

$\Rightarrow 16500x + 165000 = 18150x$ [Apply distributive property]

$\Rightarrow 1650x = 165000$ [Subtract 16500x from both sides]

$\Rightarrow x = 165000 \div 1650 = 100$ [Divide both sides by 1650]

Therefore, the amount of time it takes Turbine X to produce 1650 mega watts of electricity
$\Rightarrow 100 + 10 = 110$ hours

And, the amount of electricity generated by Turbine X in 1 hour $= \dfrac{1650}{x+10} = \dfrac{1650}{100+10} = \dfrac{1650}{110} = 15$ mw

THIS PAGE HAS BEEN INTENTIONALLY LEFT BLANK

THIS PAGE HAS BEEN INTENTIONALLY LEFT BLANK

PART 1.0: ARITHMETIC WORD PROBLEMS:

TABLE OF CONTENTS:

PART 1.0: ARITHMETIC WORD PROBLEMS:...31
    1.1: Basic Arithmetic Operations:...32
    1.2: Advanced Arithmetic Word Problems: 34
    1.3: Part-Whole Arithmetic Word Problems:...36
    1.4: Multiple Operations Arithmetic Word Problems:..37
    Practice Exercise – Questions and Answers With Explanations: Arithmetic Word Problems: 38

1.1: BASIC ARITHMETIC OPERATIONS:

(A) ADDITION:

Example #1:   If John has $2.25 and he gets another $6.25, how much money does he have?
Solution: $\Rightarrow$ $2.25 + $6.25 = $8.50

Example #2:   If John has $\$\dfrac{10}{9}$ and he gets another $\$\dfrac{15}{9}$, how much money does he have?

Solution: $\Rightarrow \dfrac{10}{9} + \dfrac{15}{9} = \dfrac{25}{9} = 2\dfrac{7}{9}$

Example #3:   If John glues a wooden piece of pine that is 11/2 inches thick with a piece of oak that is 12/5 inches thick, what is the total thickness, in inches, of the wooden table?

Solution: $\Rightarrow \dfrac{11}{2} + \dfrac{12}{5} = \dfrac{55}{10} + \dfrac{24}{10} = \dfrac{79}{10} = 7\dfrac{9}{10}$

(B) SUBTRACTION:

Example #4:   If John has $8.50 and he loses $2.25, how much money does he have left?
Solution: $\Rightarrow$ $8.50 − $2.25 = $6.25

Example #5:   If John has $25/9 and he loses $10/9, how much money does he have left?

Solution: $\Rightarrow \dfrac{25}{9} - \dfrac{10}{9} = \dfrac{15}{9} = \dfrac{5}{3} = 1\dfrac{2}{3}$

Example #6:   A wooden table is made of pine and oak and is 79/10 inches thick. If John slices the wooden table and takes out the piece of pine that is 12/5 inches thick, what is the total thickness, in inches, of the oak part of the remaining wooden table?

Solution: $\Rightarrow \dfrac{79}{10} - \dfrac{12}{5} = \dfrac{79}{10} - \dfrac{24}{10} = \dfrac{55}{10} = \dfrac{11}{2} = 5\dfrac{1}{2}$

(C) MULTIPLICATION:

Example #7:   If a mixture costs $0.50 per pound, how much should 22.5 pounds cost?
Solution: $\Rightarrow$ 22.5 × 0.50 = $11.25

Example #8:   If a mixture costs $\$\dfrac{2}{5}$ per pound, how much should $\dfrac{27}{2}$ pounds cost?

Solution: $\Rightarrow \dfrac{2}{5} \times \dfrac{27}{2} = \dfrac{54}{10} = \dfrac{27}{5} = \$5\dfrac{2}{5}$

(D) DIVISION:

Example #9:   If a mixture costs $0.50 per pound, how much can be bought for $11.25?
Solution: $\Rightarrow$ 11.25 ÷ 0.50 = 22.5 pounds

Example #10:   A worker grinds a pound of mixture in 2/5 of an hour, and if he works for 27/5 hours, how many pounds will he grind?

Solution: $\Rightarrow \dfrac{27}{5} \div \dfrac{2}{5} = \dfrac{27}{5} \times \dfrac{5}{2} = \dfrac{27}{2} = 13\dfrac{1}{2}$ pounds

(E) SIGNED NUMBERS:

Example #11: A store made a profit of $7.15 on Monday, profit of $5.10 on Tuesday, profit of $9.20 on Wednesday, profit of $2.25 on Thursday, loss of $1.11 on Friday, profit of $6.05 on Saturday, loss of $8.14 on Sunday. What was its total profit (or loss) for the whole week?

Solution: $\Rightarrow 7.15 + 5.10 + 9.20 + 2.25 + (-1.11) + 6.05 + (-8.14) = 29.75 - 9.25 = 20.50$

(F) COMPLEX FRACTIONS:

Example #12: It takes 2¼ hours to get from Washington DC to New York traveling at a constant rate of speed. What part of the distance is traveled in 1¾ hours?

Solution:
$$\Rightarrow \frac{1\frac{3}{4}}{2\frac{1}{4}} = \frac{\frac{7}{4}}{\frac{9}{4}} = \frac{7}{4} \div \frac{9}{4} = \frac{7}{\cancel{4}} \times \frac{\cancel{4}}{9} = \frac{7}{9}$$

1.2: ADVANCED ARITHMETIC WORD PROBLEMS:

NUMBER LINE:

Example #1: On a real number line, what is the midpoint of –5 and 19?
Solution: Number of units between –5 & 19 $\Rightarrow$ 19 – (–5) = 24, and half of the difference is 24 ÷ 2 = 12
Midpoint between –5 & 19 $\Rightarrow$ –5 + 12 = 7   OR   19 – 12 = 7

PLACE VALUE:

Example #2: What is the units digit of $(2)^1(15)^2(69)^3(92)^4$?
Solution:
Units digit of $(2)^1$ $\Rightarrow$ since 2 × 1 = 2 $\Rightarrow$ 2
Units digit of $(15)^2$ $\Rightarrow$ since 5 × 5 = 25 $\Rightarrow$ 5
Units digit of $(69)^3$ $\Rightarrow$ since 9 × 9 × 9 = 729 $\Rightarrow$ 9
Units digit of $(92)^4$ $\Rightarrow$ since 2 × 2 × 2 × 2 = 16 $\Rightarrow$ 6
Units digit of $(2)^1(15)^2(69)^3(92)^4$ $\Rightarrow$ since 2 × 5 × 9 × 6 = 540 $\Rightarrow$ 0

ABSOLUTE VALUE:

Example #3: Following is the set of points on a real number line, which point has the highest absolute value?
{–1.95, –0.25, 0, 0.85, 1.75}
Solution: Highest Absolute Value $\Rightarrow$ |–1.95| = 1.95

SCIENTIFIC NOTATION:

Example #4: If $x = 1.2 \times 10^7$ and $y = 5.6 \times 10^{-9}$, what is the value of xy in terms of scientific notation?
Solution: Value of xy $\Rightarrow (1.2 \times 10^7)(5.6 \times 10^{-9})$
                   $\Rightarrow (1.2 \times 5.6)(10^7 \times 10^{-9})$
                   $\Rightarrow 6.72 \times 10^{-2}$

MULTIPLES & LCM:

Example #5: John has two types of digital beepers, one that beeps every 2 seconds and the other that beeps every 9 seconds. If both beepers are turned on at exactly the same time, how many times during the next hour will both beepers beep at the same time?
Solution: LCM of 2 & 9 = 18 $\Rightarrow$ the beepers will beep together at the same time every 18 seconds.
1 Hour = 60 minutes = 3,600 Seconds.
Number of simultaneous beeps in an hour $\Rightarrow$ 3,600 ÷ 18 = 200 times

Example #6: The employees of a certain company can be separated into 16 groups with an equal number of employees in each group or into 18 groups with an equal number of employees in each group. What is the lowest possible number of employees in the company?
Solution: The lowest possible number of employees in the company is a lowest number that can be divided evenly by 16 and 18.
Prime Factors of 16 $\Rightarrow$ 2 × 2 × 2 × 2
Prime Factors of 18 $\Rightarrow$ 2 × 3 × 3
LCM of 16 & 18 $\Rightarrow$ 2 × 2 × 2 × 2 × 3 × 3 = 144
Therefore, the lowest possible number of employees in the company is 144.

FACTORS & GCF:

Example #7: If a is the greatest prime factor of 68 and b is the greatest prime factor of 100, what is the value of $a + b$?
Solution: Greatest Prime Factor of 68 $\Rightarrow a$ = 17
Greatest Prime Factor of 100 $\Rightarrow b$ = 5

Value of $a + b \Rightarrow 17 + 5 = 22$

Example #8: The product of the integers, p, q, r, s, and t is 2310, where $t > s > r > q > p > 0$. What is the value of $p + r + t$?

Solution: Since $t > s > r > q > p > 0$, it means that all five integers are positive integers and none of them can be of the same value.
Prime Factorization of 2310 $\Rightarrow$ (2)(3)(5)(7)(11) = 2310
Since there are only 5 prime factors $\Rightarrow p = 2$, $q = 3$, $r = 5$, $s = 7$, $t = 11$.
Value of $(p + r + t) = 2 + 5 + 11 = 18$

PRIME NUMBERS:

Example #9: What is the quotient of product and sum of the first five prime numbers?

Solution: Product of the first five prime numbers $\Rightarrow 2 \times 3 \times 5 \times 7 \times 11 \Rightarrow 2310$
Sum of the first five prime numbers $\Rightarrow 2 + 3 + 5 + 7 + 11 \Rightarrow 28$
Quotient of product and sum of the first five prime numbers $\Rightarrow 2310 \div 28 = 82.5$

Example #10: If x, y, and z are distinct prime numbers less than 25, what is the greatest possible value of $\dfrac{x + y}{z}$?

Solution: To find the greatest possible value of any fraction, the numerator should be the largest possible and the denominator should be the smallest possible. Keeping this point in mind, let's pick the two largest prime numbers less than 25 for x and y, which are 23 and 19, and the smallest prime number less than 25 for z, which is 2.

$$\Rightarrow \frac{x + y}{z} = \frac{23 + 19}{2} = \frac{42}{2} = 21$$

1.3: PART-WHOLE ARITHMETIC WORD PROBLEMS:

Some word problems describe how different quantities are related to one another. They typically provide some specific relationships between the two or more quantities at a given time based on their sum, difference, product, and/or quotient. These relationships need to be transformed into algebraic equations. The key to solving these types of word problems is to realize that sum of all the parts equals their whole.

These types of word problems have one or more of the information given, and you will be asked to determine the value of one or more of the quantities that are unknown.

EZ STEP-BY-STEP METHOD: Apply the following step(s) to solve any "Parts = Whole" Word Problems:

STEP 1: Assign a different letter (variable) for each quantity.

STEP 2: Establish relationships between the values of two or more quantities in the problem.

STEP 3: Transform the relationships between the values of two or more quantities into algebraic equations such that the sum of all the parts equals their whole.

STEP 4: Solve the expression/equations formed, and determine the unknowns or the missing quantities.

EZ REFERENCE: For more in-depth knowledge about part-whole relationship, refer to our Arithmetic Module.

Example #1: Jason lost one-fourth of his baseball cards, and Tyson took one-third of what was left. Tyson then gave one-half of his cards to Nelson. What fractional part of Jason's cards did Nelson have?

Solution: No. of Cards that Jason has Originally $\Rightarrow 1$

No. of Card Jason has after he Lost ¼ of his Cards $\Rightarrow 1 - \dfrac{1}{4} = \dfrac{3}{4}$

No. of Cards Jason gave to Tyson $\Rightarrow \dfrac{1}{3} \times \dfrac{3}{4} = \dfrac{1}{4}$

No. of Cards Tyson gave to Nelson $\Rightarrow \dfrac{1}{2} \times \dfrac{1}{4} = \dfrac{1}{8}$

Example #2: In a certain investment portfolio, one-half of the money is invested in stocks, one-fourth in bonds, one-sixth in mutual funds, and the remaining $15,000 in money market account, what is the total amount of the investment portfolio?

Solution: Fraction of Funds Invested in Stocks, Bonds, and Mutual Fund $\Rightarrow \dfrac{1}{2} + \dfrac{1}{4} + \dfrac{1}{6} = \dfrac{6}{12} + \dfrac{3}{12} + \dfrac{2}{12} = \dfrac{11}{12}$

Fraction of Funds Invested in Money Market $\Rightarrow 1 - \dfrac{11}{12} = \dfrac{12}{12} - \dfrac{11}{12} = \dfrac{1}{12}$

$\Rightarrow \dfrac{1}{12}x = 15,000$

$\Rightarrow x = 15,000 \times 12 = \$180,000$

Therefore, the total amount of the investment portfolio is $180,000.

1.4: MULTIPLE OPERATIONS ARITHMETIC WORD PROBLEMS:

Example #1:   John's monthly take home salary is $2,000. Every month, he pays $650 in rent, $125 in car installment, $98 in health insurance, and $27 for phone access. After paying for all these regular expenses, he evenly divides the remaining money between savings and miscellaneous expenses. How much money will he save after one year?

Solution:

Monthly Take-Home Salary	$\Rightarrow$ $2,000
Monthly Regular Expenses	$\Rightarrow$ $650 + $125 + $98 + $27 = $900
Remaining Money after paying Regular Expenses	$\Rightarrow$ $2,000 − $900 = $1,100
Miscellaneous Expenses	$\Rightarrow$ $1,100 ÷ 2 = $550
Monthly Savings	$\Rightarrow$ $1,100 ÷ 2 = $550
Annual Savings	$\Rightarrow$ $550 × 12 = $6,600

Example #2:   During a special sale, Julia buys five chairs for $199 each and 2 tables for $250 each. If she paid one-fifth of the total as down payment and the remaining in 8 equal monthly installments, what is the amount of each month's payment?

Solution:

Cost of 5 Chairs for $199 each	$\Rightarrow$ $199 × 5	$\Rightarrow$ $995
Cost of 2 Tables for $250 each	$\Rightarrow$ $250 × 2	$\Rightarrow$ +$500
Total Cost		$\Rightarrow$ $1,495
Down Payment	$\Rightarrow$ 0.20 × $1,495	$\Rightarrow$ −$299
Remaining Balance		$\Rightarrow$ $1,196
Monthly Installment for 8 months	$\Rightarrow$ $1,196 ÷ 8	$\Rightarrow$ $149.50

PRACTICE EXERCISE – QUESTIONS AND ANSWERS WITH EXPLANATIONS: ARITHMETIC WORD PROBLEMS:

Question #1: If John walks into a store and buys items worth $2.19 and $5.43, how much money did he spend?
Solution: $\Rightarrow$ $2.19 + $5.43 = $7.62

Question #2: If John has $\$\dfrac{8}{7}$ and he gets another $\$\dfrac{12}{7}$, how much money does he have?

Solution: $\Rightarrow \dfrac{8}{7} + \dfrac{12}{7} = \dfrac{20}{7} = 2\dfrac{6}{7}$

Question #3: John has baskets of apples containing 24 apples each. He gives 19 apples to his male friends and 11 apples to his female friends. How many baskets of apples did John give out to his friends?
Solution: $\Rightarrow \dfrac{19}{24} + \dfrac{11}{24} = \dfrac{30}{24} = \dfrac{5}{4} = 1\dfrac{1}{4}$

Question #4: If John walks into a store with $7.62 and walks out with $5.43, how much money did he spend?
Solution: $\Rightarrow$ $7.62 – $5.43 = $2.19

Question #5: If John has $\$\dfrac{20}{7}$ and he loses $\$\dfrac{8}{7}$, how much money does he have left?

Solution: $\Rightarrow \dfrac{20}{7} - \dfrac{8}{7} = \dfrac{12}{7} = 1\dfrac{5}{7}$

Question #6: If John walks in to a store with $\$\dfrac{79}{10}$ and walks out with $\$\dfrac{12}{5}$, how much money did he spend?

Solution: $\Rightarrow \dfrac{79}{10} - \dfrac{12}{5} = \dfrac{79}{10} - \dfrac{24}{10} = \dfrac{55}{10} = \dfrac{11}{2} = 5\dfrac{1}{2}$

Question #7: If a mixture costs $12.9 per pound, how much should 15.2 pounds cost?
Solution: $\Rightarrow$ 12.9 × 15.2 = $196.08

Question #8: A worker gets paid $\dfrac{5}{2}$ dollars per hour if he works for $\dfrac{12}{25}$ hours, how much does he make?

Solution: $\Rightarrow \dfrac{5}{2} \times \dfrac{12}{25} = \dfrac{6}{5} = 1\dfrac{1}{5}$

Question #9: If a mixture costs $12.9 per pound, how much can be bought for $196.08?
Solution: $\Rightarrow$ 196.08 ÷ 12.9 = 15.2 pounds

Question #10: A worker gets paid $\$\dfrac{5}{2}$ per hour if he makes $\$\dfrac{6}{5}$, how many hours does he work?

Solution: $\Rightarrow \dfrac{6}{5} \div \dfrac{5}{2} = \dfrac{6}{5} \times \dfrac{2}{5} = \dfrac{12}{25}$ hours

Question #11: At midnight, the temperature of a town was 56°F. A weatherman observed the following temperature changes at every two-hour period over the course of the next eight hours: a rise of 12°F, then a fall of 5°F, then a rise of 17°F, and then a fall of 2°F. What was the temperature at the end of the eight-hour period?
Solution: $\Rightarrow$ 56°F + 12°F + (–5°F) + 17°F + (–2°F) = 85°F + (–7°F) = 78°F

Question #12: It takes 2 1/5 hours to get from Washington DC to New York traveling at a constant rate of speed. What part of the distance is traveled in 1 2/5 hours?

Solution:
$$\Rightarrow \frac{1\frac{2}{5}}{2\frac{1}{5}} = \frac{\frac{7}{5}}{\frac{11}{5}} = \frac{7}{5} \div \frac{11}{5} = \frac{7}{5} \times \frac{5}{11} = \frac{7}{11}$$

Question #13: On a number line, if you start at −1 and then go 2 units to the right, then 6 units to the left, then 11 units to the right, and then 15 units to the left, where will you end up?

Solution: Starting Point $\Rightarrow -1$
Then, 2 units to the right $\Rightarrow -1 + 2 = +1$
Then, 6 units to the left $\Rightarrow +1 - 6 = -5$
Then, 11 units to the right$\Rightarrow -5 + 11 = +6$
Then, 15 units to the left $\Rightarrow +6 - 15 = -9$
Therefore, you'll end up at −9.

Question #14: What is the units digit of $(83)^4(79)^3(11)^2(9)^1$?
Solution: Units digit of $(83)^4$ $\Rightarrow$ since $3 \times 3 \times 3 \times 3 = 81$ $\Rightarrow 1$
Units digit of $(79)^3$ $\Rightarrow$ since $9 \times 9 \times 9 = 729$ $\Rightarrow 9$
Units digit of $(11)^2$ $\Rightarrow$ since $1 \times 1 = 1$ $\Rightarrow 1$
Units digit of $(9)^1$ $\Rightarrow$ since $9 \times 1 = 9$ $\Rightarrow 9$
Units digit of $(83)^4(79)^3(11)^2(9)^1$ $\Rightarrow$ since $1 \times 9 \times 1 \times 9 = 81$ $\Rightarrow 1$

Question #15: If $n = 11.5799$ and t is the decimal number obtained by rounding n to the nearest tenths and h is the decimal number obtained by rounding n to the nearest hundredths, what is the value of $t - h$?
Solution: Value of $n = 11.5799$
Round-off n to the nearest tenths $\Rightarrow t = 11.6$
Round-off n to the nearest hundredths $\Rightarrow h = 11.58$
Value of $t - h \Rightarrow 11.6 - 11.58 = 0.02$

Question #16: Following is the set of points on a real number line, which point has the highest absolute value?
{−1.99, −0.27, 0, 0.86, 1.88}
Solution: Highest Absolute value is $|-1.99| = 1.99$

Question #17: For a certain type of beverage, the amount of preservatives is 1.2×10^{-9} parts per gallon. In an effort to increase the shelf life of the beverage, the amount of preservatives in the new and improved beverage was increased by 100 times. What was the amount of the preservatives in the new beverage? (Express your answer in scientific notation.)
Solution: Amount of preservatives in the original beverage $\Rightarrow 1.2 \times 10^{-9}$ parts per gallon
Amount of preservatives in the new beverage $\Rightarrow (1.2 \times 10^{-9}) \times 100$ parts per gallon
                                                $\Rightarrow (1.2 \times 10^{-9}) \times 10^2$
                                              $\Rightarrow 1.2 \times 10^{-9+2}$
                                              $\Rightarrow 1.2 \times 10^{-7}$ parts per gallon

Question #18: Last year, a certain country had a gross income of $\$6.6 \times 10^{15}$. If the population of the country was 550 million last year, what was the gross per capita income? (Express your answer in scientific notation.)
Solution: Gross Per Capita Income $\Rightarrow$ Gross Income ÷ Population
$$\Rightarrow \frac{6.6 \times 10^{15}}{550,000,000} = \frac{6.6 \times 10^{15}}{5.5 \times 10^8} = \frac{6.6}{5.5} \times \frac{10^{15}}{10^8} = 1.2 \times 10^{15-8} = 1.2 \times 10^7$$

Question #19: Ryan has three types of digital beepers, the first one beeps every 2 minutes, the second one beeps every 6 minutes, and the third one beeps every 8 minutes. If all three beepers beep at exactly 12:00 am, after how many minutes will all three beepers beep again next at the same time?
Solution: LCM of 2, 6, & 8 = 24 $\Rightarrow$ all three beepers will beep at the same time every 24 minutes.
Therefore, all three beepers will beep again simultaneously after 24 minutes.

Question #20: A wire is cut into three equal parts. The resulting segments are then cut into 2, 6, and 8 equal parts respectively. If each of the resulting segments has an integer length, what is the minimum possible length of the wire?

Solution: Since the rope has to be divided into 3 equal parts, each with an integer length, so the minimum length must be a multiple of 3.

Now the resulting segments are further divided into 2, 6, and 8 equal parts, so the minimum length of each segment must be a multiple of 2, 6, and 8.

In short, the minimum possible length of each of the three segments of the rope must be the least common multiple (LCM) of 2, 6, and 8; which is 24.

Now since there are three such segments, the minimum possible length of the wire must be 3 × 24 = 72.

Question #21: What is the smallest positive integer greater than 1 that leaves a remainder of 1 when divided by any of the integers 5, 6, and 8?

Solution: Let's first find the least common multiple (LCM) of 5, 6, and 8, and then add 1 to it.

Prime Factors of 5   ⇒ 1 × 5
Prime Factors of 6   ⇒ 2 × 3
Prime Factors of 8   ⇒ 2 × 2 × 2
LCM of 5, 6, and 8   ⇒ 1 × 5 × 2 × 3 × 2 × 2 = 120

Therefore, the smallest integer greater than 1 that leaves a remainder of 1 when divided by any of the integers 5, 6, and 8 is 120 + 1 = 121.

Question #22: A number is "witty" if it is a multiple of 2 or 3. How many witty numbers are there between –11 and 11?

Solution: There are 15 witty numbers that are multiples of 2 or 3 between –11 and 11 ⇒ 2, 3, 4, 6, 8, 9, 10, and their opposites and 0.

Question #23: A number is "goofy if it is a multiple of 2 and 3. How many goofy numbers are there between –25 and 25?

Solution: There are 9 goofy numbers that are multiples of 2 and 3 between –25 and 25 ⇒ 6, 12, 18, 24, and their opposites and 0.

Question #24: How many multiples of 3 are there among the integers 15 through 105 inclusive?

Solution: Let's try to make a list of multiple of 3 from 15 though 105 inclusive:

⇒ 3 × 5 = 15   ⇒ 3 × 6 = 18   ⇒ 3 × 7 = 21   ⇒ 3 × 8 = 24   ⇒ 3 × 9 = 27   ⇒ 3 × 10 = 30
....   ⇒ 3 × 34 = 102 ⇒ 3 × 35 = 105

As shown above, the multiples of 3 from 15 through 105 inclusive can be obtained by multiplying 3 by each of the integers 5 through 35 inclusive. The answer to this question should be the number of integers from 5 through 35 inclusive ⇒ 35 – 5 = 30 plus 1 for the first entry, that is, there are 31 integers among the integers 5 through 35 inclusive. Therefore, the number of multiples of 3 that are there among the integers 15 through 105 inclusive is 31.

Question #25: How many multiples of 5 are there among the integers 15 through 105 inclusive?

Solution: Let's try to make a list of multiple of 5 from 15 though 105 inclusive:

⇒ 5 × 3 = 15   ⇒ 5 × 4 = 20   ⇒ 5 × 5 = 25   ⇒ 5 × 6 = 30   ⇒ 5 × 7 = 35   ⇒ 5 × 8 = 40
....   ⇒ 5 × 20 = 100 ⇒ 5 × 21 = 105

As shown above, the multiples of 5 from 15 through 105 inclusive can be obtained by multiplying 5 by each of the integers 3 through 21 inclusive. The answer to this question should be the number of integers from 3 through 21 inclusive ⇒ 21 – 3 = 18 plus 1 for the first entry, that is, there are 19 integers among the integers 3 through 21 inclusive. Therefore, the number of multiples of 5 that are there among the integers 15 through 105 inclusive is 19.

Question #26: How many multiples of 3 and 5 are there among the integers 15 through 105 inclusive?

Solution: For any integer to be a multiple of both, 3 and 5, it has to be a multiple of 3 × 5 = 15.

Now let's try to make a list of multiple of 15 from 15 though 105 inclusive:

⇒ 15 × 1 = 15   ⇒ 15 × 2 = 30   ⇒ 15 × 3 = 45   ⇒ 15 × 4 = 60   ⇒ 15 × 5 = 75   ⇒ 15 × 6 = 90
⇒ 15 × 7 = 105

As shown above, the multiples of 3 and 5 from 15 through 105 inclusive can be obtained by multiplying 15 by each of the integers 1 through 7 inclusive. The answer to this question should be the number of integers from 1 through 7 inclusive ⇒ 7 − 1 = 6 plus 1 for the first entry, that is, there are 7 integers among the integers 1 through 7 inclusive. Therefore, the number of multiples of 3 and 5 that are there among the integers 15 through 105 inclusive is 7.

Question #27: A jar of candies could be divided among 6 students, 8 students, or 10 students, with each student getting the same number of candies, and with only 1 candy left over in each case for the teacher. What is the least possible number of candies that could be in the jar?

Solution: When the candies in the jar are divided evenly among the 6, 8, or 10 students, there is always 1 candy left over for the teacher. This implies if there were no candy left for the teacher, then the number of candies in the jar should be evenly divisible by 6, 8, and 10 with no remainder. In other words, we need to find the LCM of 6, 8, and 10 and then add 1 to find the least number of candies that could be in the jar.
Prime Factorization of 6, 8, 10
Prime Factors of 6   ⇒ 2 × 3
Prime Factors of 8   ⇒ 2 × 2 × 2
Prime Factors of 10 ⇒ 2 × 5
LCM of 6,8, and 10 ⇒ 2 × 2 × 2 × 3 × 5 = 120
Therefore, the least possible number of candies that could be in the jar is 120 + 1 = 121.

Question #28: There is a stack of postcards, each with a distinct number written on them from 1 through 150, inclusive, and a winning card is the one which has a number written on it that is divisible by 2, 6, and as well as 8. How many winning cards are there?

Solution: LCM of 2, 6, and 8 = 24
No. of integers between 1 and 150 that are evenly divisible by 2, 6, & 8 are the multiples of the LCM
Therefore, there are 6 winning cards (24, 48, 72, 96, 120, 144).

Question #29: What is the LCM of 1 through 9, inclusive?
Solution: ⇒ 1 = 1^1 ⇒ 2 = 2^1 ⇒ 3 = 3^1 ⇒ 4 = 2^2 ⇒ 5 = 5^1
⇒ 6 = $2^1 × 3^1$ ⇒ 7 = 7^1 ⇒ 8 = 2^3 ⇒ 9 = 3^2
LCM of 1, 2, 3, 4, 5, 6, 7, 8, and 9 ⇒ $1^1 × 2^3 × 3^2 × 5^1 × 7^1$ = 2,520

Question #30: What is the smallest positive integer that is evenly divisible by both 18 and 28?
Solution: Prime Factors of 18 ⇒ 2 × 3 × 3
Prime Factors of 28 ⇒ 2 × 2 × 7
LCM of 18 & 28   ⇒ 2 × 3 × 3 × 2 × 7 = 252
Therefore, the smallest possible positive integer that is evenly divisible by both 18 and 28 is 252.

Question #31: It takes John exactly 20 minutes to change oil in a car and Tom only needs 15 minutes to change oil in a car. If they both start changing oil at 8 A.M. without any gap in between, what is the first time they will finish changing the oil in a car at the same time?

Solution: Since John will finish J cars after J × 20 minutes and Tom will finish T cars after T × 15 minutes, they will both finish changing oil in a car at the same time when J × 20 = T × 15. Since J ant T, which represents the number of cars, must be integers, this question is asking you to find a common multiple of 20 and 15. Since the question is asking for the first time they will finish at the same time, we essentially have to find the LEAST common multiple (LCM)
Prime factors of 20 ⇒ 2 × 2 × 5
Prime factors of 15 ⇒ 3 × 5
LCM of 20 & 15   ⇒ 2 × 2 × 5 × 3 = 60
⇒ So John and Tom will finish changing oil in a car at the same time 60 minutes after they start, or at 9 A.M. By this time, John will have changed oil in 3 cars and Tom will have changed oil in 4 cars.

Question #32: If m and n are both integers greater than 1 and if n is a factor of $m + 5$ and $m + 12$, what is the value of n?
Solution: Since n is a factor of both, $m + 5$ and $m + 12$, n must be the difference of $m + 5$ and $m + 12$
Value of n ⇒ $(m + 12) − (m + 5) = m + 12 − m − 5 = 7$

Question #33: How many positive integers are both multiples of 8 and divisors of 128?
Solution: Multiple of 8:   ⇒ 8, 16, 24, 32, 40, 48, 56, 64, 72, 80, 88, 96, 104, 112, 120, 128

Divisors of 128: $\Rightarrow$ 128, 64, 32, 16, 8
There are only 5 positive integers that are both multiples of 8 and divisors of 128 $\Rightarrow$ 8, 16, 32, 64, 128

Question #34: How many different positive integers are factors of 88?
Solution: Factor Pairs of 88 $\Rightarrow$ 1 × 88, 2 × 44, 4 × 22, 8 × 11
Different Factors of 88 $\Rightarrow$ 1, 2, 4, 8, 11, 22, 44, and 88 $\Rightarrow$ 8 different factors

Question #35: What is the greatest common prime factor of 16 and 24?
Solution: Factors of 16 $\Rightarrow$ 1, 2, 4, 8, 16
Factors of 24 $\Rightarrow$ 1, 2, 3, 4, 6, 8, 12, 24
Greatest Common Prime Factor of 16 & 24 $\Rightarrow$ 2 (note: none of the other common factors are prime)

Question #36: What is the greatest common prime factor of 56 and 98?
Solution: Factors of 56 $\Rightarrow$ 1, 2, 4, 7, 8, 14, 28, 56
Factors of 98 $\Rightarrow$ 1, 2, 7, 14, 49, 98
Greatest Common Prime Factor of 56 & 98 $\Rightarrow$ 7

Question #37: What is the greatest integer that will divide evenly into both 51 and 68?
Solution: Factors of 51 $\Rightarrow$ 1, 3, 17, 51
Factors of 68 $\Rightarrow$ 1, 2, 4, 17, 34, 68
Greatest Common of 51 & 68 $\Rightarrow$ 17

Question #38: What is the greatest positive integer n such that 2^n is a factor of 12^{10}?
Solution: Factors of 12^{10} $\Rightarrow$ $(2 \times 2 \times 3)^{10} = 2^{10} \times 2^{10} \times 3^{10} = 2^{20} \times 3^{10}$
If 2^n is a factor of 12^{10}, then n must be 20

Question #39: If 2, 7, and 11 are factors of the integer n, then what other numbers must also be factors of n?
Solution: Since the prime factors of n are 2, 7, and 11, we know that n must also be a factor of all the possible prime products:
$\Rightarrow$ 2 × 7 = 14
$\Rightarrow$ 2 × 11 = 22
$\Rightarrow$ 7 × 11 = 77
$\Rightarrow$ 2 × 7 × 11 = 154
So, without even knowing what n is, we have found 4 more of its factors: 14, 22, 77, and 154.

Question #40: How many prime less than 1000 are divisible by 11?
Solution: Since the definition of a prime number is that it should have only two distinct factors 1 and itself, there is only one prime less than 1000 that is divisible by 11, which is 11 itself. All other primes will only be divisible by 1 and themselves, and definitely not 11, or any other number.

Question #41: How many prime numbers are there between 0 and 25?
Solution: Prime Numbers between 0 – 25 $\Rightarrow$ 2, 3, 5, 7, 11, 13, 17, 19, 23 $\Rightarrow$ total of 9 prime numbers
Note: 1 is not a prime number and 2 is the smallest prime number.

Question #42: What is the sum of all the prime numbers that are greater than 80 and less than 90?
Solution: Sum of Prime Numbers between 80 and 90 $\Rightarrow$ 83 + 89 = 172

Question #43: What is the greatest integer that is a sum of four distinct prime numbers, each less than 20?
Solution: Greatest sum of four distinct prime numbers, each less than 20 $\Rightarrow$ 19 + 17 + 13 + 11 = 60

Question #44: How many integers greater than 10 and less than 20 are each the product of exactly two different numbers, both of which are prime?
Solution: First, list all the numbers between 10 and 20, and then write them as factor pairs, both of which should be prime numbers. There are only two such integers $\Rightarrow$ 14 (2 × 7) and 15 (3 × 5).

Question #45: If the sum of seven different prime numbers is an even number, what is the value of the smallest of the seven prime numbers?

Solution: To answer this question correctly, you must know the rules of odd and even numbers. If the sum of odd number of terms is even, either all terms must be even or exactly one or any other odd number of the terms must be even. Hence, the only time the sum of seven odd numbers can be even is when exactly one of them is even or three, or five, or all seven of them are even. Since we are dealing with prime numbers, there is only one even prime number, which is 2, all the rest are odd.
Therefore, 2 must be one of the seven prime numbers, for the sum of those seven prime numbers to be even, and, of course, since 2 is the smallest prime number, the value of the smallest of the seven prime numbers is 2.

Question #46: If p, q, and r are distinct positive integers less than 25, what is the greatest possible value of $\frac{p^2-q^2}{r^2}$?

Solution: To find the greatest possible value of any fraction, the numerator should be the largest possible and the denominator should be the smallest possible. Keeping this point in mind, let's pick the largest positive integer less than 25 for p, which is 24, the smallest positive integer less than 25 for r, which is 1, and the next smallest possible integer less than 25 for q, which is 2. Don't make the mistake of picking 2 for r and 1 for q, since the value of the given fraction will be the least when it is divided by the least integer, and not subtracted.

$$\Rightarrow \frac{p^2-q^2}{r^2} = \frac{24^2-2^2}{1^2} = \frac{576-4}{1} = 572$$

Question #47: A test contains 220 questions in all. If three-fourth of the questions are math questions, and two fifth of the remaining questions are verbal questions, how many questions are verbal questions?

Solution: Total No. of Questions $\Rightarrow$ 220

Total No. of Math Questions $\Rightarrow \frac{3}{4} \times 220 = 165$

Remaining No. of Questions $\Rightarrow 220 - 165 = 55$

Total No. of Verbal Questions $\Rightarrow \frac{2}{5} \times 55 = 22$

Question #48: Sonia finished one-sixth of her homework in the morning and one-half of the remaining homework in the afternoon. What fraction of her original homework would Sonia have to do in the evening in order to finish her homework?

Solution: Part of Homework done in the Morning $\Rightarrow \frac{1}{6}$

Remaining Homework $\Rightarrow 1 - \frac{1}{6} = \frac{5}{6}$

Part of Homework done in the Afternoon $\Rightarrow \frac{1}{2} \times \frac{5}{6} = \frac{5}{12}$

Remaining Homework $\Rightarrow \frac{5}{6} - \frac{5}{12} = \frac{10}{12} - \frac{5}{12} = \frac{5}{12}$

Question #49: In a certain test, two-third of the total number of questions are math questions. Of the math questions, one-fourth of the questions are word problems. If there are a total of 96 questions in the entire test, how many questions are word problems?

Solution: Total No. of Questions $\Rightarrow$ 96

No. of Math Questions $\Rightarrow \frac{2}{3}$ of Total Questions $= \frac{2}{3}$ of 96 = 64

No. of Word Problems $\Rightarrow \frac{1}{4}$ of Math Questions $= \frac{1}{4}$ of 64 = 16

Therefore, there are 16 word problems in the entire test.

Question #50: In a certain bookstore, one-half of the books are historical books and one-third of the remaining books are political books. If there are a total of 75,000 books in the bookstore, how many books are political books?

Solution: Total No. of Books $\Rightarrow$ 75,000

No. of Historical Books $\Rightarrow \frac{1}{2}$ of All Books = $\frac{1}{2}$ of 75,000 = 37,500

Remaining Books $\Rightarrow$ Total No. of Books – Historical Books = 75,000–37,500 = 37,500

No. of Political Books $\Rightarrow \frac{1}{3}$ of Remaining Books = $\frac{1}{3}$ of 37,500 = 12,500

Therefore, there are 12,500 political books.

Question #51: Tom's monthly take home salary is $2,500. Every month, he pays $650 in rent, $125 in car installment, $98 in health insurance, and $27 for phone access. After paying for all these regular expenses, he evenly divides the remaining money between savings and miscellaneous expenses. How much money will he save after one year?

Solution:
Monthly Take-Home Salary	$\Rightarrow$ $2,500
Monthly Regular Expenses	$\Rightarrow$ $650 + $125 + $98 + $27 = $900
Remaining Money after paying Regular Expenses	$\Rightarrow$ $2,500 – $900 = $1,600
Miscellaneous Expenses	$\Rightarrow$ $1,600 ÷ 2 = $800
Monthly Savings	$\Rightarrow$ $1,600 ÷ 2 = $800
Annual Savings	$\Rightarrow$ $800 × 12 = $9,600

Question #52: Maria is making lunch bags. If she puts 2 apples in each bag, she will make 50 lunch bags and have no apples left over. If instead she puts 10 apples in each lunch bag, how many lunch bags can she make?

Solution: If Maria puts 2 apples in each lunch bag, and makes 50 lunch bags with no left over:
The total number of apples must be $\Rightarrow$ 50 × 2 = 100 apples
Therefore, the total number of apples that Maria has $\Rightarrow$ 100 apples
If instead Maria puts 10 apples in each bag, she can make $\Rightarrow$ 100 ÷ 10 = 10 lunch bags

Question #53: At a local gourmet shop 99 pounds of cheese is to be divided into pouches each weighing 1.25 pounds. How many pounds of cheese are left when there isn't enough to make another whole pouch?

Solution: Let's first find the number of whole pouches that can be made: $\Rightarrow$ 99 ÷ 1.25 = 79.2
So 79 full pouches can be made, and for that, the amount of cheese required is $\Rightarrow$ 79 × 1.25 = 98.75
Amount of cheese left over: $\Rightarrow$ 99 – 98.75 = 0.25 pounds

Question #54: In a certain shop, there were 10 crates of soda bottles. Eight crates contained 12 bottles each and the remaining crates contained 8 bottles each. If a customer buys all 10 crates, how many bottles would that be?

Solution:
8 of 12-bottle Crates	$\Rightarrow$ 8 × 12	$\Rightarrow$ 96 bottles
2 of 8-bottle Crates	$\Rightarrow$ 2 × 8	$\Rightarrow$ 16 bottles
Total No. of Bottles	$\Rightarrow$ 96 + 16	$\Rightarrow$ 112 bottles

Question #55: John bought 5 pens from a bookstore. He gave the cashier a ten-dollar bill and got back two quarters in change. John realized that the cashier accidentally gave him back too much change, and he gave one of the quarters back to the cashier. What was the price of each pen?

Solution:
First, John gave the cashier	$\Rightarrow$ $10.00 for 5 pens
He immediately got back	$\Rightarrow$ 2 quarters = $0.50
At this point, John had paid	$\Rightarrow$ $10.00 – 0.50 = $9.50
Then John gave back the cashier	$\Rightarrow$ 1 quarter = $0.25
Therefore, John paid a total of	$\Rightarrow$ $9.50 + 0.25 = $9.75 for 5 pens
Cost of each pen $\Rightarrow \Rightarrow\Rightarrow\Rightarrow \Rightarrow \Rightarrow \Rightarrow$	$\Rightarrow$ $9.75 ÷ 5 = $1.95

Question #56: The toll on the Bay Bridge is $1.00 for a van and a driver, and $0.75 for each additional passenger. If the total toll paid was $6.25, how many passengers were riding in the van?

Solution:
Total Toll paid on Bay Bridge	$\Rightarrow$ $6.25
Basic Toll for Van and Driver	$\Rightarrow$ $1.00
Extra Toll for Passengers	$\Rightarrow$ $6.25 – $1.00 = $5.25
Toll per Passenger	$\Rightarrow$ $0.75
No. of Passengers	$\Rightarrow$ $5.25 ÷ $0.75 = 7

Question #57: Tickets for a concert are $6 each, or $25 for a block of 5 tickets. What is the lowest possible cost for 27 tickets?

Solution: Price for Single Tickets   ⇒ $6
Price for a Block of 5 Tickets ⇒ $25
To find the lowest price for 27 tickets, break them into two parts:
First Part   ⇒ 25 tickets at the rate of $25 for 5 tickets ⇒ 5 × $25 ⇒ $125
Second Part ⇒ 2 tickets at the rate of $6 per ticket   ⇒ 2 × $6   ⇒ <u>$12</u>
Total Lowest Possible Cost for 27 tickets ⇒ ⇒ ⇒ ⇒ ⇒ ⇒ ⇒ ⇒   ⇒ <u>$137</u>

Question #58: Tickets for a concert are $12 each if bought directly at the window, or $50 for a block of 5 tickets if bought through a distributor. What is the amount of saving if you buy 50 tickets from the distributor?

Solution: Price for 50 Tickets, if bought directly at window ($12 per ticket)   = $12 × 50 ⇒ $600
Price for 50 Tickets, if bought through distributor (10 blocks, $50 per block) = $50 × 10 ⇒ <u>$500</u>
Savings ⇒   ⇒ <u>$100</u>

Question #59: A company projects an annual sale of $975,000, with equal amount of sales each month. If, at the end of the seventh month, the total sales were $577,875, by how did the company exceed its projections?

Solution: Annual Projected Sale   ⇒ $975,000
Monthly Projected Sale   ⇒ $975,000 ÷ 12 = $81,250
Projected Sale for 7 months ⇒ $81,250 × 7 = $568,750
Actual Sale for 7 months   ⇒ $577,875
Actual Sale – Projected Sale ⇒ $577,875 – $568,750 = $9,125

Question #60: John runs from Monday to Friday. On Monday, he runs 10 miles. On Tuesday, he ran twice as much as Monday. On Wednesday, he ran 2 more mile than he did on Tuesday. On Thursday, he ran 6 fewer than he did on Wednesday. On Friday, he ran quarter the sum of what he ran on the previous four days. How many miles did he run in the entire week?

Solution: Let's translate one sentence at a time:
Monday   ⇒ he ran 10 miles   ⇒ 10 miles
Tuesday   ⇒ he ran twice as much as Monday   ⇒ 2(Monday) = 2(10) = 20
Wednesday ⇒ he ran 2 more mile than he did on Tuesday   ⇒ Tuesday + 2 = 20 + 2 = 22
Thursday   ⇒ he ran 6 fewer miles than he did on Wednesday ⇒ Wednesday – 6 = 22 – 6 = 16
On Friday, he ran quarter the sum of what he ran on the previous four days:
⇒ ¼(Monday + Tuesday + Wednesday + Thursday) = ¼(10 + 20 + 22 + 16) = ¼(68) = 17
Miles ran in the entire week   ⇒ 10 + 20 + 22 + 16 + 17 = 85 miles

Question #61: A certain type of batteries is sold in packs of 52 for $10.92 and in packs of 26 for $7.28. A customer who wants to buy 52 batteries could buy either one pack of 52 or two packs of 26. How much will the customer save for each battery if he buys the larger pack instead of the smaller pack?

Solution: Price per Battery for Large packs of 52 for $10.92   ⇒ $10.92 ÷ 52 = $0.21
Price per Battery for Small packs of 26 for $7.28   ⇒ $7.28 ÷ 26 = $0.28
Difference in Price per Battery for Large & Small pack ⇒ $0.28 – $0.21 = $0.07

Question #62: There are just enough candies in a bag to give 12 candies to each of 20 children. If 5 of the children do not want any candy, how many pieces of candies can be given to each of the remaining children?

Solution: Total No. of Candies in the Bag   ⇒ 12 × 20 = 240
Total No. of Children   ⇒ 20
No. of Children who don't want Candies   ⇒ 5
Remaining No. of Children who want Candies   ⇒ 20 – 5 = 15
No. of Candies to be given to the Remaining 15 Children ⇒ 240 ÷ 15 = 16

Question #63: A group can charter a particular aircraft at a fixed total cost. If 72 people charter the aircraft rather than 80 people, then the cost per person is greater by $12. What is the cost per person if 80 people charter the aircraft?

Solution: Since when 8 people drop out, the additional cost per person for the remaining 72 people is $12, the total additional cost to all 72 people ⇒ 12 × 72 = 864

Now this total additional cost must be the cost that those 8 people would have paid ⇒ 864 ÷ 8 = 108
Therefore, cost per person if 80 people charter the aircraft is $108

Question #64: A group of 8 people charter a ferry and agree to contribute equally towards the total charter cost of $680. If each person contributes equally to a $120 advance payment to reserve the ferry, how much will each person still have to pay to charter the ferry?

Solution:
Total Cost to Charter the Ferry   ⇒ $680
Advance Payment   ⇒ $120
Remaining Payment   ⇒ $680 – $120 = $560
Remaining Payment per Person   ⇒ $560 ÷ 8 = $70

Question #65: A certain photography store charges $1.85 for the first print and $0.75 for each additional print. How many prints of a particular photograph can one get for $20?

Solution:
Total Budget for Printing   ⇒ $20
Cost of First Print   ⇒ $1.85
Remaining Budget after the First Print ⇒ $20 – $1.85 = $18.15
Cost for each Additional Print   ⇒ $0.75
No. of Additional Prints   ⇒ $18.15 ÷ $0.75 = 24.2
Therefore, one can get 1 + 24 = 25 prints for $20.

Question #66: A certain online money transfer company imposes a surcharge of $1.25 per order on any money transfer in the amount of $25 or less, and $0.05 for each additional amount of $25 in transfer. If a man makes 2 different money transfers in the amounts of $25.50 and $127, what is the total surcharge for his money transfers?

Solution:
Surcharge for Money Transfer of $25.50   ⇒ $1.25 + 1($0.05) = $1.25 + $0.05 = $1.30
Surcharge for Money Transfer of $127   ⇒ $1.25 + 5($0.05) = $1.25 + $0.25 = $1.50
Total Surcharge for both Money Transfers ⇒ $1.30 + $1.50 = $2.80

Question #67: The sale price of a certain pen is $1.80 exclusive of sales tax. However, when 9 of these pens are bought, 1 additional pen is given for free. What is the average savings per pen for 10 pens exclusive of sales tax?

Solution:
Cost of 9 + 1 pens   ⇒ $1.80 × 9   ⇒ 16.20
Cost per Pen for 10 Pens ⇒ $16.20 ÷ 10 ⇒ $1.62
Average Saving per Pen ⇒ $1.80 – $1.62 ⇒ $0.18

Question #68: In a local election, candidate X receives one-half the number of votes candidate Y receives, and candidate Y receives one-third the number of votes candidate Z receives. If candidate Z receives 15,000 votes, how many votes did candidate X receive?

Solution:
No. of Votes that Candidate Z Received   ⇒ 15,000

No. of Votes that Candidate Y Received   ⇒ $\frac{1}{3}$ of 15,000 = 5,000

No. of Votes that Candidate X Received   ⇒ $\frac{1}{2}$ of 5,000 = 2,500

Question #69: A man has an estate worth $12 million that he will divide either equally among his 10 children or among his 10 children and 2 siblings. How much more will each of his children inherit if his 2 siblings are excluded?

Solution:
Total Estate Value ⇒ $12,000,000
If divided only among 10 Children, each one will receive ⇒ $12,000,000 ÷ 10 = $1,200,000
If divided among 10 children and 2 siblings, each one will receive ⇒ $12,000,000 ÷ 12 = $1,000,000
Amount that each child would get more if 2 siblings are excluded⇒$1,200,000–$1,000,000 = $200,000

Question #70: In an indoor garage, to park a car, it costs $6.75 for the first hour, and $1.75 for each additional hour. At an outdoor garage, to park a car, it costs $6.25 for the first hour and $1.25 for each additional hour. What is the value of the positive difference between the cost parking a car for 10 hours at the indoor garage and the outdoor garage?

Solution:
Cost of Parking a Car for 10 Hours at the Indoor Garage:

$\Rightarrow$ \$6.75 (for first hour) + \$1.75 × 9 (for next nine hours) $\Rightarrow$ \$6.75 + \$15.75 = \$22.50
Cost of Parking a Car for 10 Hours at the Outdoor Garage:
$\Rightarrow$ \$6.25 (for first hour) + \$1.25 × 9 (for next nine hours) $\Rightarrow$ \$6.25 + \$11.25 = \$17.50
Value of the positive difference between the cost of parking a car for 10 hours at the indoor garage and the outdoor garage $\Rightarrow$ \$22.50 – \$17.50 = \$5

THIS PAGE HAS BEEN INTENTIONALLY LEFT BLANK

PART 2.0: ALGEBRAIC WORD PROBLEMS:

TABLE OF CONTENTS:

PART 2.0: ALGEBRAIC WORD PROBLEMS: 49
    2.1: Equation Based Word Problems: 50
    2.2: Inequality Based Word Problems: 51
    Practice Exercise – Questions and Answers With Explanations: Algebraic Word Problems: 52

2.1: EQUATION BASED WORD PROBLEMS:

Equation problems are similar to other word problems. They usually involve forming one or more equations like in regular word problems, and are generally quite easy to solve; however, some of them can be quite tricky. These types of inequality word problems may become even more complicated and challenging when you fall into the wrong track. Moreover, use of multiple unknowns or multiple equations makes them some of the most difficult word problems.

The best way to solve equation word problems is by converting them into equations. Once the equations are formed, simply try to solve for what's being asked in the problem. You may have to do a little bit of manipulation in the process, but make sure that you adhere to the rules of equations.

Example #1:   John's house costs 5 times as much as Tom's house. Tom's house costs half as much as Nick's house. Nick's house costs $250,000. How much does John's house costs?

Solution: Let, the cost of John's house $\Rightarrow J$
And, the cost of Tom's house $\Rightarrow T$
And, the cost of Nick's house $\Rightarrow N$

John's house costs 5 times as much as Tom's house	$\Rightarrow J = 5T$	$\Rightarrow$ Equation #1
Tom's house costs half as much as Nick's house	$\Rightarrow T = \frac{1}{2}N$	$\Rightarrow$ Equation #2
Nick's house costs $250,000	$\Rightarrow N = 250,000$	$\Rightarrow$ Equation #3
Substitute the value of N from Equation #3 into #2	$\Rightarrow T = \frac{1}{2}N$	[Rewrite Equation #2]
	$\Rightarrow T = \frac{1}{2}(250,000)$	[Substitute $N = 250,000$]
	$\Rightarrow T = 125,000$	[Do the multiplication]
Substitute the value of T in Equation #1	$\Rightarrow J = 5T$	[Rewrite Equation #1]
	$\Rightarrow J = 5 \times 125,000$	[Substitute $T = 125,000$]
	$\Rightarrow J = 625,000$	[Do the multiplication]

Therefore, John's house costs $625,000

Example #2:   By the end of the second quarter, ¼ of the vacancies were filled, but as soon as 10 more candidates were hired, 1/3 of the vacancies would have been filled. What was the original number of vacancies?

Solution: Let the original number of vacancies = x

$\Rightarrow$ ¼ of vacancies + 10 = 1/3 of vacancies

$\Rightarrow \dfrac{1}{4}x + 10 = \dfrac{1}{3}x$ [Translate and convert the words into an algebraic equation]

$\Rightarrow (12)\dfrac{1}{4}x + (12)10 = (12)\dfrac{1}{3}x$ [Multiply both sides by the LCM of 3 & 4, which is 12]

$\Rightarrow 3x + 120 = 4x$ [Simplify both sides of the equation]

$\Rightarrow x = 120$ [Subtract 3x from both sides to isolate x]

Therefore, there was a total vacancy of 120 people.

2.2: INEQUALITY BASED WORD PROBLEMS:

Inequality problems are similar to other word problems. The only difference is that inequality word problems usually involve forming one or more inequalities instead of equations like in regular word problems, and are generally quite easy to solve; however, some of them can be quite tricky. These types of inequality word problems may become even more complicated and challenging when you fall into the wrong track. Moreover, use of multiple unknowns or multiple inequalities makes them some of the most difficult word problems.

The best way to solve inequality word problems is by converting them into inequalities. Once the inequalities are formed, simply try to solve for what's being asked in the problem. You may have to do a little bit of manipulation in the process, but make sure that you adhere to the rules of inequalities.

EZ REFERENCE: For more in-depth knowledge about inequalities, refer to our Algebra Module.

Example #1:   If the sum of three consecutive integers is less than 60, what is the greatest possible value of the smallest of the three integers?

Solution: Let, the three consecutive numbers be n, $n + 1$, $n + 2$; Then:
EZ Problem Set-Up $\Rightarrow$ Sum of three consecutive integers is less than 60
$\Rightarrow n + (n + 1) + (n + 2) < 60$ [Set up the inequality]
$\Rightarrow 3n + 3 < 60$ [Combine like-terms]
$\Rightarrow 3n < 57$ [Subtract 3 from both sides]
$\Rightarrow n < 19$ [Divide both sides by 3]
Therefore, the greatest possible value of the smallest of the three integers $\Rightarrow n = 18$

Example #2:   If $1 < x < 3$ and $2 < y < 4$, what is the largest integer value of $x + y$?

Solution: Largest possible integer value of x $\Rightarrow 2$
Largest possible integer value of y $\Rightarrow 3$
Largest possible integer value of $x + y \Rightarrow 2 + 3 = 5$
However, the question does not say that x and y have to be integers, only $x + y$ must be an integer, therefore, both x and y can be non-integer numbers.
Now, we know that x must be less than 3 and y must be less than 4, and 3 + 4 = 7; therefore our answer must be less than 7 and there is only one integer between 5 & 7, which is 6.
Largest possible integer value of $x + y \Rightarrow 2.1 + 3.9 = 6$

PRACTICE EXERCISE – QUESTIONS AND ANSWERS WITH EXPLANATIONS: ALGEBRAIC WORD PROBLEMS:

Question #1: A car rental company charges $99 per week plus $0.10 per mile for a mid-size car. How many miles can one travel on a maximum budget of $250?

Solution: Let, the No. of miles traveled $\Rightarrow n$

Then, the amount spent on traveling n miles at $0.10 per mile $\Rightarrow 0.10n$

Total maximum budget $\Rightarrow$ $250

Fixed rental fee $\Rightarrow$ $99

EZ Problem Set-Up $\Rightarrow$ Fixed Rental Fee + Mileage = Total Maximum Budget

$\Rightarrow 99 + 0.10n = 250$ [Set up the equation]

$\Rightarrow 0.10n = 151$ [Subtract 99 from both sides]

$\Rightarrow n = 1,510$ miles   [Divide both sides by 0.10]

Therefore, one can travel a maximum of 1,510 miles under the given conditions.

Question #2: If the price of x screws priced at the rate of 15 cents each equals the price of $x - 8$ nuts priced at the rate of 21 cents each, then what is the value of x?

Solution: EZ Problem Set-Up $\Rightarrow$ Price of x screws at 15 cents each = Price of $x - 8$ nuts at 21 cents each

$\Rightarrow 0.15x = (x - 8)(0.21)$ [Set up the equation]

$\Rightarrow 0.15x = 0.21x - 1.68$ [Apply distributive property]

$\Rightarrow 0.06x = 1.68$ [Subtract 0.15x from both sides]

$\Rightarrow x = 28$ [Divide both sides by 0.06]

Question #3: A 120-inch long string is cut into two pieces. If one piece is 12 inches longer than the other is, what is the length, in inches, of the longer piece?

Solution: Let the length of the shorter piece of the string $\Rightarrow n$ inches

Then, the length of the longer piece of the string $\Rightarrow n + 12$

EZ Problem Set-Up $\Rightarrow$ Shorter Piece + Longer Piece = Total Length of the String

$\Rightarrow n + (n + 12) = 120$ [Set up the equation]

$\Rightarrow 2n + 12 = 120$ [Combine like-terms]

$\Rightarrow 2n = 108$ [Subtract 12 from both sides]

$\Rightarrow n = 54$ [Divide both sides by 2]

Length of the shorter piece of string $\Rightarrow n = 54$

Length of the longer piece of string $\Rightarrow n + 12 = 54 + 12 = 66$

Question #4: A school has 27 students. If there are 7 more girls than boys in the school, how many students are boys?

Solution: Let, the No. of boys in the school $\Rightarrow n$

Then, the No. of girls in the school $\Rightarrow n + 7$

Total No. of Students $\Rightarrow 27$

EZ Problem Set-Up $\Rightarrow$ No. of Boys + No. of Girls = Total No. of students

$\Rightarrow n + (n + 7) = 27$ [Set up the equation]

$\Rightarrow 2n + 7 = 27$ [Combine like-terms]

$\Rightarrow 2n = 20$ [Subtract 7 from both sides]

$\Rightarrow n = 10$ [Divide both sides by 2]

No. of boys in the class $\Rightarrow n = 10$

No. of girls in the class $\Rightarrow n + 7 = 10 + 7 = 17$

Question #5: A theater sells children's tickets for half the adult ticket price. If 5 adult tickets and 8 children's tickets cost a total of $99, what is the cost of a children's ticket?

Solution: Let, the price of children's ticket $\Rightarrow C$

And, the price of adult's ticket $\Rightarrow A$

Children's Tickets cost half the Adult Ticket Price $\Rightarrow C = \frac{1}{2}A$ $\Rightarrow$ Equation #1

5 Adult Tickets & 8 Children's Tickets cost $99 $\Rightarrow 5A + 8C = 99$ $\Rightarrow$ Equation #2

Substitute the value of C form Equation #1 into #2 $\Rightarrow 5A + 8(\frac{1}{2}A) = 99$ [Substitute $C = \frac{1}{2} A$]
$\Rightarrow 5A + 4A = 99$ [Apply distributive property]
$\Rightarrow 9A = 99$ [Combine like-terms]
$\Rightarrow A = 11$ [Divide both sides by 9]
Substitute the value of A in Equation #1 $\Rightarrow C = \frac{1}{2}A$ [Rewrite Equation #1]
$\Rightarrow C = \frac{1}{2}(11)$ [Substitute $A = 11$]
$\Rightarrow C = 5.500$ [Apply distributive property]
Therefore, the cost of a children's ticket is $5.50

Question #6: The total fare for 2 adults and 3 children on a park ride is $21. If each child's fare is one-half of each adult's fare, what is the adult fare?

Solution: Let, the price of children's fare $\Rightarrow C$
And, the price of adult's fare $\Rightarrow A$
Total fare for 2 adults & 3 children is $21 $\Rightarrow 2A + 3C = 21$ $\Rightarrow$ Equation #1
Each child's fare is one-half of each adult's fare $\Rightarrow C = 0.5A$ $\Rightarrow$ Equation #2
Substitute the value of C from Equation #2 into #1 $\Rightarrow 2A + 3(0.5A) = 21$ [Substitute $C = 0.5A$]
$\Rightarrow 2A + 1.5A = 21$ [Apply distributive property]
$\Rightarrow 3.5A = 21$ [Combine like-terms]
$\Rightarrow A = 6$ [Divide both sides by 3.5]
Therefore, the adult's fare is $6

Question #7: A certain book costs $12 more in hardcover than in paperback. If the paperback price is 1/3 of the hardcover price, how much does the book cost in hardcover?

Solution: Let, the price of Hardcover book = H
And, the price of Paperback book = P
Hardcover costs $12 more than Paperback $\Rightarrow H = \$12 + P$ $\Rightarrow$ Equation #1
Paperback price is 1/3 of the Hardcover price $\Rightarrow P = 1/3H$ $\Rightarrow$ Equation #2

Substitute the value of P from Equation #2 into #1 $\Rightarrow H = 12 + \dfrac{1}{3}H$ [Substitute $P = 1/3H$]

$\Rightarrow H - \dfrac{1}{3}H = 12$ [Subtract 1/3H from both sides]

$\Rightarrow \dfrac{2}{3}H = 12$ [Combine like-terms]

$\Rightarrow H = 18$ [Multiply both sides by 3/2]

Question #8: Mary's monthly salary is $85 less than Nancy's, whose monthly salary is $25 more than Susan's. If Susan earns $775 per month, how much does Mary earn per month?

Solution: Mary's monthly salary is $85 less than Nancy's $\Rightarrow M = N - 85$ $\Rightarrow$ Equation #1
Nancy's monthly salary is $25 more than Susan's $\Rightarrow N = S + 25$ $\Rightarrow$ Equation #2
Susan earns $775 per month $\Rightarrow S = 775$ [Subtract 25 from both sides]
Substitute the value of S in Equation #2 $\Rightarrow N = S + 25 = 775 + 25 = 800$
Substitute the value of N in Equation #1 $\Rightarrow M = N - 85 = 800 - 85 = 715$
Therefore, Mary's monthly salary is $715

Question #9: Peter's salary is 80 percent more than Hector's salary, and Hector's salary is 20 percent less than Victor's salary. What percent of Victor's salary is Peter's salary?

Solution: Peter's salary is 80 percent more than Hector's salary $\Rightarrow P = H + 0.80H = 1.80H$ $\Rightarrow$ Equation #1
Hector's salary is 20 percent less than Victor's salary $\Rightarrow H = V - 0.20V = 0.80V$ $\Rightarrow$ Equation #2
Substitute the value of H from equation #2 into #1 $\Rightarrow P = 1.80H = 1.80(0.80V) = 1.44V$
Therefore, Peter's salary is 144% of Victor's salary.

Question #10: John has 5 times as much money as Tom has. If John gifts Tom $60, Tom will then have 2 times as much as John has. How much money do the two of them have together?

Solution: At the beginning: Tom $\Rightarrow n$ John $\Rightarrow 5n$
After the gift: Tom $\Rightarrow n + 60$ John $\Rightarrow 5n - 60$
EZ Problem Set-Up $\Rightarrow$ After the gift, Tom will have 2 times as much as John

$\Rightarrow n + 60 = 2(5n - 60)$ [Set up the equation]
$\Rightarrow n + 60 = 10n - 120$ [Apply distributive property]
$\Rightarrow 60 = 9n - 120$ [Subtract n from both sides]
$\Rightarrow 9n = 180$ [Add 120 to both sides]
$\Rightarrow n = 20$ [Divide both sides by 9]

Therefore, Tom has $20 and John has ($20 × 5) = $100, and they together have ($20 + $100) = $120.

Question #11: John has five times more money than what Tom has. Tom has half of what Peter has. Peter has $10 more than Bob has. Bob has $15 less than what Michael has. If Michael has $117, how much does John have?

Solution: Convert each sentence into an equation, and then try to connect the equations and solve for what's been asked for in the question:

Michael has $117	$\Rightarrow M = \$117$	$\Rightarrow$ Equation #1
Bob has $15 less than what Michael has	$\Rightarrow B = M - \$15$	$\Rightarrow$ Equation #2
Substitute the value of M from #1 into #2	$\Rightarrow B = \$117 - \$15 = \$102$	$\Rightarrow$ Equation #3
Peter has $10 more than what Bob has	$\Rightarrow P = B + \$10$	$\Rightarrow$ Equation #4
Substitute the value of B from #3 into #4	$\Rightarrow P = \$102 + \$10 = \$112$	$\Rightarrow$ Equation #5
Tom has half of what Peter has	$\Rightarrow T = \tfrac{1}{2}P$	$\Rightarrow$ Equation #6
Substitute the value of P from #5 into #6	$\Rightarrow T = \tfrac{1}{2}(\$112) = \$56$	$\Rightarrow$ Equation #7
John has 5 times more than what Tom has	$\Rightarrow J = 5T$	$\Rightarrow$ Equation #8
Substitute the value of T from #7 into #8	$\Rightarrow J = 5 \times \$56 = \$280$	

Therefore, John has $280.

Question #12: In a small family, father's salary is 125% of son's salary. Mother's salary is 80% of son's salary. The combined salary of all three is $61,000. What is Mother's salary?

Solution: Let, Son's Salary $\Rightarrow S$
Combined Salary $\Rightarrow \$61,000$
Father's salary is 125% of son's salary $\Rightarrow F = 125\% \times S$

$$\Rightarrow F = \frac{125}{100}S = \frac{5}{4}S$$

Mother's salary is 80% of son's salary $\Rightarrow M = 80\% \times S$

$$\Rightarrow M = \frac{80}{100}S = \frac{4}{5}S$$

EZ Problem Set-Up $\Rightarrow$ Father's Salary + Mother's Salary + Son's Salary = Combined Salary

$$\Rightarrow \frac{5}{4}S + \frac{4}{5}S + S = \$61,000 \qquad \text{[Set up the equation]}$$

$$\Rightarrow \frac{25}{20}S + \frac{16}{20}S + \frac{20}{20}S = \$61,000 \qquad \text{[Scale-Up all the fractions to their LCD]}$$

$$\Rightarrow \frac{61}{20}S = \$61,000 \qquad \text{[Combine like-terms]}$$

$$\Rightarrow S = \$61,000 \times \frac{20}{61} = 20,000 \qquad \text{[Multiply both sides by 20/61]}$$

Son's salary $\Rightarrow S = \$20,000$

Father's salary $\Rightarrow F = \dfrac{5}{4}S = \dfrac{5}{4} \times 20,000 = \$25,000$

Mother's salary $\Rightarrow M = \dfrac{4}{5}S = \dfrac{4}{5} \times 20,000 = \$16,000$

Question #13: John's team won 7 more games than Tom's team. Nick's team won twice as many games as Tom's team. Tom's team won 5 games. How many more wins did John's team have than Nick's team?

Solution: Let, John's team $\Rightarrow J$
And, Tom's team $\Rightarrow T$
And, Nick's team $\Rightarrow N$
John's team won 7 more games than Tom's team $\Rightarrow J = T + 7$ $\Rightarrow$ Equation #1

Nick's team won twice as many games as Tom's team $\Rightarrow N = 2T$ $\Rightarrow$ Equation #2
Tom's team won 5 games $\Rightarrow T = 5$
Substitute the value of T into #2 $\Rightarrow N = 2T$ [Rewrite Equation #2]
$\Rightarrow N = 2(5)$ [Substitute $T = 5$]
$\Rightarrow N = 10$ [Do the multiplication]
Substitute the value of T into #1 $\Rightarrow J = T + 7$ [Rewrite Equation #`]
$\Rightarrow J = 5 + 7$ [Substitute $T = 5$]
$\Rightarrow J = 12$ [Combine like-terms]
No. of more wins that John's team have than Nick's team $\Rightarrow J - N = ?$ [Find the difference]
$\Rightarrow 12 - 10 = 2$ [Substitute $J = 12$; $N = 12$]
Therefore, John's team won 2 more games than Nick's team.

Question #14: In a farm, there are only cows and people. If we counted 70 heads and 198 legs in the entire farm, how many cows and how many people are in the farm?
Solution: Let, the No. of people in the farm $\Rightarrow n$
Since each person and a cow has only one head, total No. of people and cows $\Rightarrow 70$
Therefore, the No. of cows $\Rightarrow 70 - n$
Since people have 2 legs, the total No. of human legs $\Rightarrow 2n$
Since cows have 4 legs, the total No. of cow legs $\Rightarrow 4(70 - n)$
Total No. of legs $\Rightarrow 198$
EZ Problem Set-Up $\Rightarrow$ Total No. of Human Legs + Total No. of Cow Legs = Total No. of Legs
$\Rightarrow 2n + 4(70 - n) = 198$ [Set up the equation]
$\Rightarrow 2n + 280 - 4n = 198$ [Apply distributive property]
$\Rightarrow -2n + 280 = 198$ [Combine like-terms]
$\Rightarrow -2n = -82$ [Subtract 280 from both sides]
$\Rightarrow n = 41$ [Divide both sides by -2]
No. of humans in the farm $\Rightarrow n = 41$
No. of cows in the farm $\Rightarrow 70 - n = 70 - 41 = 29$

Question #15: Nick, Rick, Mack, and Jack shared a $1,225 bonus. Rick has twice as much as Nick, Mack has 6 times as much as Nick, and Jack has $100. How much, in dollars, did Nick get?
Solution: Let's assume Nick has N $\Rightarrow N = N$
Rick has twice as much as Nick $\Rightarrow R = 2N$
Mack has 6 times as mush as Nick $\Rightarrow M = 6N$
Jack has $100 $\Rightarrow J = \$100$
EZ Problem Set-Up $\Rightarrow$ Total share of Nick, Rick, Mack, and Jack in the bonus = $1,225
$\Rightarrow N + R + M + J = \$1,225$ [Set up the equation]
$\Rightarrow N + 2N + 6N + \$100 = \$1,225$ [Substitute the value of $N, R, M,$ and J]
$\Rightarrow 9N + 100 = 1,225$ [Combine like-terms]
$\Rightarrow 9N = 1,125$ [Subtract 100 from both sides]
$\Rightarrow N = \$125$ [Divide both sides by 9]
Therefore, Nick's share in the bonus $\Rightarrow N = \$125$

Question #16: The sum of Amber and Helen's income is $1,575. If twice the income of Amber is $120 more than Helen's income, what is Helen's income?
Solution: Sum of Amber and Helen's income is $1,575 $\Rightarrow A + H = \$1,575$ $\Rightarrow$ Equation #1
Twice the income of Amber is $120 more than Helen's income $\Rightarrow 2A = H + \$120$
$\Rightarrow 2A - H = \$120$ $\Rightarrow$ Equation #2
Add Equation #1 and Equation #2 $A + H = \$1,575$ [Rewrite Equation #1]
$+ \quad 2A - H = \$120$ [Rewrite Equation #2]
$3A \quad = \$1,695$ [Add both equations]
$A \quad = \$565$ [Divide both sides by 3]
Substitute the value of A in Equation #1 $\Rightarrow A + H = \$1,575$ [Rewrite Equation #1]
$\Rightarrow \$565 + H = \$1,575$ [Substitute $A = \$565$]
$\Rightarrow H = \$1,010$ [Subtract $565 from both sides]
Therefore, Helen's income is $1,010.

Question #17: During a certain shopping spree, Victoria spent twice as much as Susan, who spent eight times as much as Nancy. If Victoria and Nancy together spent $255, how much did Susan spend?

Solution:

Victoria spent twice as much as Susan	$\Rightarrow V = 2S$	$\Rightarrow$ Equation #1
Susan spent eight times as much as Nancy	$\Rightarrow S = 8N$	$\Rightarrow$ Equation #2
Victoria and Nancy together spent $255	$\Rightarrow V + N = \$255$	$\Rightarrow$ Equation #3
Substitute the value of V from #1 into #3	$\Rightarrow 2S + N = \$255$	$\Rightarrow$ Equation #4
Substitute the value of S from #2 into #4	$\Rightarrow 2(8N) + N = \$255$	[Substitute $S = 8N$]
	$\Rightarrow 16N + N = \$255$	[Apply distributive property]
	$\Rightarrow 17N = \$255$	[Combine like-terms]
	$\Rightarrow N = \$15$	[Divide both sides by 17]
Substitute the value of N in #2	$\Rightarrow S = 8N$	[Rewrite Equation #2]
	$\Rightarrow S = 8(15)$	[Substitute $N = \$15$]
	$\Rightarrow S = \$120$	[Do the multiplication]

Therefore, Susan spent $120

Question #18: In a certain year, Florida produced one-half and Alabama produced one-seventh of all the oranges produced in the United States. If all the other states combined produced 60 million tons of oranges that year, how many million tons did Alabama alone produce that year?

Solution:

Let, the total Production of Oranges in United States	$\Rightarrow x$ million tons
Fraction of Oranges produced by Florida	$\Rightarrow \dfrac{1}{2}$
Fraction of Oranges produced by Alabama	$\Rightarrow \dfrac{1}{7}$
Fraction of Oranges produced by Florida & Alabama	$\Rightarrow \dfrac{1}{2} + \dfrac{1}{7} = \dfrac{9}{14}$
Fraction of Oranges produced by Other States	$\Rightarrow 1 - \dfrac{9}{14} = \dfrac{5}{14}$
Total Production of Oranges by Other States	$\Rightarrow \dfrac{5}{14}$ of $x = 60$
	$\Rightarrow x = 60 \times \dfrac{14}{5} = 168$
Amount of Oranges produced by Alabama	$\Rightarrow \dfrac{1}{7} \times 168 = 24$ million tons

Question #19: A jar contains only red, blue, and green marbles. The number of red marbles is four-fifth the number of blue marbles, and the number of blue marbles is three-fourth the number of green marbles. If there are a total of 564 marbles in the jar, how many of them are red?

Solution:

Let, the No. of green marbles	$\Rightarrow g$
Then, the No. of blue marbles	$\Rightarrow \dfrac{3}{4}g$
And, the No. of red marbles	$\Rightarrow \dfrac{\cancel{4}}{5}\left(\dfrac{3}{\cancel{4}}\right)g = \dfrac{3}{5}g$

EZ Problem Set-Up $\Rightarrow$ No. of green marbles + No. of blue marbles + No. of red marbles = Total No. of Marbles

$\Rightarrow g + \dfrac{3}{4}g + \dfrac{3}{5}g = 564$	[Set up the equation]
$\Rightarrow \dfrac{20}{20}g + \dfrac{15}{20}g + \dfrac{12}{20}g = 564$	[Scale-Up all the fractions to their LCD]
$\Rightarrow \dfrac{47}{20}g = 564$	[Combine like-terms]
$\Rightarrow g = 564 \times \dfrac{20}{47} = 240$	[Multiply both sides by 20/47]

No. of green marbles $\Rightarrow g = 240$

No. of blue marbles $\Rightarrow \dfrac{3}{4}g = \dfrac{3}{4} \times 240 = 180$

No. of red marbles $\Rightarrow \dfrac{3}{5}g = \dfrac{3}{5} \times 240 = 144$

Question #20: Mary finishes the first half of a test in two-thirds the time it takes her to finish the second half. If the whole test takes her an hour, how many minutes does she spend on the first half of the test?

Solution: Let, the time taken on Second Half of the Test $\Rightarrow n$

Then, the time taken on First Half of the Test $\Rightarrow \dfrac{2}{3}n$

Total Time taken to finish the Whole Test $\Rightarrow$ 1 hour = 60 minutes
EZ Problem Set-Up $\Rightarrow$ Time on First Half + Time on Second Half = Total Time on Whole Test

$\Rightarrow n + \dfrac{2}{3}n = 60$ [Set up the equation]

$\Rightarrow \dfrac{3}{3}n + \dfrac{2}{3}n = 60$ [Scale-Up all the fractions to their LCD]

$\Rightarrow \dfrac{5}{3}n = 60$ [Combine like-terms]

$\Rightarrow n = 60 \times \dfrac{3}{5} = 36$ [Multiply both sides by 3/5]

Time spent on Second Half of the test $\Rightarrow n = 36$ minutes

Time spent on First Half of the test $\Rightarrow \dfrac{2}{3}n = \dfrac{2}{3} \times 36 = 24$ minutes

Question #21: If Mary gives Nancy 7 dollars and Nancy gives Susan 2 dollars, the three girls will have the same amount of money. How much more money does Mary have than Nancy?

Solution: After Mary gives Nancy 7 dollars $\Rightarrow$ Mary = $M - 7$ & $\Rightarrow$ Nancy = $N + 7$
After Nancy gives Susan 2 dollars $\Rightarrow$ Nancy = $N + 7 - 2$ & $\Rightarrow$ Susan = $S + 2$
Now, the three girls will have the same amount of money $\Rightarrow M - 7 = N + 5$
$\Rightarrow M = N + 12$

Therefore, Mary has $12 more than Nancy does.

Question #22: John's monthly salary is $70 less than Tom's, and $50 more than Victor's. If Victor earns $575 per month, how much does Tom earn per month?

Solution:
John's monthly salary is $70 less than Tom's	$\Rightarrow J = T - 70$	$\Rightarrow$ Equation #1	
John's monthly salary is $50 more than Victor's	$\Rightarrow J = V + 50$	$\Rightarrow$ Equation #2	
Victor earns $575 per month	$\Rightarrow V = 575$	[Given]	
Substitute the value of V in Equation #2	$\Rightarrow J = V + 50$	[Rewrite Equation #2]	
	$\Rightarrow J = 575 + 50$	[Substitute $V = 575$]	
	$\Rightarrow J = 625$	[Combine like-terms]	
Substitute the value of J in Equation #1	$\Rightarrow J = T - 70$	[Rewrite Equation #1]	
	$\Rightarrow 625 = T - 70$	[Substitute $J = 625$]	
	$\Rightarrow T = 695$	[Add 70 to both sides]	

Therefore, Tom's monthly salary is $695

Question #23: At a carnival, a candy stand sells hard candies at 20 cents each and soft candies at 50 cents each. If in the entire carnival the candy stand sells 120 candies and raises $27, how many hard candies did they sell?

Solution: Let, the Hard Candies $\Rightarrow h$
And, the Soft Candies $\Rightarrow s$
Total No. of candies sold is 120 $\Rightarrow h + s = 120$ $\Rightarrow$ Equation #1
Total amount generated by sales is $27 $\Rightarrow 20h + 50s = 2,700$ $\Rightarrow$ Equation #2
(convert everything in cents)

Multiply Equation #1 by (−20)	$\Rightarrow -20h - 20s = -2,400$	$\Rightarrow$ Equation #3
Add Equation #2 and Equation #3	$-20h + (-20s) = -2,400$	[Rewrite Equation #2]
	$+20h + (50s) = 2,700$	[Rewrite Equation #3]
	$\Rightarrow \quad\quad 30s = 300$	[Add both equations]
	$\Rightarrow \quad\quad\quad s = 10$	[Divide both sides by 30]
Substitute the value of s in Equation #1	$\Rightarrow h + s = 120$	[Rewrite Equation #1]
	$\Rightarrow h + 10 = 120$	[Substitute $s = 10$]
	$\Rightarrow h = 110$	[Subtract 10 from both sides]

Question #24: A widow received one-tenth of her husband's estate, and each of her six children received one-tenth of the balance. If the widow and one of her children received a total of $118,750 from the estate, what was the total amount of the estate?

Solution:

Let, the total amount of estate $\Rightarrow x$

Widow's share of the estate $\Rightarrow \dfrac{1}{10}x$

Remaining value of the estate after the widow's share $\Rightarrow x - \dfrac{1}{10}x = \dfrac{10}{10}x - \dfrac{1}{10}x = \dfrac{9}{10}x$

Each child's share of the estate $\Rightarrow \dfrac{1}{10}\left(\dfrac{9}{10}x\right) = \dfrac{9}{100}x$

Total amount received from the estate $\Rightarrow \$118,750$

EZ Problem Set-Up $\Rightarrow$ Widow's share + Each child's share = Total amount received from the estate

$\Rightarrow \dfrac{1}{10}x + \dfrac{9}{100}x = \$118,750$	[Set up the equation]
$\Rightarrow \dfrac{10}{100}x + \dfrac{9}{100}x = \$118,750$	[Scale-Up all the fractions to their LCD]
$\Rightarrow \dfrac{19}{100}x = \$118,750$	[Combine like-terms]
$\Rightarrow x = \$118,750 \times \dfrac{100}{19} = \$625,000$	[Multiply both sides by 100/19]

Question #25: If $1 < x < 7$ and $2 < y < 9$, what is the largest integer value of $x + y$?

Solution:
Largest possible integer value of x $\Rightarrow 6$
Largest possible integer value of y $\Rightarrow 8$
Largest possible integer value of $x + y \Rightarrow 6 + 8 = 14$
However, the question does not say that x and y have to be integers, only $x + y$ must be an integer, therefore, both x and y can be non-integer numbers.
Now we know that x must be less than 7 and y must be less than 9, and $7 + 9 = 16$; therefore our answer must be less than 16 and there is only one integer between 14 & 16.
Largest possible integer value of $x + y \Rightarrow 6.1 + 8.9 = 15$

Question #26: If $1 < x < 6$ and $2 < y < 8$, what is the largest integer value of $x + y$?

Solution:
Largest possible integer value of x $\Rightarrow 5$
Largest possible integer value of y $\Rightarrow 7$
Largest possible integer value of $x + y \Rightarrow 5 + 7 = 12$
However, the question does not say that x and y have to be integers, only $x + y$ must be an integer, therefore, both x and y can be non-integer numbers.
Now we know that x must be less than 6 and y must be less than 8, and $6 + 8 = 14$; therefore our answer must be less than 14 and there is only one integer between 12 & 14.
Largest possible integer value of $x + y \Rightarrow 5.1 + 7.9 = 13$

Question #27: If $-7 \le m \le 7$ and $-5 \le n \le 5$, what is the greatest possible value of $n - m$?

Solution:
In order to make $n - m$ as large as possible, pick n to be as large as possible, and pick m to be as small as possible, and then subtract the two numbers.
Largest possible value of n $\Rightarrow 5$
Smallest possible value of m $\Rightarrow -7$

Greatest possible value of $n - m$ $\Rightarrow 5 - (-7) = 12$

Question #28: If $-7 \le m \le 7$ and $-5 \le n \le 5$, what is the least possible value of $n - m$?

Solution: In order to make $n - m$ as small as possible, pick n to be as small as possible, and pick m to be as large as possible, and then subtract the two numbers.

Smallest possible value of n $\Rightarrow -5$
Largest possible value of m $\Rightarrow 7$
Least possible value of $n - m$ $\Rightarrow (-5) - 7 = -12$

Question #29: If the sum of three consecutive integers is less than 75, what is the greatest possible value of the smallest of the three integers?

Solution: Let the three consecutive numbers be n, $n + 1$, and $n + 2$

EZ Problem Set-Up $\Rightarrow$ Sum of three consecutive integers is less than 75
$\Rightarrow n + (n + 1) + (n + 2) < 75$ [Set up the inequality]
$\Rightarrow 3n + 3 < 75$ [Combine like-terms]
$\Rightarrow 3n < 72$ [Subtract 3 from both sides]
$\Rightarrow n < 24$ [Divide both sides by 3]

Therefore, the greatest possible value of the smallest of the three integers is 23.

Question #30: If the sum of three consecutive integers is less than 78, what is the greatest possible value of the smallest of the three integers?

Solution: Let the three consecutive numbers be n, $n + 1$, and $n + 2$

EZ Problem Set-Up $\Rightarrow$ Sum of three consecutive integers is less than 78
$\Rightarrow n + (n + 1) + (n + 2) < 78$ [Set up the inequality]
$\Rightarrow 3n + 3 < 78$ [Combine like-terms]
$\Rightarrow 3n < 75$ [Subtract 3 from both sides]
$\Rightarrow n < 25$ [Divide both sides by 3]

Therefore, the greatest possible value of the smallest of the three integers is 24.

THIS PAGE HAS BEEN INTENTIONALLY LEFT BLANK

PART 3.0: NUMERAL PROBLEMS:

TABLE OF CONTENTS:

PART 3.0: NUMERAL PROBLEMS: 61
   3.1: Number Problems: 62
   3.2: Consecutive Integers: 63
   3.3: Non-Consecutive Integers:...65
   3.4: Coin Problems:...66
   Practice Exercise – Questions and Answers With Explanations: Numeral Word Problems:................67

3.1: NUMBER PROBLEMS:

Numeral word problems describe how several numbers are related to one another. They typically provide some specific relationships between two or more numbers based on their sum, difference, product, quotient, etc. Those relationships need to be transformed into algebraic equations. All number related word problems have one or more of the information given, and you will be asked to determine the value of one or more of the numbers that are unknown.

EZ STEP-BY-STEP METHOD: Apply the following step(s) to solve any Integer Word Problem:

STEP 1: Assign a different letter (variable) for each unknown number.

STEP 2: Establish relationships among the numbers in the problem.

STEP 3: Transform the relationships among the numbers into algebraic equations that justify those relationships.

STEP 4: Solve the formed equations, and determine the value of the unknowns or the missing numbers.

EZ TIP: Also, make use of our EZ Step-by-Step Strategy for solving Word Problems, and the translation/conversion table given at the beginning of this unit.

EZ REFERENCE: For more in-depth knowledge about rules of numbers, refer to our Arithmetic Module.

Example #1:   One tenth is what part of two-sevenths?

Solution: Let the value of that part = x

EZ problem Set-Up $\Rightarrow$ One tenth is what part of two-sevenths

$$\Rightarrow \frac{1}{10} = x \bullet \frac{2}{7}$$ [Set up the equation]

$$\Rightarrow 20x = 7$$ [Cross multiply]

$$\Rightarrow x = \frac{7}{20}$$ [Dive both sides by 20]

Example #2:   If subtracting 10 from a number is the same as taking $\frac{2}{7}$ of the number, what is the number?

Solution: Let the value of that number = x

EZ problem Set-Up $\Rightarrow$ Subtracting 10 from a number is the same as taking $\frac{2}{7}$ of the number

$$\Rightarrow x - 10 = \frac{2}{7}x$$ [Set up the equation]

$$\Rightarrow x - \frac{2}{7}x - 10 = 0$$ [Subtract 2/7x from both sides]

$$\Rightarrow x - \frac{2}{7}x = 10$$ [Add 10 to both sides]

$$\Rightarrow \frac{5}{7}x = 10$$ [Combine like-terms]

$$\Rightarrow x = 10 \times \frac{7}{5} = 14$$ [Multiply both sides by 7/5]

3.2: CONSECUTIVE INTEGERS:

Example #1:   If the sum of two consecutive integers is 51, what is the value of the bigger integer?
Solution: Let, the value of first integer $\Rightarrow n$
Then, the value of second integer $\Rightarrow n + 1$
EZ Problem Set-Up $\Rightarrow$ Sum of two consecutive integers is 51
$\Rightarrow n + (n + 1) = 51$ [Set up the equation]
$\Rightarrow 2n + 1 = 51$ [Combine like-terms]
$\Rightarrow 2n = 50$ [Subtract 1 from both sides]
$\Rightarrow n = 25$ [Divide both sides by 2]
Value of first Integer (smaller) $\Rightarrow n = 25$
Value of second integer (bigger) $\Rightarrow n + 1 = 25 + 1 = 26$

Example #2:   If the sum of three consecutive integers is 51, what is the value of the middle integer?
Solution: Let, the value of first integer $\Rightarrow n$
Then, the value of second integer $\Rightarrow n + 1$
And, the value of third integer $\Rightarrow n + 2$
EZ Problem Set-Up $\Rightarrow$ Sum of three consecutive integers is 51
$\Rightarrow n + (n + 1) + (n + 2) = 51$ [Set up the equation]
$\Rightarrow 3n + 3 = 51$ [Combine like-terms]
$\Rightarrow 3n = 48$ [Subtract 3 from both sides]
$\Rightarrow n = 16$ [Divide both sides by 3]
Value of first integer (smallest) $\Rightarrow n = 16$
Value of second integer (middle) $\Rightarrow n + 1 = 16 + 1 = 17$
Value of third integer (biggest) $\Rightarrow n + 2 = 16 + 2 = 18$

Example #3:   If the sum of two even consecutive integers is 50, what is the value of the bigger integer?
Solution: Let, the value of first even integer $\Rightarrow n$
Then, the value of second even integer $\Rightarrow n + 2$
EZ Problem Set-Up $\Rightarrow$ Sum of two even consecutive integers is 50
$\Rightarrow n + (n + 2) = 50$ [Set up the equation]
$\Rightarrow 2n + 2 = 50$ [Combine like-terms]
$\Rightarrow 2n = 48$ [Subtract 2 from both sides]
$\Rightarrow n = 24$ [Divide both sides by 2]
Value of first even integer (smaller) $\Rightarrow n = 24$
Value of second even integer (bigger) $\Rightarrow n + 2 = 26$

Example #4:   If the sum of three even consecutive integers is 54, what is the value of the middle number?
Solution: Let, the value of first even integer $\Rightarrow n$
Then, the value of second even integer $\Rightarrow n + 2$
And, the value of third even integer $\Rightarrow n + 4$
EZ Problem Set-Up $\Rightarrow$ Sum of three even consecutive integers is 54
$\Rightarrow n + (n + 2) + (n + 4) = 54$ [Set up the equation]
$\Rightarrow 3n + 6 = 54$ [Combine like-terms]
$\Rightarrow 3n = 48$ [Subtract 6 from both sides]
$\Rightarrow n = 16$ [Divide both sides by 3]
Value of first even integer (smallest) $\Rightarrow n = 16$
Value of second even integer (middle) $\Rightarrow n + 2 = 16 + 2 = 18$
Value of third even integer (biggest) $\Rightarrow n + 4 = 16 + 4 = 20$

Example #5:   A teacher wrote three consecutive even integers on the board. She then multiplied the first by 2, the second by 5, and the third by 7. Finally, she added all six numbers and got a sum of 214. What was the middle number that she wrote?
Solution: Let, the value of first even integer $\Rightarrow n$
Then, the value of second even integer $\Rightarrow n + 2$

And, the value of third even integer $\Rightarrow n + 4$
EZ Problem Set-Up $\Rightarrow$ Sum of n, $n + 2$, $n + 4$, $2n$, $5(n + 2)$, and $7(n + 4)$ is 214
$\Rightarrow n + (n + 2) + (n + 4) + 2n + 5(n + 2) + 7(n + 4) = 214$ [Set up the equation]
$\Rightarrow 17n + 44 = 214$ [Combine like-terms]
$\Rightarrow 17n = 170$ [Subtract 44 from both sides]
$\Rightarrow n = 10$ [Divide both sides by 17]
Value of first even integer (smallest) $\Rightarrow n = 10$
Value of second even integer (middle) $\Rightarrow n + 2 = 10 + 2 = 12$
Value of third even integer (biggest) $\Rightarrow n + 4 = 10 + 4 = 14$

Example #6: If the sum of five consecutive integers is 760, what is the sum of the next five consecutive integers?
Solution: Let, the value of five consecutive integers $\Rightarrow n$, $n + 1$; $n + 2$, $n + 3$; and $n + 4$
EZ Problem Set-Up $\Rightarrow$ Sum of five consecutive integers is 760
$\Rightarrow n + (n + 1) + (n + 2) + (n + 3) + (n + 4) = 760$ [Set up the equation]
$\Rightarrow 5n + 10 = 760$ [Combine like-terms]
$\Rightarrow 5n = 750$ [Subtract 10 from both sides]
$\Rightarrow n = 150$ [Divide both sides by 5]
Value of first five consecutive integers $\Rightarrow$ 150, 151, 152, 153, and 154
Value of next five consecutive integers $\Rightarrow$ 155, 156, 157, 158, and 159
Sum of next five consecutive integers $\Rightarrow$ 155 + 156 + 157 + 158 + 159 = 785

3.3: NON-CONSECUTIVE INTEGERS:

Example #1: If the product of 2 and 7 more than a certain integer is 9 times that integer, what is the value of that integer?

Solution: Let the value of that certain integer = n

EZ Problem Set-Up $\Rightarrow$ Product of 2 and 7 more than a certain integer is 9 times that integer

$\Rightarrow 2(7 + n) = 9n$ [Set up the equation]
$\Rightarrow 14 + 2n = 9n$ [Apply distributive property]
$\Rightarrow 14 = 7n$ [Subtract $2n$ from both sides]
$\Rightarrow n = 2$ [Divide both sides by 7]

Value of that certain integer $\Rightarrow 2$

Example #2: If sum of two integers is 111, and one of the integers is 9 less than 7 times the other integer, what is the value of the bigger of the two integers?

Solution: Let, the value of one of the integer $\Rightarrow n$
Then, the value of the other integer $\Rightarrow 7n - 9$

EZ Problem Set-Up $\Rightarrow$ Sum of one integer and another integer, which is 9 less than 7 times the first integer is 111

$\Rightarrow n + (7n - 9) = 111$ [Set up the equation]
$\Rightarrow 8n - 9 = 111$ [Combine like-terms]
$\Rightarrow 8n = 120$ [Add 9 to both sides]
$\Rightarrow n = 15$ [Divide both sides by 8]

Value of one of the integers (smaller) $\Rightarrow n = 15$
Value of the other integers (bigger) $\Rightarrow 7n - 9 = 7(15) - 9 = 105 - 9 = 96$

Example #3: If 7 times an integer less 5 times the integer is 200, what is the value of the integer?

Solution: Let, the value of the integer be $\Rightarrow n$

EZ Problem Set-Up $\Rightarrow$ 7 times an integer less 5 times the integer is 200

$\Rightarrow 7n - 5n = 200$ [Set up the equation]
$\Rightarrow 2n = 200$ [Combine like-terms]
$\Rightarrow n = 100$ [Divide both sides by 2]

Value of the integer $\Rightarrow n = 100$

Example #4: If the difference between two integers is 10 and their sum is 110, what are the values of those two integers?

Solution: Let the value of first integer $\Rightarrow x$
And, the value of second number $\Rightarrow y$

The difference between x & y is 10 $\Rightarrow x - y = 10$ $\Rightarrow$ Equation #1
The sum of x & y is 110 $\Rightarrow \underline{x + y = 110}$ $\Rightarrow$ Equation #2
Add Equation #1 and #2 $\Rightarrow 2x \quad\;\; = 120$ [Add both equations]
                                  $\Rightarrow x \quad\quad = 60$ [Divide both sides by 2]
Substitute value of x in Equation #1 $\Rightarrow x - y = 10$ [Rewrite Equation #1]
                                  $\Rightarrow 60 - y = 10$ [Substitute $x = 60$]
                                  $\Rightarrow -y = 10 - 60$ [Subtract 60 from both sides]
                                  $\Rightarrow -y = -50$ [Combine like-terms]
                                  $\Rightarrow y = 50$ [Multiply both sides by -1]

Value of the first integer $\Rightarrow x = 60$
Value of the second integer $\Rightarrow y = 50$

3.4: COIN PROBLEMS:

Coin Problems generally involve nickels, dimes, quarters, half dollars, and dollars, something with which you must already be familiar.
Following are the basic coin conversions that you must know:
- 1 Dollar   = 100 Cents
- 1 Half Dollar   = 50 Cents
- 1 Quarter   = 25 Cents
- 1 Dime   = 10 Cents
- 1 Nickel   = 5 Cents

While solving coin problems, the best strategy is to convert everything into a common denomination, and the easiest way is to change the value into cents before writing any equation or trying to solve anything.
- The number of nickels must be multiplied by 5 to get the value in cents.
- The number of dimes must be multiplied by 10 to get the value in cents.
- The number of quarters must be multiplied by 25 to get the value in cents.
- The number of half dollars must be multiplied by 50 to get the value in cents.
- The number of dollars must be multiplied by 100 to get the value in cents.

Example #1: Monika has $1.75, consisting of nickels and dimes. If she has 11 more nickels than dimes, how many nickels does she have?

Solution: Let, the No. of dimes $\Rightarrow d$
Then, the No. of nickels $\Rightarrow d + 11$
Since each dime is worth 10 cents $\Rightarrow$ Value of dimes in cents = $10d$
Since each nickel is worth 5 cents $\Rightarrow$ Value of nickels in cents = $5(d + 11) = 5d + 55$
Total value of money = $1.75 or 175 cents
EZ Problem Set-Up $\Rightarrow$ Value of dimes in cents + Value of nickels in cents = 175 cents

$\Rightarrow 10d + 5d + 55 = 175$	[Substitute the value of dimes & nickels in cents]
$\Rightarrow 15d + 55 = 175$	[Combine like-terms]
$\Rightarrow 15d = 120$	[Subtract 55 from both sides]
$\Rightarrow d = 8$	[Divide both sides by 15]

Therefore, Monika has 8 dimes and 8 + 11 = 19 nickels

Example #2: Maria has $6.50 in nickels and dimes. If the number of dimes is 2 times the number of nickels, how many dimes does she have?

Solution: Let, the No. of nickels $\Rightarrow n$
Then, the No. of dimes $\Rightarrow 2n$
Since each nickel is worth 5 cents $\Rightarrow$ Value of nickels in cents = $5n$
Since each dime is worth 10 cents $\Rightarrow$ Value of dimes in cents = $10(2n) = 20n$
Total value of money = $6.50 or 650 cents
EZ Problem Set-Up $\Rightarrow$ Value of nickels in cents + Value of dimes in cents = 650 cents

$\Rightarrow 5n + 20n = 650$	[Substitute the value of nickels & dimes in cents]
$\Rightarrow 25n = 650$	[Combine like-terms]
$\Rightarrow n = 26$	[Divide both sides by 25]

Therefore, Maria has 26 nickels and 2 × 26 = 52 dimes

PRACTICE EXERCISE – QUESTIONS AND ANSWERS WITH EXPLANATIONS: NUMERAL WORD PROBLEMS:

Question #1: One tenth is what part of two-fifths?
Solution: Let the value of that part = x
EZ problem Set-Up $\Rightarrow$ One tenth is what part of two-fifths

$\Rightarrow \dfrac{1}{10} = x \bullet \dfrac{2}{5}$ [Set up the equation]

$\Rightarrow 20x = 5$ [Cross-multiply]

$\Rightarrow x = \dfrac{1}{4}$ [Divide both sides by 20]

Question #2: If subtracting 15 from a number is the same as taking ¾ of the number, what is the number?
Solution: Let the value of that number = x
EZ problem Set-Up $\Rightarrow$ Subtracting 15 from a number is the same as taking ¾ of the number

$\Rightarrow x - 15 = \dfrac{3}{4}x$ [Set up the equation]

$\Rightarrow x - \dfrac{3}{4}x - 15 = 0$ [Subtract 3/4x from both sides]

$\Rightarrow x - \dfrac{3}{4}x = 15$ [Add 15 to both sides]

$\Rightarrow \dfrac{1}{4}x = 15$ [Combine like-terms]

$\Rightarrow x = 60$ [Multiply both sides by 4]

Question #3: If $\dfrac{2}{11}$ of a number is 25, what is $\dfrac{8}{5}$ of that number?
Solution: Let the value of that number = x

EZ problem Set-Up $\Rightarrow \dfrac{2}{11}$ of a number is 25

$\Rightarrow \dfrac{2}{11}x = 25$ [Set up the equation]

$\Rightarrow x = 25 \times \dfrac{11}{2}$ [Multiply both sides by 11/2]

Value of $\dfrac{8}{5}x$ $\Rightarrow 25 \times \dfrac{11}{2} \times \dfrac{8}{5} = 220$ [Multiply both sides by 8/5]

Question #4: $\dfrac{5}{7}$ of 14 is equal to $\dfrac{2}{5}$ of what number?
Solution: Let the value of that number = x

EZ problem Set-Up $\Rightarrow \dfrac{5}{7}$ of 14 is equal to $\dfrac{2}{5}$ of what number

$\Rightarrow \dfrac{5}{7} \times 14 = \dfrac{2}{5}x$ [Set up the equation]

$\Rightarrow 10 = \dfrac{2}{5}x$ [Simplify the left hand side]

$\Rightarrow x = 10 \times \dfrac{5}{2} = 25$ [Multiply both sides by 5/2]

Question #5: Eleven has how many fifths of eleven?
Solution: EZ Problem Set-Up $\Rightarrow$ Eleven has how many fifths of eleven

$$\Rightarrow 11 = n \times \frac{1}{5} \times 11 \qquad \text{[Set up the equation]}$$

$$\Rightarrow 11 = \frac{11}{5}n \qquad \text{[Simplify right side]}$$

$$\Rightarrow n = 5 \qquad \text{[Multiply both sides by 5/11]}$$

Therefore, eleven has 5 one-fifths of eleven.

Question #6: Hundred has how many fifths of twenty-five?
Solution: EZ Problem Set-Up $\Rightarrow$ Hundred has how many fifths of twenty-five

$$\Rightarrow 100 = n \times \frac{1}{5} \times 25 \qquad \text{[Set up the equation]}$$

$$\Rightarrow 100 = 5n \qquad \text{[Simplify right side]}$$
$$\Rightarrow n = 20 \qquad \text{[Divide both sides by 5]}$$

Therefore, hundred has 20 one-fifths of twenty-five.

Question #7: When a certain number is multiplied by 8, the result is 192. What is that number?
Solution: Let the value of that certain number = x
EZ problem Set-Up $\Rightarrow$ When a number is multiplied by 8, the result is 192
$$\Rightarrow 8x = 192 \qquad \text{[Set up the equation]}$$
$$\Rightarrow x = 24 \qquad \text{[Divide both sides by 8]}$$

Question #8: When a certain number is divided by 8, the result is 24. What is that number?
Solution: Let the value of that certain number = x
EZ problem Set-Up $\Rightarrow$ When a number is divided by 8, the result is 24

$$\Rightarrow \frac{x}{8} = 24 \qquad \text{[Set up the equation]}$$

$$\Rightarrow x = 192 \qquad \text{[Multiply both sides by 8]}$$

Question #9: If a certain number is doubled and the result is increased by 5, the result obtained in 19. What is the original number?
Solution: Let the value of the original number = x
EZ Problem Set-Up $\Rightarrow$ If x is doubled and 5 is added to it, the result is 19
$$\Rightarrow 2(x) + 5 = 19 \qquad \text{[Set up the equation]}$$
$$\Rightarrow 2x = 14 \qquad \text{[Subtract 5 from both sides]}$$
$$\Rightarrow x = 7 \qquad \text{[Divide both sides by 2]}$$

Question #10: The product of two numbers is 900. One number is tripled. In order for the product to remain the same, the other number must be multiplied by what number?
Solution: Product of two numbers $\Rightarrow$ 900
Let those two numbers be 100 and 9, then $\Rightarrow$ 100 × 9 = 900
Now, one of the numbers, let's say 100 is tripled $\Rightarrow$ 300 × n = 900
                                                        $\Rightarrow$ 300 × 3 = 900

3 is 1/3 of 9 $\Rightarrow 9 \times \frac{1}{3} = \frac{9}{3} = 3$

Therefore, the other number, in this case 9, must be multiplied by 1/3 or divided by 3, in order for the product to remain the same. Note: multiplying by 1/3 is the same as dividing by 3

Question #11: The product of two numbers is 800. One number is quadrupled. In order for the product to remain the same, the other number must be multiplied by what number?
Solution: Product of two numbers $\Rightarrow$ 800
Let those two numbers be 100 and 8, then $\Rightarrow$ 100 × 8 = 800
Now, one of the numbers, let's say 100 is quadrupled $\Rightarrow$ 400 × n = 800
                                                           $\Rightarrow$ 400 × 2 = 800

2 is ¼ of 8 $\Rightarrow 8 \times \frac{1}{4} = \frac{8}{4} = 2$

Therefore, the other number, in this case 8, must be multiplied by ¼ or divided by 4, in order for the product to remain the same. Note: multiplying by ¼ is the same as dividing by 4

Question #12: What is the sum of the product and the quotient of 8 and 8?
Solution: Product of 8 and 8 $\Rightarrow 8 \times 8 = 64$
                  Quotient of 8 and 8 $\Rightarrow 8 \div 8 = 1$
                  Sum of Product and Quotient $\Rightarrow$ Product + Quotient
                                              $\Rightarrow 64 + 1 = 65$

Question #13: What is the sum of the product and the quotient of 7 and 7?
Solution: Product of 7 and 7 $\Rightarrow 7 \times 7 = 49$
                  Quotientof 7 and 7 $\Rightarrow 7 \div 7 = 1$
                  Sum of Product and Quotient $\Rightarrow$ Product + Quotient
                                              $\Rightarrow 49 + 1 = 50$

Question #14: How much greater than $n - 2$ is $n + 7$?
Solution: EZ Problem Set-Up $\Rightarrow$ Find the difference between $n - 2$ and $n + 7$,
                                Or, what should be added to $n - 2$ to get $n + 7$.
                  $\Rightarrow n + 7 - (n - 2)$ [Set up the expression]
                  $\Rightarrow n + 7 - n + 2$ [Eliminate the parentheses]
                  $\Rightarrow 9$ [Combine like-terms]

Question #15: The number 1,000 is how many times the number 0.1?
Solution: EZ Problem Set-Up $\Rightarrow$ 1,000 is how many times 0.1
                  $\Rightarrow 1000 = 0.1x$ [Set up the equation]
                  $\Rightarrow x = 10,000$ [Divide both sides by 0.1]
                  Therefore, the number 1,000 is 10,000 times the number 0.1.

Question #16: The number 765 is how many times the number 0.15?
Solution: EZ Problem Set-Up $\Rightarrow$ 765 is how many times 0.15
                  $\Rightarrow 765 = 0.15x$ [Set up the equation]
                  $\Rightarrow x = 5,100$ [Divide both sides by 0.15]
                  Therefore, the number 765 is 5,100 times the number 0.15

Question #17: The value of $-2 - (-11)$ is how much greater than the value of $-11 - (-2)$?
Solution: Value of $-2 - (-11) \Rightarrow -2 + 11 = 9$
                  Value of $-11 - (-2) \Rightarrow -11 + 2 = -9$
                  Difference in the values $\Rightarrow 9 - (-9) = 9 + 9 = 18$

Question #18: To find 600 times 20, one could multiply 12 by what number?
Solution: This problem requires you to think of 600×20 as 12 times some number.
                  Rewrite 600 times 20 as $\Rightarrow 600 \times 20 = (6 \times 100) \times (2 \times 10) = (6 \times 2) \times (100 \times 10) = 12 \times 1,000$
                  Therefore, to find 600 times 20, one could multiply 12 by 1,000

Question #19: To find 75 times 20, one could multiply 25 by what number?
Solution: This problem requires you to think of 75×20 as 25 times some number.
                  Rewrite 75 times 20 as $\Rightarrow 75 \times 20 = (5 \times 15) \times (5 \times 4) = (5 \times 5) \times (15 \times 4) = 25 \times 60$
                  Therefore, to find 75 times 20, one could multiply 25 by 60

Question #20: To find 2.1×10^5, one could multiply 20 by what number?
Solution: This problem requires you to think of 2.1×10^5 as 20 times some number.
                  Rewrite 2.1×10^5 as $\Rightarrow 210,000$
                  Now, let's divide the result by 20 $\Rightarrow 210,000 \div 20 = 10,500$
                  Therefore, to find 2.1×10^5, one could multiply 20 by 10,500

Question #21: If the sum of two consecutive integers is 101, what is the value of the bigger number?
Solution: Let, the value of first integer $\Rightarrow n$

Then, the value of second integer ⇒ $n + 1$
EZ Problem Set-Up ⇒ Sum of two consecutive integers is 101
⇒ $n + (n + 1) = 101$ [Set up the equation]
⇒ $2n + 1 = 101$ [Combine like-terms]
⇒ $2n = 100$ [Subtract 1 from both sides]
⇒ $n = 50$ [Divide both sides by 2]
Value of first integer (smaller)   ⇒ $n = 50$
Value of second integer (bigger)   ⇒ $n + 1 = 50 + 1 = 51$

Question #22: If the sum of three consecutive integers is 177, what is the value of the middle number?
Solution: Let, the value of first integer   ⇒ n
Then, the value of second integer ⇒ $n + 1$
And, the value of third integer   ⇒ $n + 2$
EZ Problem Set-Up ⇒ Sum of three consecutive integers is 177
⇒ $n + (n + 1) + (n + 2) = 177$ [Set up the equation]
⇒ $3n + 3 = 177$ [Combine like-terms]
⇒ $3n = 174$ [Subtract 3 from both sides]
⇒ $n = 58$ [Divide both sides by 3]
Value of first integer (smallest)   ⇒ $n = 58$
Value of second integer (middle)   ⇒ $n + 1 = 58 + 1 = 59$
Value of third integer (biggest)   ⇒ $n + 2 = 58 + 2 = 60$

Question #23: If the sum of two even consecutive integers is 150, what is the value of the bigger number?
Solution: Let, the value of first even integer   ⇒ n
Then, the value of second even integer   ⇒ $n + 2$
EZ Problem Set-Up ⇒ Sum of two even consecutive integers is 150
⇒ $n + (n + 2) = 150$ [Set up the equation]
⇒ $2n + 2 = 150$ [Combine like-terms]
⇒ $2n = 148$ [Subtract 2 from both sides]
⇒ $n = 74$ [Divide both sides by 2]
Value of first even integer (smaller)   ⇒ $n = 74$
Value of second even integer (bigger) ⇒ $n + 2 = 74 + 2 = 76$

Question #24: If the sum of two odd consecutive integers is 152, what is the value of the bigger number?
Solution: Let, the value of first odd integer   ⇒ n
Then, the value of second odd integer ⇒ $n + 2$
EZ Problem Set-Up ⇒ Sum of two odd consecutive integers is 152
⇒ $n + (n + 2) = 152$ [Set up the equation]
⇒ $2n + 2 = 152$ [Combine like-terms]
⇒ $2n = 150$ [Subtract 2 from both sides]
⇒ $n = 75$ [Divide both sides by 2]
Value of first odd integer (smaller)   ⇒ $n = 75$
Value of second odd integer (bigger) ⇒ $n + 2 = 75 + 2 = 77$

Question #25: If the sum of three odd consecutive integers is 171, what is the value of the middle number?
Solution: Let, the value of first odd integer   ⇒ n
Then, the value of second odd integer ⇒ $n + 2$
And, the value of third odd integer   ⇒ $n + 4$
EZ Problem Set-Up ⇒ Sum of three odd consecutive integers is 171
⇒ $n + (n + 2) + (n + 4) = 171$ [Set up the equation]
⇒ $3n + 6 = 171$ [Combine like-terms]
⇒ $3n = 165$ [Subtract 6 from both sides]
⇒ $n = 55$ [Divide both sides by 3]
Value of first odd integer (smallest)   ⇒ $n = 55$
Value of second odd integer (middle)   ⇒ $n + 2 = 55 + 2 = 57$
Value of third odd integer (biggest)   ⇒ $n + 4 = 55 + 4 = 59$

Question #26: If the sum of three consecutive integers is 198, what is the sum of the next three consecutive integers?
Solution: Let, the value of first integer $\Rightarrow n$
Then the value of second integer $\Rightarrow n + 1$
And, the value of third integer $\Rightarrow n + 2$
EZ Problem Set-Up $\Rightarrow$ Sum of three consecutive integers is 198
$\Rightarrow n + (n + 1) + (n + 2) = 198$ [Set up the equation]
$\Rightarrow 3n + 3 = 198$ [Combine like-terms]
$\Rightarrow 3n = 195$ [Subtract 3 from both sides]
$\Rightarrow n = 65$ [Divide both sides by 3]
Value of first three consecutive integers $\Rightarrow$ 65, 66, and 67
Value of next three consecutive integers $\Rightarrow$ 68, 69, and 70
Sum of next three consecutive integers $\Rightarrow$ 68 + 69 + 70 = 207

Question #27: A teacher wrote three consecutive even integers on the board. She then multiplied the first by 5, the second by 7, and the third by 9. Finally, she added all six numbers and got a sum of 296. What was the value of the middle integer she wrote?
Solution: Let, the value of first even integer $\Rightarrow n$
Then, the value of second even integer $\Rightarrow n + 2$
And, the value of third even integer $\Rightarrow n + 4$
EZ Problem Set-Up $\Rightarrow$ Sum of three consecutive even integers and 5 times the first integer, 7 times the second integer, 9 times the third integer is 296
$\Rightarrow n + (n + 2) + (n + 4) + 5n + 7(n + 2) + 9(n + 4) = 296$ [Set up the equation]
$\Rightarrow n + n + 2 + n + 4 + 5n + 7n + 14 + 9n + 36 = 296$ [Apply distributive property]
$\Rightarrow 24n + 56 = 296$ [Combine like-terms]
$\Rightarrow 24n = 240$ [Subtract 56 from both sides]
$\Rightarrow n = 10$ [Divide both sides by 24]
Value of the first (smallest) integer $\Rightarrow n = 10$
Value of the second (middle) integer $\Rightarrow n + 2 = 10 + 2 = 12$
Value of the third (biggest) integer $\Rightarrow n + 4 = 10 + 4 = 14$

Question #28: If the sum of three consecutive integers is 20 more than the middle integer, what is the value of the smallest of the three?
Solution: Let, the value of smallest integer $\Rightarrow n$
Then, the value of middle integer $\Rightarrow n + 1$
And, the value of biggest integer $\Rightarrow n + 2$
EZ Problem Set-Up $\Rightarrow$ Sum of three consecutive integers is 20 more than the middle integer
$\Rightarrow n + (n + 1) + (n + 2) = 20 + (n + 1)$ [Set up the equation]
$\Rightarrow 3n + 3 = 21 + n$ [Combine like-terms]
$\Rightarrow 2n + 3 = 21$ [Subtract n from both sides]
$\Rightarrow 2n = 18$ [Subtract 3 from both sides]
$\Rightarrow n = 9$ [Divide both sides by 2]
Value of the smallest integer $\Rightarrow n = 9$
Value of the middle integer $\Rightarrow n + 1 = 9 + 1 = 10$
Value of the biggest integer $\Rightarrow n + 2 = 9 + 2 = 11$

Question #29: If $2n - 8$ is an odd integer, what is the value of the next larger even integer?
Solution: Since an even integer follow an odd integer, simply add 1 to the odd integer to find the next larger even integer $\Rightarrow (2n - 8) + 1 = 2n - 7$

Question #30: If $2n - 10$ is an odd integer, what is the value of the next larger odd integer?
Solution: Since odd integers follow with a difference of 2, simply add 2 to the odd integer to find the next larger odd integer $\Rightarrow (2n - 10) + 2 = 2n - 8$

Question #31: If the product of 5 and 18 more than a certain integer is 11 times that integer, what is the value of that integer?

Solution: Let, the value of that integer $\Rightarrow n$

EZ Problem Set-Up $\Rightarrow$ Product of 5 and 18 more than a certain integer is 11 times that integer

$\Rightarrow 5(18 + n) = 11n$	[Set up the equation]
$\Rightarrow 90 + 5n = 11n$	[Apply distributive property]
$\Rightarrow 90 = 6n$	[Subtract $5n$ from both sides]
$\Rightarrow n = 15$	[Divide both sides by 6]

Value of that integer $\Rightarrow n = 15$

Question #32:   If sum of two integers is 79, and one of the integers is 7 more than five times the other integer, what is the value of the bigger of the two integers?

Solution: Let, the value of one of the integers $\Rightarrow n$

Then, the value of other integer $\Rightarrow 5n + 7$

EZ Problem Set-Up $\Rightarrow$ Sum of one integer and another integer, which is 7 more than 5 times the first integer is 79

$\Rightarrow n + (5n + 7) = 79$	[Set up the equation]
$\Rightarrow 6n + 7 = 79$	[Combine like-terms]
$\Rightarrow 6n = 72$	[Subtract 7 from both sides]
$\Rightarrow n = 12$	[Divide both sides by 6]

Value of one of the integers $\Rightarrow n = 12$

Value of the other integer $\Rightarrow 5n + 7 = 5(12) + 7 = 67$

Question #33:   If the sum of two integers is 77, and one of the integers is 1 less than twice the other integer, what is the value of the bigger of the two integers?

Solution: Let, the value of one of the integers $\Rightarrow n$

Then, the value of the other integer $\Rightarrow 2n - 1$

EZ Problem Set-Up $\Rightarrow$ Sum of one integer and another integer, which is 1 less than twice the first integer is 77

$\Rightarrow n + (2n - 1) = 77$	[Set up the equation]
$\Rightarrow 3n - 1 = 77$	[Combine like-terms]
$\Rightarrow 3n = 78$	[Add 1 to both sides]
$\Rightarrow n = 26$	[Divide both sides by 3]

Value of one of the integers $\Rightarrow n = 26$

Value of the other integer $\Rightarrow 2n - 1 = 2(26) - 1 = 52 - 1 = 51$

Question #34:   If the sum of two integers is 149, and one of the integers is one less than twice the other integer, what is the value of the bigger of the two integers?

Solution: Let, the value of one of the integers $\Rightarrow n$

Then, the value of the other integer $\Rightarrow 2n - 1$

EZ Problem Set-Up $\Rightarrow$ Sum of one integer and another integer, which is 1 less than twice the first integer is 149

$\Rightarrow n + (2n - 1) = 149$	[Set up the equation]
$\Rightarrow 3n - 1 = 149$	[Combine like-terms]
$\Rightarrow 3n = 150$	[Add 1 to both sides]
$\Rightarrow n = 50$	[Divide both sides by 3]

Value of one of the integers $\Rightarrow n = 50$

Value of the other integer $\Rightarrow 2n - 1 = 2(50) - 1 = 100 - 1 = 99$

Question #35:   If sum of two integers is 127, and one of the integer is 7 more than five times the other integer, what is the value of the bigger of the two integers?

Solution: Let, the value of one of the integers $\Rightarrow n$

Then, the value of the other integer $\Rightarrow 5n + 7$

EZ Problem Set-Up $\Rightarrow$ Sum of one integer and another integer, which is 7 more than 5 times the first integer is 127

$\Rightarrow n + (5n + 7) = 127$	[Set up the equation]
$\Rightarrow 6n + 7 = 127$	[Combine like-terms]
$\Rightarrow 6n = 120$	[Subtract 7 from both sides]

$\Rightarrow n = 20$ [Divide both sides by 6]

Value of one of the integers (smaller) $\Rightarrow n = 20$

Value of the other integers (bigger) $\Rightarrow 5n + 7 = 5(20) + 7 = 100 + 7 = 107$

Question #36: If 7 times an integer less 5 times the integer is 50, what is the value of the integer?

Solution: Let, the value of the integer be $\Rightarrow n$

EZ Problem Set-Up $\Rightarrow$ 7 times an integer less 5 times the integer is 50

$\Rightarrow 7n - 5n = 50$ [Set up the equation]

$\Rightarrow 2n = 50$ [Combine like-terms]

Value of the integer $\Rightarrow n = 25$ [Divide both sides by 2]

Question #37: If the difference between two integers is 2 and their sum is 50, what are the values of those two integers?

Solution: Let, the value of the first integer $\Rightarrow x$

And, the value of the second integer $\Rightarrow y$

Difference between two integers is 2 $\Rightarrow x - y = 2$ $\Rightarrow$ Equation #1

Sum of two integers is 50 $\Rightarrow \underline{x + y = 50}$ $\Rightarrow$ Equation #2

$2x = 52$ [Add both equations]

$x = 26$ [Divide both sides by 2]

Substitute the value of x into Eq #1 $\Rightarrow x - y = 2$ [Rewrite Equation #1]

$\Rightarrow 26 - y = 2$ [Substitute $x = 26$]

$\Rightarrow -y = -24$ [Subtract 26 from both sides]

$\Rightarrow y = 24$ [Multiply both sides by −1]

Value of the first integer $\Rightarrow x = 26$

Value of the first integer $\Rightarrow y = 24$

Question #38: If the difference between two integers is 5 and their sum is 155, what are the values of those two integers?

Solution: Let, the value of the first integer $\Rightarrow x$

And, the value of the second integer $\Rightarrow y$

Difference between two integers is 5 $\Rightarrow x - y = 5$ $\Rightarrow$ Equation #1

Sum of two integers is 155 $\Rightarrow \underline{x + y = 155}$ $\Rightarrow$ Equation #2

$2x = 160$ [Add both the equations]

$x = 80$ [Divide both sides by 2]

Substitute the value of x into Eq #1 $\Rightarrow x - y = 5$ [Rewrite Equation #1]

$\Rightarrow 80 - y = 5$ [Substitute $x = 80$]

$\Rightarrow -y = -75$ [Subtract 80 from both sides]

$\Rightarrow y = 75$ [Multiply both sides by −1]

Value of the first integer $\Rightarrow x = 80$

Value of the first integer $\Rightarrow y = 75$

Question #39: If the difference between two integers is 20 and their sum is 2, what are the values of those two integers?

Solution: Let, the value of the first integer $\Rightarrow x$

And, the value of the second integer $\Rightarrow y$

Difference between two integers is 20 $\Rightarrow x - y = 20$ $\Rightarrow$ Equation #1

Sum of two integers is 2 $\Rightarrow \underline{x + y = 2}$ $\Rightarrow$ Equation #2

$2x = 22$ [Add both equations]

$x = 11$ [Divide both sides by 2]

Substitute the value of x into Eq #1 $\Rightarrow x - y = 20$ [Rewrite Equation #1]

$\Rightarrow 11 - y = 20$ [Substitute $x = 11$]

$\Rightarrow -y = 9$ [Subtract 11 from both sides]

$\Rightarrow y = -9$ [Multiply both sides by −1]

Value of the first integer $\Rightarrow x = 11$

Value of the first integer $\Rightarrow y = -9$

Question #40: If the difference between two integers is 128 and their sum is 26, what are the values of those two integers?

Solution: Let, the value of the first integer $\Rightarrow x$
And, the value of the second integer $\Rightarrow y$

Difference between two integers is 128	$\Rightarrow$	$x - y = 128$	$\Rightarrow$ Equation #1
Sum of two integers is 26	$\Rightarrow$	$x + y = 26$	$\Rightarrow$ Equation #2
Add both the equations		$2x = 154$	[Add both equations]
		$x = 77$	[Divide both sides by 2]

Substitute the value of x into Equation #1 $\Rightarrow x - y = 128$ [Rewrite Equation #1]
                                         $\Rightarrow 77 - y = 128$ [Substitute $x = 77$]
                                           $\Rightarrow -y = 51$ [Subtract 77 from both sides]
                                           $\Rightarrow y = -51$ [Multiply both sides by −1]

Value of the first integer $\Rightarrow x = 77$
Value of the first integer $\Rightarrow y = -51$

Question #41: Monika has $1.90, consisting of nickels and dimes. If she has 11 more nickels than dimes, how many nickels does she have?

Solution: Let, the No. of dimes $\Rightarrow d$
Then, the No. of nickels $\Rightarrow d + 11$
Since each dime is worth 10 cents $\Rightarrow$ Value of dimes in cents = $10d$
Since each nickel is worth 5 cents $\Rightarrow$ Value of nickels in cents = $5(d + 11) = 5d + 55$
Total value of money $\Rightarrow$ $1.90 or 190 cents
EZ Problem Set-Up $\Rightarrow$ Value of dimes in cents + Value of nickels in cents = 190 cents
                         $\Rightarrow 10d + 5d + 55 = 190$ [Substitute the value of dimes & nickels in cents]
                         $\Rightarrow 15d + 55 = 190$ [Combine like-terms]
                         $\Rightarrow 15d = 135$ [Subtract 55 from both sides]
                         $\Rightarrow d = 9$ [Divide both sides by 15]
Therefore, Monika has 9 dimes and 9 + 11 = 20 nickels

Question #42: Monika has $5.85, consisting of nickels and quarter. If she has 9 more quarters than nickels, how many nickels does she have?

Solution: Let, the No. of nickels $\Rightarrow n$
Then, the No. of quarters $\Rightarrow n + 9$
Since each nickel is worth 5 cents $\Rightarrow$ Value of nickels in cents = $5n$
Since each quarter is worth 25 cents $\Rightarrow$ Value of quarters in cents = $25(n + 9) = 25n + 225$
Total value of money $\Rightarrow$ $5.85 or 585 cents
EZ Problem Set-Up $\Rightarrow$ Value of nickels in cents + Value of quarters in cents = 585 cents
                         $\Rightarrow 5n + 25n + 225 = 585$ [Substitute the value of nickels & quarters in cents]
                         $\Rightarrow 30n + 225 = 585$ [Combine like-terms]
                         $\Rightarrow 30n = 360$ [Subtract 225 from both sides]
                         $\Rightarrow n = 12$ [Divide both sides by 30]
Therefore, Monika has 12 nickels and 12 + 9 = 21 quarters

Question #43: Monika has $7.35, consisting of dimes and quarter. If she has 7 more quarters than dimes, how many dimes does she have?

Solution: Let, the No. of dimes $\Rightarrow d$
Then, the No. of quarters $\Rightarrow d + 7$
Since each dime is worth 10 cents $\Rightarrow$ Value of dimes in cents = $10d$
Since each quarter is worth 25 cents $\Rightarrow$ Value of quarters in cents = $25(d + 7) = 25d + 175$
Total value of money $\Rightarrow$ $7.35 or 735 cents
EZ Problem Set-Up $\Rightarrow$ Value of dimes in cents + Value of quarters in cents = 735 cents
                         $\Rightarrow 10d + 25d + 175 = 735$ [Substitute the value of dimes & quarters in cents]
                         $\Rightarrow 35d + 175 = 735$ [Combine like-terms]
                         $\Rightarrow 35d = 560$ [Subtract 175 from both sides]
                         $\Rightarrow d = 16$ [Divide both sides by 35]
Therefore, Monika has 16 dimes and 16 + 7 = 23 quarters

Question #44:   Maria has $6.75 in nickels and dimes. If the number of dimes is 2 times the number of nickels, how many dimes does she have?

Solution: Let, the No. of nickels $\Rightarrow n$
Then, the No. of dimes $\Rightarrow 2n$
Since each nickel is worth 5 cents $\Rightarrow$ Value of nickels in cents = $5n$
Since each dime is worth 10 cents $\Rightarrow$ Value of dimes in cents = $10(2n) = 20n$
Total value of money $\Rightarrow$ $6.75 or 675 cents
EZ Problem Set-Up $\Rightarrow$ Value of nickels in cents + Value of dimes in cents = 675 cents
$\quad\quad\quad\quad\quad \Rightarrow 5n + 20n = 675$ [Substitute the value of nickels & dimes in cents]
$\quad\quad\quad\quad\quad \Rightarrow 25n = 675$ [Combine like-terms]
$\quad\quad\quad\quad\quad \Rightarrow n = 27$ [Divide both sides by 25]
Therefore, Maria has 27 nickels and 2 × 27 = 54 dimes

Question #45:   Maria has $6.05 in nickels and quarters. If the number of quarters is 2 times the number of nickels, how many quarters does she have?

Solution: Let, the No. of nickels $\Rightarrow n$
Then, the No. of quarters $\Rightarrow 2n$
Since each nickel is worth 5 cents $\Rightarrow$ Value of nickels in cents = $5n$
Since each quarter is worth 25 cents $\Rightarrow$ Value of quarters in cents = $25(2n) = 50n$
Total value of money $\Rightarrow$ $6.05 or 605 cents
EZ Problem Set-Up $\Rightarrow$ Value of nickels in cents + Value of quarters in cents = 605 cents
$\quad\quad\quad\quad\quad \Rightarrow 5n + 50n = 605$ [Substitute the value of nickels & quarters in cents]
$\quad\quad\quad\quad\quad \Rightarrow 55n = 605$ [Combine like-terms]
$\quad\quad\quad\quad\quad \Rightarrow n = 11$ [Divide both sides by 55]
Therefore, Maria has 11 nickels and 2 × 11 = 22 quarters

Question #46:   Maria has $2.70 in dimes and quarters. If the number of quarters is 5 times the number of dimes, how many quarters does she have?

Solution: Let, the No. of dimes $\Rightarrow d$
Then, the No. of quarters $\Rightarrow 5d$
Since each dime is worth 10 cents $\Rightarrow$ Value of dimes in cents = $10d$
Since each quarter is worth 25 cents $\Rightarrow$ Value of quarters in cents = $25(5d) = 125d$
Total value of money $\Rightarrow$ $2.70 or 270 cents
EZ Problem Set-Up $\Rightarrow$ Value of dimes in cents + Value of quarters in cents = 270 cents
$\quad\quad\quad\quad\quad \Rightarrow 10d + 125d = 270$ [Substitute the value of dimes & quarters in cents]
$\quad\quad\quad\quad\quad \Rightarrow 135d = 270$ [Combine like-terms]
$\quad\quad\quad\quad\quad \Rightarrow d = 2$ [Divide both sides by 135]
Therefore, Maria has 2 dimes and 2 × 5 = 10 quarters

Question #47:   In a piggy bank containing nickels and dimes, the ratio of nickels to dimes is 2:5. If there are 84 coins in all, what is the value of the nickels?

Solution: Since the ratio of nickels to dime is 2:5 $\Rightarrow$ Let the No. of nickels = $2x$
$\quad\quad\quad\quad\quad\quad\quad\quad\quad\quad\quad\quad\quad\quad\quad \Rightarrow$ And, the No. of dimes = $5x$
Since there are a total of 84 coins $\Rightarrow 2x + 5x = 84$
$\quad\quad\quad\quad\quad\quad\quad\quad\quad\quad \Rightarrow 7x = 84$
$\quad\quad\quad\quad\quad\quad\quad\quad\quad\quad \Rightarrow x = 12$
Therefore, there are 12 × 2 = 24 nickels, with a value of 24 × $0.05 = $1.20

Question #48:   A piggy bank has 100 coins, all of which are either nickels or dimes, worth a total of $7.75. How many dimes are there?

Solution: Let, the No. of dimes $\Rightarrow d$
Then, the No. of nickels $\Rightarrow 100 - d$
Since each dime is worth 10 cents $\Rightarrow$ Value of dimes in cents = $10d$
Since each nickel is worth 5 cents $\Rightarrow$ Value of nickels in cents = $5(100 - d) = 500 - 5d$
Total value of money = $7.75 or 775 cents

EZ Problem Set-Up $\Rightarrow$ Value of dimes in cents + Value of nickels in cents = 775 cents
                           $\Rightarrow 10d + 500 - 5d = 775$ [Substitute the value of dimes and nickels in cents]
                           $\Rightarrow 5d + 500 = 775$ [Combine like-terms]
                           $\Rightarrow 5d = 275$ [Subtract 500 from both sides]
                           $\Rightarrow d = 55$ [Divide both sides by 5]
Therefore, there are 55 dimes and $100 - 55 = 45$ nickels in the piggy bank.

Alternate Method:
Let, the No. of nickels $\Rightarrow n$
And, the No. of dimes $\Rightarrow d$
Total No. of coins (nickels & dimes) is 100 $\Rightarrow n + d = 100$ $\Rightarrow$ Equation #1
Each nickel = 5 cents & each dime = 10 cents $\Rightarrow 5n + 10d = 775$ $\Rightarrow$ Equation #2
Multiply Equation #1 by 10 $\Rightarrow 10n + 10d = 1{,}000$ $\Rightarrow$ Equation #3
Subtract Equation #2 from Equation #3 $10n \quad + \quad 10d \quad = 1{,}000$
                                            $\underline{-5n \quad - \quad 10d \quad = -775}$
                                       $5n \qquad\qquad\qquad = 225$
                                 $\Rightarrow n = 225 \div 5 = 45$
Substitute the value of $n = 45$ in Equation #1 $\Rightarrow 45 + d = 100$
                                       $\Rightarrow d = 100 - 45 = 55$
Therefore, there are 45 nickels and 55 dimes in the piggy bank.

PART 4.0: LITERAL EXPRESSIONS:

TABLE OF CONTENTS:

PART 4.0: LITERAL EXPRESSIONS: 77
    4.1: Communicating with Letters:..78
    Practice Exercise – Questions and Answers With Explanations: Literal Expressions:...79

4.1: COMMUNICATING WITH LETTERS:

Many students who have no problem computing with numbers become quite terrified when it comes to letters. Dealing with letters is completely different from computing with numbers; however, the fundamentals are still the same. If you understand the concepts of a problem in which numbers are given, you simply need to apply the same concepts to the letters. The computational procedures are similar, just determine what you would do if you had numbers instead, and do exactly the same thing with the given letters.

Example #1:   If p pencils cost c cents, what is the cost of one pencil?

Solution: Cost of p Pencils $\Rightarrow c$ cents

            Cost of 1 Pencil $\Rightarrow \dfrac{c}{p}$

Example #2:   If it takes t tablespoons of tea to make c cups of tea, how many tablespoons of tea are needed to make d cups of tea?

Solution: No. of Tablespoons of Tea needed to make c cups of tea $\Rightarrow t$

            No. of Tablespoons of Tea needed to make 1 cup of tea $\Rightarrow \dfrac{t}{c}$

            No. of Tablespoons of Tea needed to make d cups of tea $\Rightarrow \dfrac{td}{c}$

Example #3:   If 1 notebook costs d dollars, what is the cost, in dollars, of n notebooks?

Solution: Cost of 1 Notebook $\Rightarrow d$ dollars
            Cost of n Notebooks $\Rightarrow nd$ dollars

Example #4:   The cost for developing and printing a roll of film is m cents for processing the roll and n cents for each print. How much will it cost, in cents, to develop and print a roll of film with 25 exposures?

Solution: Cost of Developing a Roll $\Rightarrow m$ cents
            Cost of Printing 1 Picture $\Rightarrow n$ cents
            Cost of Printing 25 Pictures $\Rightarrow 25n$ cents
            Total Cost of Developing & Printing $\Rightarrow m + 25n$ cents

Example #5:   The cost of renting a car is d dollars per day and c cents per mile. What is the total cost of renting a car, in dollars, for 5 days and driving 1,000 miles?

Solution: Cost of Daily Charges = d dollars/day $\Rightarrow$ Cost of Daily Charges for 5 Days = $5d$ dollars
            Cost for Driving 1 Mile = c cents $\Rightarrow$ Cost for Driving 1,000 Miles = $1,000c$ cents = $10c$ dollars
            Total Cost for 5 Days and 1,000 Miles = $5d + 10c$ dollars

Example #6:   Hector gave Stacy x marbles. He then gave Tracy one marble more than he gave Stacy. Next, he gave Macy two marbles fewer than he gave Tracy. Finally, he gave Lacy twice the number of marbles he gave Stacy. In terms of x, altogether how many marbles did Hector give out all four girls?

Solution: No. of marbles given to Stacy $\Rightarrow x$
            No. of marbles given to Tracy $\Rightarrow x + 1$
            No. of marbles given to Macy $\Rightarrow (x + 1) - 2 = x - 1$
            No. of marbles given to Lacy $\Rightarrow 2x$
            Total No. of marbles given out $\Rightarrow x + (x + 1) + (x - 1) + 2x = 5x$

PRACTICE EXERCISE – QUESTIONS AND ANSWERS WITH EXPLANATIONS: LITERAL EXPRESSIONS:

Question #1: If a car covers m miles in h hours, what is the number of miles it covers in one hour?

Solution: In h hours, the car covers $\Rightarrow m$ miles

In 1 hour, the car covers $\Rightarrow \dfrac{m}{h}$ miles

Question #2: A certain state teachers association has a total of t teachers from c counties. If each county has the same number of teachers, how many teachers does each county have?

Solution: No. of teachers in c counties $\Rightarrow t$

No. of teachers in each county $\Rightarrow \dfrac{t}{c}$

Question #3: If a car covers m miles in h hours, what is the number of miles it covers in n hour?

Solution: In h hours, the car covers $\Rightarrow m$ miles

In 1 hour, the car covers $\Rightarrow \dfrac{m}{h}$ miles

In n hours, the car covers $\Rightarrow \dfrac{mn}{h}$ miles

Question #4: If g gallons of gasoline cost d dollars, what is the cost of h gallons of gasoline?

Solution: Cost of g gallons of gasoline $\Rightarrow d$ dollars

Cost of 1 gallon of gasoline $\Rightarrow \dfrac{d}{g}$ dollars

Cost of h gallons of gasoline $\Rightarrow \dfrac{dh}{g}$

Question #5: If p pills cost c cents, then at this rate how many cents will 5 pills cost?

Solution: Cost of p pills $\Rightarrow c$ cents

Cost of 1 pill $\Rightarrow \dfrac{c}{p}$ cents

Cost of 5 pills $\Rightarrow \dfrac{5c}{p}$ cents

Question #6: If it takes an athlete 7 minutes to run x meters, how many meters can he run in y minutes, at the same rate?

Solution: No. of Meters ran in 7 minutes $\Rightarrow x$ meters

No. of Meters ran in 1 minute $\Rightarrow \dfrac{x}{7}$ meters

No. of Meters ran in y minutes $\Rightarrow \dfrac{xy}{7}$ meters

Question #7: How many minutes will it take to type y words at the rate of x word per every 5 minutes?

Solution: No. of Minutes it takes to type x words $\Rightarrow 5$ minutes

No. of Minutes it takes to type 1 word $\Rightarrow \dfrac{5}{x}$ minutes

No. of Minutes it takes to type y word $\Rightarrow \dfrac{5y}{x}$ minutes

Question #8: If the cost of d dozen roses is r dollars, what is the cost of one rose?

Solution:

Cost of d dozen Roses $\Rightarrow r$ dollars

Cost of 1 dozen Roses $\Rightarrow \dfrac{r}{d}$ dollars

Cost of 1 Rose $\Rightarrow \dfrac{r}{12d}$

Question #9: If e erasers cost c cents, how many erasers can be bought for d dollars?

Solution:

No. of Erasers that can be bought with c cents $\Rightarrow e$

No. of Erasers that can be bought with 1 cent $\Rightarrow \dfrac{e}{c}$

No. of Erasers that can be bought with 100 cents or 1 dollar $\Rightarrow \dfrac{100e}{c}$

No. of Erasers that can be bought with d dollars $\Rightarrow \dfrac{100de}{c}$

Question #10: In a certain school, there are c classes with s students in each class. If a total of n notebooks are distributed equally among all students, how many notebooks will each student get?

Solution:

No. of classes in the school $\Rightarrow c$

No. of students in each class $\Rightarrow s$

Total No. of students in the school $\Rightarrow cs$

Total No. of notebooks distributed $\Rightarrow n$

No. of notebooks for each student $\Rightarrow \dfrac{n}{cs}$

Question #11: Richard can type a full thesis in h hours. At this rate, how many theses can he type in m minutes?

Solution:

No. of Theses typed in h hours $\Rightarrow 1$

No. of Theses typed in 1 hour $\Rightarrow \dfrac{1}{h}$

No. of Theses typed in 60 minutes $\Rightarrow \dfrac{1}{h}$

No. of Theses typed in 1 minute $\Rightarrow \dfrac{1}{60h}$

No. of Theses typed in m minutes $\Rightarrow \dfrac{m}{60h}$

Question #12: If x workers can build a house in z days, how many days will it take y workers, working at the same rate, to build 5 similar houses?

Solution:

No. of days, x workers will take to build a house $\Rightarrow z$

No. of days, 1 worker will take to build a house $\Rightarrow zx$

No. of days, y workers will take to build a house $\Rightarrow \dfrac{xz}{y}$

No. of days, y workers will take to build 5 houses $\Rightarrow \dfrac{5xz}{y}$

Question #13: Macy has n marbles, which is 5 times as many as Nancy has and ½ as many as Tracy has. How many marbles do the three of them have in total, in terms of n?

Solution:

No. of marbles Macy has $\Rightarrow n$

No. of marbles Nancy has $\Rightarrow \dfrac{n}{5}$

No. of marbles Tracy has $\Rightarrow 2n$

Total No. of marbles $\Rightarrow n + \dfrac{n}{5} + 2n = \dfrac{5n}{5} + \dfrac{n}{5} + \dfrac{10n}{5} = \dfrac{16n}{5}$

Question #14: What is the number of days in *n* weeks and *n* days?
Solution: Since 1 week has 7 days ⇒ *n* weeks will have 7*n* days
Add *n* additional days   ⇒ *n* Weeks and *n* Days will have = 7*n* + *n* = 8*n* days

Question #15: The cost of a ferry ride is *d* dollars for the car and driver and *c* cents for each additional passenger. What is the charge, in dollars, for a car containing five passengers?
Solution: Charges for Car and Driver   ⇒ *d* dollars
Charges for each Additional Passenger   ⇒ *c* cents
Charges for 5 Additional Passengers   ⇒ 5*c* cents = 5*c* ÷ 100 = 0.05 *c* dollars
Total Charges for Car + Driver + 5 Passengers ⇒ *d* + 0.05*c* dollars

Question #16: What is the total cost, in cents, of *b* books at *d* dollars each and *n* books at *c* cents each?
Solution: Cost for 1 Book = *d* dollars each ⇒ Cost of *b* Books = *bd* dollars = 100*bd* cents
Cost of 1 Book = *c* cents each   ⇒ Cost of *n* Books = *nc* cents
Total Cost of *b* Books + *n* Books ⇒ (100*bd* + *nc*) cents

Question #17: What is the total cost of a long distance call of *m* minutes if the charge is *c* cents for the first 5 minutes and *d* cents for each additional minute, if *m* is greater than 5?
Solution: Cost for first 5 minutes   ⇒ *c* cents
Cost for additional minutes over 5 minutes   ⇒ *d* cents per minutes = *d*(*m* − 5)
Total cost of a call of *m* minutes   ⇒ *c* + *d*(*m* − 5) = *c* + *dm* − 5*d*

Question #18: What is the total cost of mailing a package of *p* pound if the charge is *n* dollars for the first *q* pounds and *m* dollars for each additional pound, if *p* is greater than *q*?
Solution: Cost for first *q* pounds   ⇒ *n* dollars
Cost for additional pounds over *q* pounds   ⇒ *m* dollars per pound = *m*(*p* − *q*)
Total cost of sending a package of *p* pounds ⇒ *n* + *m*(*p* − *q*) = *n* + *mp* − *mq*

Question #19: What is the number of seats in an auditorium if there are *r* rows with *m* seats each and *s* rows with *n* seats each?
Solution: Total No. of seats in *r* rows with *m* seats each ⇒ *rm* seats
Total No. of seats in *s* rows with *n* seats each ⇒ *sn* seats
Total No. of seats in the whole movie theater ⇒ *rm* + *sn* seats

Question #20: What is the number of seats in a movie theater if there are *r* rows with *s* seats each and *s* rows with *r* seats each?
Solution: Total No. of seats in *r* rows with *s* seats each ⇒ *rs* seats
Total No. of seats in *s* rows with *r* seats each ⇒ *sr* seats
Total No. of seats in the whole movie theater ⇒ *rs* + *sr* = 2*rs* seats

Question #21: At a certain store, a decorative brick costs *d* dollars and *c* cents. What is the cost, in cents, of *b* bricks?
Solution: Cost of 1 brick   ⇒ *d* dollars + *c* cents = 100*d* cents + *c* cents = 100*d* + *c* cents
Cost of *b* bricks ⇒ *b*(100*d* + *c*) = 100*bd* + *bc* cents

Question #22: The cost of 100 kilograms of cement is *x* dollars, and one kilogram of cement costs the same as *y* kilogram of gravel. What is the cost, in dollars, of one kilogram of gravel?
Solution: Price of 100 kg of cement   ⇒ *x* dollars

Price of 1 kg of cement   ⇒ $\frac{x}{100}$ dollars

Price of *y* kg of gravel   ⇒ $\frac{x}{100}$ dollars

Price of 1 kg of gravel   ⇒ $\frac{x}{100y}$ dollars

Question #23: What is the total cost of sending a telegram of *w* words if the charge is *c* cents for the first 25 words and *d* cents for each additional word, if *w* is greater than 25?

Solution: Cost for first 25 words $\Rightarrow c$ cents
Cost for additional words over 25 words $\Rightarrow d$ cents per word $= d(w - 25)$
Total cost of sending a telegram of w words $\Rightarrow c + d(w - 25) = c + dw - 25d$

Question #24: What is the number of minutes in h hours and m minutes?
Solution: Since 1 hour has 60 minutes $\Rightarrow h$ hours will have $60h$ minutes
Add m additional minutes $\Rightarrow h$ Hours and m Minutes will have $= 60h + m$ minutes

Question #25: How many nickels are equivalent to d dimes and q quarters?
Solution: Since, 1 Dime = 10 cents $\Rightarrow d$ Dimes $= 10d$ cents
Since, 1 Quarter = 25 cents $\Rightarrow q$ Quarters $= 25q$ cents
Therefore, d Dimes and q Quarters $\Rightarrow 10d + 25q$ cents

No. of Nickels in d Dimes and q Quarters $\Rightarrow \dfrac{10d + 25q}{5} = \dfrac{10d}{5} + \dfrac{25q}{5} = 2d + 5q$

Question #26: How many dimes are equivalent to n nickels and q quarters?
Solution: Since, 1 nickel = 5 cents $\Rightarrow n$ Nickels $= 5n$ cents
Since, 1 quarter = 25 cents $\Rightarrow q$ Quarters $= 25q$ cents
Therefore, n Nickels and q Quarters $\Rightarrow 5n + 25q$ cents

No. of Dimes in n Nickels and q Quarters $\Rightarrow \dfrac{5n + 25q}{10} = \dfrac{5n}{10} + \dfrac{25q}{10} = \dfrac{n}{2} + \dfrac{5q}{2} = \dfrac{n + 5q}{2}$

Question #27: What is the total cost of posting a print advertisement of w words if the charge is n dollars for the first 50 words and m dollars for each additional word, if w is greater than 50?
Solution: Cost for first 50 words $\Rightarrow n$ dollars
Cost for additional words over 50 words $\Rightarrow m$ dollars per word $= m(w - 50)$
Total cost of sending a telegram of w words $\Rightarrow n + m(w - 50) = n + mw - 50m$

Question #28: If 8 pencils cost p cents, and 6 erasers cost e cents, then what is the cost, in cents, of 2 pencils and 2 erasers?

Solution: Cost of 8 pencils $\Rightarrow p$ cents   Cost of 1 pencil $\Rightarrow \dfrac{p}{8}$ cents

Cost of 6 erasers $\Rightarrow e$ cents   Cost of 1 eraser $\Rightarrow \dfrac{e}{6}$

Cost of 2 pencils + 2 erasers $\Rightarrow (2)\dfrac{p}{8} + (2)\dfrac{e}{6} = \dfrac{p}{4} + \dfrac{e}{3} = \dfrac{3p}{12} + \dfrac{4e}{12} = \dfrac{3p + 4e}{12}$

Question #29: The amount of oil in a tank is halved by removing 12 gallons of oil from it. If g gallons of oil are then added to the tank, how many gallons of oil are there in the tank?
Solution: Half Capacity of the Tank $\Rightarrow 12$ Full Capacity of the tank $\Rightarrow 2(12) = 24$ gallons
Amount of oil in the tank after removing half the oil $\Rightarrow 12$ gallons
Amount of oil in the tank after adding g gallons $\Rightarrow (12 + g)$ gallons

Question #30: Henry and Roger go for dinner. If Henry pays h dollars and Roger pays r dollars to pay off the bill, what percent of the total bill does Henry pay?
Solution: Amount of bill that Henry pays $\Rightarrow h$ dollars
Amount of bill that Roger pays $\Rightarrow r$ dollars
Total Amount of the bill $\Rightarrow h + r$ dollars

Part of the bill that Henry pays $\Rightarrow \dfrac{h}{h + r}$

Percent of the bill that Henry pays $\Rightarrow \dfrac{100h}{h + r}\%$

PART 5.0: AGE & WEIGHT PROBLEMS:

TABLE OF CONTENTS:

PART 5.0: AGE & WEIGHT PROBLEMS: **83**
5.1: Age Related Word Problems:...84
5.2: Weight Related Word Problems:..86
Practice Exercise – Questions and Answers With Explanations: Age/Weight Problems: 88

5.1: AGE RELATED WORD PROBLEMS:

Age related problems are problems that ask to find the age of an individual at a certain point in time, given some information about other people's ages, at the same or different times. Age word problems also describe how ages of several people are related to one another. They typically provide some specific relationships between the ages of two or more people in different years based on their sum, difference, product, quotient, etc. These relationships need to be transformed into algebraic equations. All age related word problems have one or more of the information given, and you will be asked to determine the value of one or more of the ages that are unknown.

EZ SPOT: These problems are easy to spot. Any problem that involves age in years, months, etc., or any other age related terminology, at different time-periods, is most likely an age word problem. All these problems require you to have the knowledge of how to solve word problems.

EZ STEP-BY-STEP METHOD: Apply the following step(s) to solve any Age Problem:
STEP 1: Assign a different letter (variable) for each person's age.
STEP 2: Establish relationships between the ages of two or more people in the problem.
STEP 3: Transform the relationships between the ages of two or more people into algebraic equations that justify those relationships.
STEP 4: Solve the equations formed, and determine the unknowns or the missing ages.

EZ TIP: Also, make use of our EZ Step-by-Step Strategy for solving Word Problems, and the translation/conversion table, given at the beginning of this unit.

EZ REFERENCE: For more in-depth knowledge about solving equations, refer to our Algebra Module.

EZ HINT: In problems involving ages, you are usually required to represent a person's age at the present time, several years from now, or several years ago. The two phrases that you will find in almost all of the age problems are "*years ago*" and "*years from now*". Make sure not to get confused between the two as they both mean different things. Always remember the following:
(A) "*years ago*" $\Rightarrow$ means you need to subtract.
                              (A person's age "n years ago" is found by subtracting n from his/her present age.)
(B) "*years from now*" $\Rightarrow$ means you need to add.
                              (A person's age "n years from now" is found by adding n to his/her present age.)

Example #1:   Monika is 27 years old and Susan is 19 years old. How many years ago was Monika twice as old as Susan?

Solution: Organize all the given information in the following grid:
                   Let n be the number of years ago when Monika was twice as old as Susan.

Year	Monika	Susan
Now	27	19
n years ago	$27 - n$	$19 - n$

EZ Problem Set-Up $\Rightarrow$ Monika's age n years ago = 2(Susan's age n years ago)
$\Rightarrow 27 - n = 2(19 - n)$ [Set up the equation]
$\Rightarrow 27 - n = 38 - 2n$ [Apply distributive property]
$\Rightarrow 27 + n = 38$ [Add 2n to both sides]
$\Rightarrow n = 11$ [Subtract 27 form both sides]
Therefore, 11 years ago Monika was twice as old as Susan.

Example #2:   Monika is 50 years old and Susan is 15 years old. How many years from now will Monika be twice as old as Susan?

Solution: Organize all the given information in the following grid:
                   Let n be the number of years from now when Monika will be twice as old as Susan.

Year	Monika	Susan
Now	50	15
n years from now	$50 + n$	$15 + n$

EZ Problem Set-Up $\Rightarrow$ Monika's age n years from now = 2(Susan's age n years from now)

$\Rightarrow 50 + n = 2(15 + n)$ [Set up the equation]

$\Rightarrow 50 + n = 30 + 2n$ [Apply distributive property]

$\Rightarrow 50 = 30 + n$ [Subtract n from both sides]

$\Rightarrow n = 20$ [Subtract 30 form both sides]

Therefore, 20 years from now Monika will be twice as old as Susan.

Example #3:   If in 7 years, Monika will be twice as old as she was 9 years ago, how old is Monika now?

Solution: Let, Monika's present age $\Rightarrow x$

Then, Monika's age in 7 years from now $\Rightarrow x + 7$

And, Monika's age 9 years ago $\Rightarrow x - 9$

EZ Problem Set-Up $\Rightarrow$ Monika's age after 7 years = 2 (Monika's age 9 years ago)

$\Rightarrow x + 7 = 2(x - 9)$ [Set up the equation]

$\Rightarrow x + 7 = 2x - 18$ [Apply distributive property]

$\Rightarrow 7 = x - 18$ [Subtract x from both sides]

$\Rightarrow x = 25$ [Add 18 to both sides]

Example #4:   In a family, the son is 20 years younger than the mother. The son is 1/6th the age of the father. Father is 5 years older than the mother. How old is the son?

Solution: Let, Son' age $\Rightarrow S$

And, Mother's age $\Rightarrow M$

And, Father's age $\Rightarrow F$

Son is 20 years younger than his mother $\Rightarrow S = M - 20$ $\Rightarrow$ Equation #1

Son is 1/6th the age of his father $\Rightarrow S = \dfrac{1}{6}(F)$ $\Rightarrow$ Equation #2

Father is 5 years older than the mother $\Rightarrow F = M + 5$ $\Rightarrow$ Equation #3

Substitute the value of F from #3 into #2 $\Rightarrow S = \dfrac{1}{6}(M + 5)$ $\Rightarrow$ Equation #4

Equate Equation #1 and Equation #4: $\Rightarrow M - 20 = \dfrac{1}{6}(M + 5)$ [Equation #1 = Equation #4]

$\Rightarrow 6(M - 20) = M + 5$ [Multiply both sides by 6]

$\Rightarrow 6M - 120 = M + 5$ [Apply distributive property]

$\Rightarrow 5M - 120 = 5$ [Subtract M from both sides]

$\Rightarrow 5M = 125$ [Add 120 to both sides]

$\Rightarrow M = 25$ [Divide both sides by 5]

Substitute the value of M in Equation #1: $\Rightarrow S = M - 20$ [Rewrite Equation #1]

$\Rightarrow S = 25 - 20 = 5$ [Substitute $M = 25$]

Substitute the value of M in Equation #3: $\Rightarrow F = M + 5$ [Rewrite Equation #3]

$\Rightarrow F = 25 + 5 = 30$ [Substitute $M = 25$]

Therefore: Father's age $\Rightarrow F = 30$

Mother's age $\Rightarrow M = 25$

Son's age $\Rightarrow S = 5$

5.2: WEIGHT RELATED WORD PROBLEMS:

Weight related problems are problems that ask you to find the weight of an individual, given some information about other people's weights. Weight word problems also describe how weights of several people are related to one another. They typically provide some specific relationships between the weights of two or more people at a given time based on their sum, difference, product, and/or quotient. Those relationships need to be transformed into algebraic equations. All weight related word problems have one or more of the information given, and you will be asked to determine the value of one or more of the weights that are unknown.

EZ SPOT: These problems are easy to spot. Any problem that involves weight in pounds, kilograms, etc., or any other weight related terminology of different people is most likely a weight word problem. All these problems require you to have is the knowledge of how to solve word problems.

EZ STEP-BY-STEP METHOD: Apply the following step(s) to solve any Weight Problem:
STEP 1: Assign a different letter (variable) for each person's weight.
STEP 2: Establish relationships between the weights of two or more people in the problem.
STEP 3: Transform the relationships between the weights of two or more people into algebraic equations that justify those relationships.
STEP 4: Solve the equations formed, and determine the unknowns or the missing weights.

EZ TIP: Also, make use of our EZ Step-by-Step Strategy for solving Word Problems, and the translation/conversion table, given at the beginning of this unit.

EZ REFERENCE: For more in-depth knowledge about solving equations, refer to our Algebra Module.

Example #1: If the wife weighs $\frac{5}{6}$ as much as the husband weighs, and the total weigh of the couple is 220 pounds, how much does the wife weighs?

Solution: Let, the Husband's Weight $\Rightarrow x$

Then, the Wife's Weight $\Rightarrow \frac{5}{6}x$

Total Weight (husband + wife)$\Rightarrow 220$
EZ Problem Set-Up $\Rightarrow$ Weight of the husband + Weight of the wife = Total Weight of the couple

$\Rightarrow x + \frac{5}{6}x = 220$ [Set up the equation]

$\Rightarrow 6(x + \frac{5}{6}x) = 6(220)$ [Multiply both sides by 6 to eliminate fractions]

$\Rightarrow 6x + 5x = 1320$ [Apply distributive property]
$\Rightarrow 11x = 1320$ [Combine like-terms]
$\Rightarrow x = 120$ [Divide both sides by 11]

Therefore: Husband's Weight $\Rightarrow x = 120$ pounds

Wife's Weight $\Rightarrow \frac{5}{6}x = \frac{5}{6} \times 120 = 100$ pounds

Example #2: In a small family of three, the father weighs 6 times as much as the child, and the mother weighs ¾ as much as the father does. If the total weight of all three of them is 230 pounds, how much does the mother weigh?

Solution: Let, Child's Weight $\Rightarrow x$
Then, Father's Weight $\Rightarrow 6x$
And, Mother's Weight $\Rightarrow ¾(6x)$
Total Weight of Family $\Rightarrow 230$
EZ Problem Set-Up $\Rightarrow$ Weight of Child + Weight of Father + Weight of Mother = Total Family Weight
$\Rightarrow x + 6x + ¾(6x) = 230$ [Set up the equation]

$\Rightarrow 4[x + 6x + ¾(6x)] = 4(230)$ [Multiply both sides by 4 to eliminate fractions]
$\Rightarrow 4x + 24x + 18x = 920$ [Apply distributive property]
$\Rightarrow 46x = 920$ [Combine like-terms]
$\Rightarrow x = 20$ [Divide both sides by 46]

Therefore: Child's Weight $\Rightarrow x = 20$ pounds
            Father's Weight $\Rightarrow 6x = 6 \times 20 = 120$ pounds
            Mother's Weight $\Rightarrow ¾(6x) = ¾ \times 120 = 90$ pounds

PRACTICE EXERCISE – QUESTIONS AND ANSWERS WITH EXPLANATIONS: AGE/WEIGHT PROBLEMS:

Question #1: John was 25 years old y years ago. How old will he be in z years?
Solution:
John's age y years ago $\Rightarrow$ 25 years   [Given]
John's age now $\Rightarrow$ 25 + y years   [Add y]
John's age after z years $\Rightarrow$ 25 + y + z years   [Add z]

Question #2: John was a years old b years ago. How old will he be in c years?
Solution:
John's age b years ago $\Rightarrow$ a years   [Given]
John's age now $\Rightarrow$ a + b years   [Add b]
John's age after c years $\Rightarrow$ a + b + c years   [Add c]

Question #3: Two years from now, Monika's age will be $2n + 1$. What was her age two years ago?
Solution:
Monika's age 2 years from now $\Rightarrow 2n + 1$ [Given]
Monika's age now $\Rightarrow (2n + 1) - 2 = 2n - 1$ [Subtract 2]
Monika's age 2 years ago $\Rightarrow (2n - 1) - 2 = 2n - 3$ [Subtract 2 again]

Question #4: Two years ago, Monika's age was $2n + 1$. What will be her age two years from now?
Solution:
Monika's age 2 year ago $\Rightarrow 2n + 1$ [Given]
Monika's age now $\Rightarrow (2n + 1) + 2 = 2n + 3$ [Add 2]
Monika's age 2 years from now $\Rightarrow (2n + 3) + 2 = 2n + 5$ [Add 2 again]

Question #5: Susan was $2n$ years old n years ago. What will be her age, n years from now?
Solution:
Susan's age n years ago $\Rightarrow 2n$ [Given]
Susan's age now $\Rightarrow 2n + n = 3n$ [Add n]
Susan's age n years from now $\Rightarrow 3n + n = 4n$ [Add n again}

Question #6: In terms of m and n, how old will a person be in exactly 1 year from now if exactly m years ago the person was n years old?
Solution:
Age of the person m years ago $\Rightarrow n$ years
Age of the person today $\Rightarrow n + m$
Age of the person 1 year from now $\Rightarrow n + m + 1$

Question #7: If Monika is 5 times older than Susan and if the difference between their ages is 60, how old is Monika?
Solution:
Let, Susan's age $\Rightarrow x$
Then, Monika's age $\Rightarrow 5x$
EZ Problem Set-Up $\Rightarrow$ Monika's age – Susan's age = 60
                       $\Rightarrow 5x - x = 60$ [Set up the equation]
                       $\Rightarrow 4x = 60$ [Combine like-terms]
                       $\Rightarrow x = 15$ [Divide both sides by 4]
Therefore, Susan's age is 15 and Monika's age = 5(15) = 75

Question #8: If Monika is 5 years older than Susan and if the sum of their ages is 55, how old is Monika?
Solution:
Let, Susan's age $\Rightarrow x$
Then, Monika's age $\Rightarrow (x + 5)$
EZ Problem Set-Up $\Rightarrow$ Monika's age + Susan's age = 55
                       $\Rightarrow (x + 5) + x = 55$ [Set up the equation]
                       $\Rightarrow 2x + 5 = 55$ [Combine like-terms]
                       $\Rightarrow 2x = 50$ [Subtract 5 from both sides]
                       $\Rightarrow x = 25$ [Divide both sides by 2]
Therefore, Susan's age is 25 and Monika's age = 25 + 5 = 30

Question #9: John is 16 years old and twice as old as Tom. What is the sum of John and Tom's age?

Solution: John is 16 years old $\Rightarrow J = 16$ [Given]
                  John is twice as old as Tom $\Rightarrow J = 2T$ [Given]
                  Tom is half as old as John $\Rightarrow T = J \div 2$ [Divide both sides by 2]
                                                $\Rightarrow T = 16 \div 2 = 8$ [Substitute $J = 16$]
                  EZ Problem Set-Up $\Rightarrow$ John's Age + Tom's Age = Sum of the ages
                                    $\Rightarrow 16 + 8$ [Substitute $J = 16$ and $T = 8$]
                                    $\Rightarrow 24$ years   [Do the addition]

Question #10: John is n years old. Mike is 7 years younger than John and 2 years older than Tom. What is the sum of the ages of all three of them?

Solution: John's age $\Rightarrow n$ [Given]
                  Mike's age $\Rightarrow$ John's age $- 7 = n - 7$ [Subtract 7 from John's age]
                  Tom's age $\Rightarrow$ Mike's age $- 2 = n - 7 - 2 = n - 9$ [Subtract 2 from Mike's age]
                  EZ Problem Set-Up $\Rightarrow$ John's Age + Mike's age + Tom's Age = Sum of the ages of all three of them
                                    $\Rightarrow (n) + (n - 7) + (n - 9)$ [Substitute all three ages]
                                    $\Rightarrow 3n - 16$ [Combine like-terms]

Question #11: If Nancy were twice as old as she is, she would be 70 years older than Vivian would. If Vivian is 12 years younger than Nancy is, how old is Nancy?

Solution: Let, Vivian's age $\Rightarrow V$
                  And, Nancy's age $\Rightarrow N$
                  Vivian is 12 years younger than Nancy $\Rightarrow V = N - 12$ $\Rightarrow$ Equation #1
                  Twice of Nancy's ages is 70 yrs plus Vivian's age $\Rightarrow 2N = V + 70$ $\Rightarrow$ Equation #2
                  Substitute the value of V from Equation #1 into #2 $\Rightarrow 2N = (N - 12) + 70$ [Substitute $V = N - 12$]
                                                                $\Rightarrow 2N = N + 58$ [Combine like-terms]
                                                                $\Rightarrow N = 58$ [Subtract N from both sides]
                  Therefore, Nancy is 58 years old.

Question #12: Mary has three sons, two of whom are twins. The sum of the ages of all three sons is 25, and the son who is not a twin is 9 years old. How old is each of the twins?

Solution: Let, the twin son's age $\Rightarrow T$
                  And, the other son's age $\Rightarrow S = 9$
                  EZ Problem Set-Up $\Rightarrow$ Ages of twin sons + Age of other son = 25
                                    $\Rightarrow T + T + S = 25$ [Set up the equation]
                                    $\Rightarrow T + T + 9 = 25$ [Substitute $S = 9$]
                                    $\Rightarrow 2T + 9 = 25$ [Combine like-terms]
                                    $\Rightarrow 2T = 16$ [Subtract 9 from both sides]
                                    $\Rightarrow T = 8$ [Divide both sides by 2]
                  Therefore, each of the twins is 8 years old.

Question #13: Monika is 23 years old and Susan is 17 years old. How many years ago was Monika twice as old as Susan?

Solution: Organize all the given information in the following grid:
                  Let the number of years ago when Monika was twice as old as Susan be n

Year	Monika	Susan
Now	23	17
n years ago	$23 - n$	$17 - n$

                  EZ Problem Set-Up $\Rightarrow$ Monika's age n years ago = 2(Susan's age n years ago)
                                    $\Rightarrow 23 - n = 2(17 - n)$ [Set up the equation]
                                    $\Rightarrow 23 - n = 34 - 2n$ [Apply distributive property]
                                    $\Rightarrow 23 + n = 34$ [Add $2n$ to both sides]
                                    $\Rightarrow n = 11$ [Subtract 23 from both sides]
                  Therefore, 11 years ago Monika was twice as old as Susan.

Question #14: Monika is 52 years old and Susan is 18 years old. How many years from now will Monika be twice as old as Susan?

Solution: Organize all the given information in the following grid:

Let the number of years from now when Monika will be twice as old as Susan be n

Year	Monika	Susan
Now	52	18
n years later	$52 + n$	$18 + n$

EZ Problem Set-Up $\Rightarrow$ Monika's age n years later = 2(Susan's age n years later)

$\Rightarrow 52 + n = 2(18 + n)$ [Set up the equation]
$\Rightarrow 52 + n = 36 + 2n$ [Apply distributive property]
$\Rightarrow 52 = 36 + n$ [Subtract n to both sides]
$\Rightarrow n = 16$ [Subtract 36 from both sides]

Therefore, 16 years from now Monika will be twice as old as Susan.

Question #15: Veronica is now 20 years old and her sister, Stacy is 14. How many years ago was Veronica three times as old as Stacy was then?

Solution: Organize all the given information in the following grid:

Year	Veronica	Stacy
Now	20	14
n years ago	$20 - n$	$14 - n$

EZ Problem Set-Up $\Rightarrow$ Veronica's age n years ago = 3(Stacy's age n years ago)

$\Rightarrow 20 - n = 3(14 - n)$ [Set up the equation]
$\Rightarrow 20 - n = 42 - 3n$ [Apply distributive property]
$\Rightarrow 20 + 2n = 42$ [Add $3n$ to both sides]
$\Rightarrow 2n = 22$ [Subtract 20 from both sides]
$\Rightarrow n = 11$ [Divide both sides by 2]

Question #16: Stacy was 24 years old in 1960, when her son, Henry, was born. In what year will Stacy be exactly three times as old as Henry?

Solution: Organize all the given information in the following grid:
Let Henry's age now be x

Year	Stacy	Henry
1960	24	0
$1960 + x$	$24 + x$	x

EZ Problem Set-Up $\Rightarrow$ Stacy's age after x years = 3(Henry's age after x years)

$\Rightarrow 24 + x = 3x$ [Set up the equation]
$\Rightarrow 2x = 24$ [Subtract x from both sides]
$\Rightarrow x = 12$ [Divide both sides by 2]

Stacy will be 3 times as old as Henry, 12 years after 1960, in 1972 (when they will be 36 and 12, respectively)

Question #17: Susan is now twice as old as John is, but 6 years ago, she was 5 times as old as he was. How old is Susan now?

Solution: Organize all the given information in the following grid:
Let John's age now be x

Year	John	Susan
Now	x	$2x$
6 years ago	$x - 6$	$2x - 6$

EZ Problem Set-Up: $\Rightarrow$ Susan's age six years ago = 5(John's age six years ago)

$\Rightarrow 2x - 6 = 5(x - 6)$ [Set up the equation]
$\Rightarrow 2x - 6 = 5x - 30$ [Apply distributive property]
$\Rightarrow -6 = 3x - 30$ [Subtract $2x$ from both sides]
$\Rightarrow 0 = 3x - 24$ [Add 6 to both sides]
$\Rightarrow 3x = 24$ [Add 24 to both sides]
$\Rightarrow x = 8$ [Divide both sides by 3]

Therefore, John is now 8 years old.
And, Susan is now twice as old as John or, $2x = 2 \times 8 = 16$ years old.

Question #18: If ½x years ago, Monika was 12, and ½x years from now she will be 2x years old, how old will she be 4x years from now?

Solution:

Monika's age ½x years ago	$\Rightarrow 12$	[Given]
Monika's age now	$\Rightarrow 12 + ½x$	[Add ½x]
Monika's age ½x years from now	$\Rightarrow 12 + ½x + ½x = 12 + x$	[Again add ½x]
Monika's age ½x years from now will be 2x	$\Rightarrow 12 + x = 2x$	[Given]
	$\Rightarrow x = 12$	[Subtract x from both sides]
Therefore, Monika's age now	$\Rightarrow 12 + ½x$	[As per above]
	$\Rightarrow 12 + ½(12)$	[Substitute x = 12]
	$\Rightarrow 12 + 6 = 18$	[Solve for the age]
And, Monika's age 4x years from now	$\Rightarrow 18 + 4x$	[Monika's age now plus 4x]
	$\Rightarrow 18 + 4(12)$	[Substitute x = 12]
	$\Rightarrow 18 + 48 = 66$	[Solve for the age]

Question #19: In 1950, Nancy was 7 times as old as Tiffany, but in 1960 Nancy was only twice as old as Tiffany was. How old was Tiffany in 1975?

Solution: Organize all the given information in the following grid:

Let Susan's age in 1975 be x

Year	Nancy	Tiffany
1950	7x	x
1960	7x + 10	x + 10

EZ Problem Set-Up $\Rightarrow$ Nancy's age in 1950 = 2(Tiffany's age in 1960)

$\Rightarrow 7x + 10 = 2(x + 10)$	[Set up the equation]
$\Rightarrow 7x + 10 = 2x + 20$	[Apply distributive property]
$\Rightarrow 5x + 10 = 20$	[Subtract 2x from both sides]
$\Rightarrow 5x = 10$	[Subtract 10 from both sides]
$\Rightarrow x = 2$	[Divide both sides by 5]

Therefore, Tiffany's age in 1950 was 2 years. However, 2 is not the correct answer. The question asks for Tiffany's age in 1975. Substitute the value of x to find any age in any year. Since Tiffany's age was 2 in 1950, she will be (2 + 25) in 1975, so the correct answer is 27. The question may have asked for some other information, which can be easily determined by plugging in the value of x in the first table to form the following new table.

Year	Nancy	Tiffany
1950	7x = 14	x = 2
1960	7x + 10 = 24	x + 10 = 12
1975	39	27
1995	59	47

Question #20: Henry is now 16 years younger than Kevin. If in 9 years, Kevin will be twice as old as Henry, how old will Henry be in 5 years?

Solution:
Let, Henry's age = H
And, Kevin's age = K

Henry is now 16 years younger than Kevin	$\Rightarrow H = K - 16$	$\Rightarrow$ Equation #1
In 9 years, Kevin will be twice as old as Henry	$\Rightarrow K + 9 = 2(H + 9)$	$\Rightarrow$ Equation #2

Solve the two equations simultaneously:

$\Rightarrow$	K	+	9	= 2(H + 9)	[Rewrite Equation #2]
$\Rightarrow -($	K	−	16	= H)	[Rewrite Equation #1]
$\Rightarrow$			25	= H + 18	[Subtract Equation #1 from Equation #2]
$\Rightarrow$			H	= 7	[Subtract 18 from both sides]

Henry's age now	$\Rightarrow H = 7$
Henry's age after five years	$\Rightarrow H + 5 = 7 + 5 = 12$

Question #21: George is twice John's age. John is 5 years older than Tom. Tom just turned 21 years old. How old is George?

Solution:

Let, George's age	$\Rightarrow G$	
And, John's age	$\Rightarrow J$	
And, Tom's age	$\Rightarrow T$	
George is twice John's age	$\Rightarrow G = 2J$	$\Rightarrow$ Equation #1

John is 5 years older than Tom $\Rightarrow J = T + 5$ $\Rightarrow$ Equation #2
Tom just turned 21 years old $\Rightarrow T = 21$ [Given]
Substitute $T = 21$ into Equation #2$\Rightarrow J = T + 5$ [Rewrite Equation #2]
                                     $\Rightarrow J = 21 + 5$ [Substitute $T = 21$]
                                       $\Rightarrow J = 26$ [Do the addition]
Substitute $J = 26$ in Equation #1 $\Rightarrow G = 2J$ [Rewrite Equation #1]
                                       $\Rightarrow G = 2 \times 26$ [Substitute $J = 26$]
                                       $\Rightarrow G = 52$ [Do the multiplication]
Therefore: George's Age $\Rightarrow G = 52$ years
              John's Age $\Rightarrow J = 26$ years
              Tom's Age $\Rightarrow T = 21$ years

Question #22: If the wife weighs ¾ as much as the husband weighs, and the total weight of the couple is 280 pounds, how much does the wife weigh?

Solution: Let, Husband's Weight $\Rightarrow x$
Then, Wife's Weight $\Rightarrow$ ¾ x
Total Weight $\Rightarrow 280$ pounds
EZ Problem Set-Up $\Rightarrow$ Weight of the husband + Weight of the wife = Total Weight of the couple

$$\Rightarrow x + \frac{3}{4}x = 280 \qquad \text{[Set up the equation]}$$

$$\Rightarrow \frac{7}{4}x = 280 \qquad \text{[Combine like-terms]}$$

$$\Rightarrow x = 280 \times \frac{4}{7} = 160 \qquad \text{[Multiply both sides by 4/7]}$$

Therefore;   Husband's Weight $\Rightarrow x = 160$ pounds
             Wife's Weight $\Rightarrow$ ¾$x = 160 \times$ ¾ $= 120$ pounds

Question #23: In a small family of three, the father weighs 8 times as much as the child, and the mother weighs ¾ as much as the father. If the total weight of all three of them is 270 pounds, how much does the mother weigh?

Solution: Let, Child's Weight $\Rightarrow x$
Then, Father's Weight $\Rightarrow 8x$
And, Mother's Weight $\Rightarrow$ ¾ $(8x)$
Total Weight $\Rightarrow 270$ pounds
EZ Problem Set-Up $\Rightarrow$ Weight of Child + Weight of Father + Weight of Mother = Total Family Weight
                             $\Rightarrow x + 8x +$ ¾$(8x) = 270$ [Set up the equation]
                             $\Rightarrow x + 8x + 6x = 270$ [Apply distributive property]
                             $\Rightarrow 15x = 270$ [Combine like-terms]
                             $\Rightarrow x = 18$ [Divide both sides by 15]
Therefore: Child's Weight $\Rightarrow x = 18$ pounds
             Father's Weight $\Rightarrow 8x = 8 \times 18 = 144$ pounds
             Mother's Weight $\Rightarrow$ ¾$(8x) =$ ¾ $\times 144 = 108$ pounds

Question #24: In a small family of three, the father weighs 12 times as much as the child, and the mother weighs ¾ as much as the father. If the total weight of all three of them is 528 pounds, how much does the mother weigh?

Solution: Let, Child's Weight $\Rightarrow x$
Then, Father's Weight $\Rightarrow 12x$
And, Mother's Weight $\Rightarrow$ ¾ $(12x)$
Total Weight $\Rightarrow 528$ pounds
EZ Problem Set-Up $\Rightarrow$ Weight of Child + Weight of Father + Weight of Mother = Total Family Weight
                             $\Rightarrow x + 12x +$ ¾$(12x) = 528$ [Set up the equation]
                             $\Rightarrow x + 12x + 9x = 528$ [Apply distributive property]
                             $\Rightarrow 22x = 528$ [Combine like-terms]
                             $\Rightarrow x = 24$ [Divide both sides by 22]

Therefore: Child's Weight $\Rightarrow x = 24$ pounds
Father's Weight $\Rightarrow 12x = 12 \times 24 = 288$ pounds
Mother's Weight $\Rightarrow \frac{3}{4}(8x) = \frac{3}{4} \times 288 = 216$ pounds

Question #25: If Monika weighs $\frac{6}{5}$ as much as Susan, and Nancy weighs ¼ as much as Monika, and the total weight of Monika, Susan and Nancy is 500 pounds, how much does Nancy weigh?

Solution: Let, Susan's Weight $\Rightarrow x$

Then, Monika's Weight $\Rightarrow \frac{6}{5}x$

And, Nancy's Weight $\Rightarrow \frac{1}{4}\left(\frac{6}{5}x\right)$

Total Weight $\Rightarrow 500$ pounds
EZ Problem Set-Up $\Rightarrow$ Weight of Susan + Weight of Monika + Weight of Nancy = Total Weight

$\Rightarrow x + \frac{6}{5}x + \frac{1}{4}\left(\frac{6}{5}x\right) = 500$ [Set up the equation]

$\Rightarrow x + \frac{6}{5}x + \frac{6}{20}x = 500$ [Apply distributive property]

$\Rightarrow \frac{20}{20}x + \frac{24}{20}x + \frac{6}{20}x = 500$ [Scale-up the fractions to their LCD,]

$\Rightarrow \frac{50}{20}x = 500$ [Combine like-terms]

$\Rightarrow \frac{5}{2}x = 500$ [Reduce the fraction to its lowest terms]

$\Rightarrow x = 500 \times \frac{2}{5} = 200$ [Multiply both sides by 2/5]

Therefore: Susan's Weight $\Rightarrow x = 200$ pounds

Monika's Weight $\Rightarrow \frac{6}{5}x = \frac{6}{5} \times 200 = 240$ pounds

Nancy's Weight $\Rightarrow \frac{1}{4}\left(\frac{6}{5}x\right) = \frac{1}{4} \times 240 = 60$ pounds

Question #26: If Monika weighs $\frac{7}{5}$ as much as Susan, and Nancy weighs ¼ as much as Monika, and the total weight of Monika, Susan and Nancy is 550 pounds, how much does Nancy weigh?

Solution: Let, Susan's Weight $\Rightarrow x$

Then, Monika's Weight $\Rightarrow \frac{7}{5}x$

And, Nancy's Weight $\Rightarrow \frac{1}{4}\left(\frac{7}{5}x\right)$

Total Weight $\Rightarrow 550$ pounds
EZ Problem Set-Up $\Rightarrow$ Weight of Susan + Weight of Monika + Weight of Nancy = Total Weight

$\Rightarrow x + \frac{7}{5}x + \frac{1}{4}\left(\frac{7}{5}x\right) = 550$ [Set up the equation]

$\Rightarrow x + \frac{7}{5}x + \frac{7}{20}x = 550$ [Apply distributive property]

$\Rightarrow \frac{20}{20}x + \frac{28}{20}x + \frac{7}{20}x = 550$ [Scale-up the fractions to their LCD, which is 20]

$\Rightarrow \frac{55}{20}x = 550$ [Combine like-terms]

$$\Rightarrow x = 550 \times \frac{20}{55} = 200 \qquad \text{[Multiply both sides by 20/55]}$$

Therefore: Susan's Weight $\Rightarrow x = 200$ pounds

Monika's Weight $\Rightarrow \dfrac{7}{5}x = \dfrac{7}{5} \times 200 = 280$ pounds

Nancy's Weight $\Rightarrow \dfrac{1}{4}\left(\dfrac{7}{5}x\right) = \frac{1}{4} \times 280 = 70$ pounds

PART 6.0: WORK PROBLEMS:

TABLE OF CONTENTS:

PART 6.0: WORK PROBLEMS: **95**
6.1: Work Problems Involving Simple Rates: 96
6.2: Work Problems Involving Multiple Workers:..98
Practice Exercise – Questions and Answers With Explanations: Work Problems: 103

6.1: WORK PROBLEMS INVOLVING SIMPLE RATES:

RATE OF WORK OR QUANTITY:

Work related rate problems are just another type of rate problems. They are essentially like motion problems because just like all other rate problems, they also involve three elements: the working rate, time, distance.

The only difference is that in work problems, the rate, time, and distance refer to slightly different things:

Rate: In motion problems, the rate is a ratio of distance to time, or the amount of distance traveled in one time unit. In work problems, the rate is a ratio of work to time, or the amount of work completed in one time unit.

Time: In motion problems, the time refers to the time spent traveling. In work problems, the time refers to the time spent working.

Distance or Work: In motion problems, the distance refers to the distance traveled. In work problems, distance is replaced by work, which refers to the job performed, i.e., the number of jobs completed or the number of items produced.

Rate Defined: A rate is a ratio that compares quantities represented by different units. If two numbers measure different quantities, their quotient is usually called a rate. So a rate is a ratio that is a comparison of two different things with different units. A rate compares the number of units of one item to one unit of another item. A rate is a ratio that relates two different kinds of quantities. Rate can be expressed in a fraction form or word form. When a rate is expressed in fraction form, its denominator is always one unit. In terms of word form, rates are often expressed by using the word *"per"*. For instance, as in "miles per hour", "cost per item", etc. Since per means *"for one"*, or *"for each"*, we express the rates as ratios or fractions reduced to a denominator of 1. These are types of proportion problems that ask you to find the rate.

For example, speed is an example of rate, which is the ratio of distance traveled to time elapsed. If a man travels 100 miles in 2 hours, his average rate of speed $= \dfrac{100\,miles}{2\,hours} = 50$ miles per hour

To determine the Rate of Work or Quantity by using the actual numbers – first identify the quantity and the units to be compared, and then write the rate in terms of a fraction where the quantity before *per* goes on top, and the quantity after *per* goes on the bottom.

$$\text{RATE} \Rightarrow \frac{quantity\ before\ "per"}{quantity\ after\ "per"}$$

Note: Make sure that the units of the quantities are in accordance.

Example #1: If a man can type 6,750 words in 1½ hours, what is his rate in words per minute?
Solution:

Time	$\Rightarrow$ 1.5 hours = 90 minutes	[Given]
Words	$\Rightarrow$ 6,750 words	[Given]

$$\text{Rate of words per minute} \Rightarrow \frac{Words}{Minutes} \qquad \text{[Write the appropriate formula]}$$

$$\Rightarrow \frac{6,750\,Words}{90\,Minutes} \qquad \text{[Substitute the values]}$$

$$\Rightarrow 75 \text{ words per minute} \qquad \text{[Simplify the expression]}$$

EZ REFERENCE: For more in-depth knowledge about rate, ratios, and proportions, refer to our Algebraic Applications Module.

AVERAGE RATE OF WORK: (AVERAGE *A* PER *B*)

To determine the Average Rate of Work or Quantity by using the actual numbers – first identify the quantities and the units to be compared and convert them into totals, and then write the rate in terms of a fraction where the total quantity before *per* goes on top, and the total quantity after *per* goes on the bottom.

$$\text{Average Rate of "A" per "B"} \Rightarrow \frac{Total\ A}{Total\ B}$$

Example #2:   If a man travels 100 miles in 8 hours and then 50 miles in 2 hours, what is his average speed in miles per hour?

Solution: Total Miles ⇒ 100 + 50 = 150   [Find the total miles]

Total Hours ⇒ 8 + 2 = 10   [Find the total time]

Average (miles per hour) ⇒ $\dfrac{Total\ Miles}{Total\ Hour}$ [Write the appropriate formula]

⇒ $\dfrac{(100 + 50)}{(8 + 2)}$ [Substitute the values]

⇒ $\dfrac{150}{10}$ [Simplify within parentheses]

⇒ 15 miles per hour   [Simplify the expression]

6.2: Work Problems Involving Multiple Workers:

Work problems generally involve two or more workers or machines, working together, usually at different rates, to complete the same job or task. These problems usually give the rate at which certain people or machines work individually, i.e., the amount of time it takes to complete a particular job working alone, and ask to find out the rate at which they work jointly, i.e., how long it will take to complete the same job working together, or vice versa. You may also be asked to predict how long it will take to complete a job if the number of workers is increased or decreased.

EZ Spot: These problems are easy to spot. Any problem that involves two or more workers, machines, pipes, etc., or any other job related terminology, working at different rates, is most likely a work problem. All these problems require you to have the knowledge of the work formula, and how to apply it in different variations and under different circumstances.

Using simple logic to solve work problems: If you can use simple logic to determine how changing the parameters or constraints affect the time it takes to do a job, you can usually solve these problems using simple logic.

EZ Tips: Keep in mind the following useful tips:

Tip #1: The greater the rate of work $\Rightarrow$ the faster you work $\Rightarrow$ the sooner you get the job done

Tip #2: The lesser the rate of work $\Rightarrow$ the slower you work $\Rightarrow$ the later you get the job done

Tip #3: Greater the number of workers $\Rightarrow$ lesser the time it takes to finish the job
(More workers can finish the same job in less time.)

Tip #4: Fewer the number of workers $\Rightarrow$ greater the time it takes to finish the job
(Fewer workers can finish the same job in more time.)

Breaking Down the Work on Hour-by-Hour Basis:

In work problems, the trick is not to think about how long it takes to do an entire job, but rather how much of the job can be done in 1 hour. So it's better to break down the work on an hour-by-hour basis.

In most work problems, a job is broken up into several parts, each representing a fractional portion of the entire job performed by each worker. For each part or fraction represented, the numerator represents the whole job, which is 1, while the denominator represents the total time needed for the worker to do the job alone. The sum of all individual fractions must always be equal to 1 for the whole job to be completed. Then determine the combined rate of all the workers working together. The combined rate of all the workers working together is equal to the sum of all the individual working rates.

Work problems usually require you to set up a proportion of two or more ratios. Recall from the ratios and proportions that ratios involving work are usually inversely related, i.e., the more workers we have, the less time it takes to get the job done.

(A) If it takes k workers 1 hour to do a particular job, then each worker does $\dfrac{1}{k}$ of the job in an hour or works at the rate

of $\dfrac{1}{k}$ of the job per hour.

(B) And, if it takes m workers h hours to finish a particular job, then each worker does $\dfrac{1}{m}$ of the job in h hours or does

$\dfrac{1}{h}$ of $\dfrac{1}{m}$ in an hour. Therefore, each worker works at the rate of $\dfrac{1}{mh}$ of the job per hour.

EZ Hint: The above logic may make more sense if you try easy numbers. For instance, if it takes 2 hours to complete the whole job, the amount of work done in 1 hour is the inverse of 2, or ½. Likewise, if one can do ½ of a job in 1 hour, the amount of time to complete the whole job will take inverse of ½ or 2 hours.

For Example: If Susan can paint a room in 2 hours, and Nancy can paint the same room in 7 hours, how many hours will it take Susan and Nancy to paint the same room if they work together, though independently at these given rates?

Solution: Determine how much work Susan can do in a certain unit of time (an easy choice is one hour), and how much work Nancy can do in that same hour, then add the results to find how much work they can do together in an hour. Then from that, find how long it will take them to finish the whole job.

Susan takes 2 hours to paint the room, i.e., she works at the rate of $\frac{1}{2}$ of the job per hour.

Nancy takes 7 hours to paint the room, i.e., she works at the rate of $\frac{1}{7}$ of the job per hour.

Together, they average a rate of $\frac{1}{2} + \frac{1}{7} = \frac{7}{14} + \frac{2}{14} = \frac{9}{14}$ of the job per hour.

To figure out how long it will take them to do the whole job working at that rate, simply flip the fraction.

So, let's say it takes them x hours working at the rate of $\frac{9}{14}$ of the job per hour to complete the job.

$\Rightarrow \frac{9}{14}x = 1$ job

$\Rightarrow x = \frac{14}{9}$ hours or $1\frac{5}{9}$ hours

If they do $\frac{9}{14}$ of the job in 1 hour, it will take them the inverse of $\frac{9}{14}$, or $\frac{14}{9}$ hours to complete the job.

Therefore, it will take Susan and Nancy $1\frac{5}{9}$ hours to paint the room working together.

EZ ALTERNATIVE METHOD: The same problem explained above can be much easily solved by taking help of the following work problem formula:

THE WORK PROBLEM FORMULA STATES: The inverse of the time it would take everyone working together equals the sum of the inverses of the time it would take each working individually. Following is the general work formula that can be used to find out how long it takes a number of people working together to complete a task:

WORK PROBLEM FORMULA: $\frac{1}{x} + \frac{1}{y} = \frac{1}{z}$

Where: $\Rightarrow$ "x" & "y" represent the number of units (hours, days, etc.) it would take each person or machine to complete a particular job working "alone," respectively.
     $\Rightarrow$ "z" represents the total number of units (hours, days, etc.) it would take "x" & "y" to complete the same job working "jointly".

If there are more than two people/machines involved, then use the following work formula: $\Rightarrow \frac{1}{a} + \frac{1}{b} + \frac{1}{c} = \frac{1}{z}$

EZ STEP-BY-STEP METHOD: Apply the following step(s) to solve any Work Problems:

STEP 1: Assign a different letter (variable), such as, x, y, z, which represents the number of units (hours, days, etc) it takes the people or objects to complete the particular job, individually and/or jointly.

STEP 2: Use the formula given above for Work-Problem, and substitute the value of the given variables in the problem.

STEP 3: Solve the equations formed and determine the unknown or the missing quantity.

Note: In general, with work problems, it is safe to assume that each person or machine in the same category works constantly at the same given rate, either working alone or jointly with some other people or machines. Don't worry about any time that they might spend not working or any breakdowns. This is the reason that some questions include the phrase "working jointly but independently at their respective rates".

EZ TIP: Also make use of our EZ Step-by-Step Strategy for solving Word Problems, and the translation/conversion table, given at the beginning of this unit.

EZ REFERENCE: For more in-depth knowledge about rate, ratios, and proportions, refer to our Algebraic Applications Module.

Example #1: If Susan can paint a room in 2 hours, and Nancy can paint the same room in 7 hours, how many hours will it take Susan and Nancy to paint the same room if they work together at these given rates?

Solution: The No. of hours in which Susan alone can paint a room $\Rightarrow x = 2$
The No. of hours in which Nancy alone can paint a room $\Rightarrow y = 7$
Let, the No. of hours in which Susan & Nancy together can paint a room working together $= z$

$\Rightarrow \dfrac{1}{x} + \dfrac{1}{y} = \dfrac{1}{z}$ [Write the appropriate formula]

$\Rightarrow \dfrac{1}{2} + \dfrac{1}{7} = \dfrac{1}{z}$ [Substitute the known values]

$\Rightarrow \dfrac{7}{14} + \dfrac{2}{14} = \dfrac{1}{z}$ [Scale-up the fractions to their LCD, which is 14]

$\Rightarrow \dfrac{9}{14} = \dfrac{1}{z}$ [Combine like-terms]

$\Rightarrow 9z = 14$ [Cross-multiply]

$\Rightarrow z = \dfrac{14}{9} = 1\dfrac{5}{9}$ hours   [Divide both sides by 9]

Therefore, it will take Susan and Nancy $1\dfrac{5}{9}$ hours to paint the room working together.

Example #2: If Machine-A can print 100 copies in 1 hours, and Machine-B can print 100 copies in 2 hours, how many hours will it take Machine-A and Machine-B to print 1000 copies if they operate together at these given rates?

Solution: The No. of hours in which Machine-A alone can print 100 copies $\Rightarrow x = 1$
The No. of hours in which Machine-A alone can print 100 copies $\Rightarrow y = 2$
Let, the No. of hours in which Machine-A and Machine-B together can print 1000 copies $= z$

$\Rightarrow \dfrac{1}{x} + \dfrac{1}{y} = \dfrac{1}{z}$ [Write the appropriate formula]

$\Rightarrow \dfrac{1}{1} + \dfrac{1}{2} = \dfrac{1}{z}$ [Substitute the known values]

$\Rightarrow \dfrac{2}{2} + \dfrac{1}{2} = \dfrac{1}{z}$ [Scale-up the fractions to their LCD, which is 2]

$\Rightarrow \dfrac{3}{2} = \dfrac{1}{z}$ [Combine like-terms]

$\Rightarrow 3z = 2$ [Cross-multiply]

$\Rightarrow z = \dfrac{2}{3}$ hours   [Divide both sides by 3]

Therefore, it will take Machine-A & Machine-B $\dfrac{2}{3}$ hours or 40 minutes to print 100 copies operating together.

Example #3: If John can mow his lawn in 6 hours working alone, and with his little brother's help he can finish the same job in 4 hours, how long will it take the little brother to mow the entire lawn alone?

Solution: The No. of hours in which John alone can mow his lawn $\Rightarrow x = 6$
The No. of hours in which John and his brother together can mow his lawn $\Rightarrow z = 4$
Let, the No. of hours in which the Brother alone can mow his lawn $= y$

$\Rightarrow \dfrac{1}{x} + \dfrac{1}{y} = \dfrac{1}{z}$ [Write the appropriate formula]

$\Rightarrow \dfrac{1}{6} + \dfrac{1}{y} = \dfrac{1}{4}$ [Substitute the known values]

$\Rightarrow \dfrac{1}{y} = \dfrac{1}{4} - \dfrac{1}{6}$ [Subtract 1/6 from both sides]

$\Rightarrow \dfrac{1}{y} = \dfrac{3}{12} - \dfrac{2}{12}$ [Scale-up the fractions to their LCD, which is 12]

$\Rightarrow \dfrac{1}{y} = \dfrac{1}{12}$ [Combine like-terms]

$\Rightarrow y = 12$ [Cross-multiply]

Therefore, it will take the little brother 12 hours to mow the lawn working alone.

Example #4: If John can type a project report in 20 hours working alone, and with his co-worker's help he can finish the same report in 6 hours, how long will it take the co-worker to type the same report alone?

Solution: The No. of hours in which John alone can type the project report $\Rightarrow x = 20$
The No. of hours in which John and the co-worker together can type the project report $\Rightarrow z = 6$
Let, the No. of hours in which the co-worker alone can type the project report $= y$

$\Rightarrow \dfrac{1}{x} + \dfrac{1}{y} = \dfrac{1}{z}$ [Write the appropriate formula]

$\Rightarrow \dfrac{1}{20} + \dfrac{1}{y} = \dfrac{1}{6}$ [Substitute the known values]

$\Rightarrow \dfrac{1}{y} = \dfrac{1}{6} - \dfrac{1}{20}$ [Subtract 1/20 from both sides]

$\Rightarrow \dfrac{1}{y} = \dfrac{10}{60} - \dfrac{3}{60}$ [Scale-up the fractions to their LCD, which is 60]

$\Rightarrow \dfrac{1}{y} = \dfrac{7}{60}$ [Combine like-terms]

$\Rightarrow 7y = 60$ [Cross-multiply]

$\Rightarrow y = \dfrac{60}{7} = 8\dfrac{4}{7}$ [Divide both sides by 7]

Therefore, it will take the co-worker $8\dfrac{4}{7}$ hours to type the project report working alone.

Example #5: If a man can fix the broken roof in 2 hours, his wife can do it 4 hours, and his son can do it in 8 hours, how many hours will it take the man, his wife and son working together to fix the broken roof at these rates?

Solution: The No. of hours in which the man alone can fix the broken roof $\Rightarrow a = 2$
The No. of hours in which the wife alone can fix the broken roof $\Rightarrow b = 4$
The No. of hours in which the son alone can fix the broken roof $\Rightarrow c = 8$
Let, the No. of hours in which the man, wife, and son together an fix the broken roof $= z$

$\Rightarrow \dfrac{1}{a} + \dfrac{1}{b} + \dfrac{1}{c} = \dfrac{1}{z}$ [Write the appropriate formula]

$\Rightarrow \dfrac{1}{2} + \dfrac{1}{4} + \dfrac{1}{8} = \dfrac{1}{z}$ [Substitute the known values]

$\Rightarrow \dfrac{4}{8} + \dfrac{2}{8} + \dfrac{1}{8} = \dfrac{1}{z}$ [Scale-up the fractions to their LCD, which is 8]

$\Rightarrow \dfrac{7}{8} = \dfrac{1}{z}$ [Combine like-terms]

$\Rightarrow 7z = 8$ [Cross-multiply]

$\Rightarrow z = \dfrac{8}{7} = 1\dfrac{1}{7}$ [Divide both sides by 7]

Therefore, it will take the man, wife, and son $1\dfrac{1}{7}$ hours to fix the broken roof working jointly.

TANK AND PIPE PROBLEMS:

Work problems may also involve determining how fast pipes can fill or empty a full or part of tanks. In solving tanks and pipe problems, you must think of the pipes as workers.

Example #6: There are two taps, tap-1 and tap-2, in a tank. If both taps are opened, the tank will be completely drained in 15 minutes. If tap-1 is closed and tap-2 is open, the tank will be completely drained in 20 minutes. If tap-1 is open and tap-2 is closed, how long will it take to completely drain the tank?

Solution: We can use the same formula to solve this problem. The only difference is that instead of machines or people, this time it's the taps that are doing the work, which is draining the tank.

Let, the No. of minutes in which tap-1 alone can drain the tank = x

The No. of minutes in which tap-2 alone can drain the tank $\Rightarrow y = 20$

The No. of minutes in which tap-1 and tap-2 together can drain the tank $\Rightarrow z = 15$

$\Rightarrow \dfrac{1}{x} + \dfrac{1}{y} = \dfrac{1}{z}$ [Write the appropriate formula]

$\Rightarrow \dfrac{1}{x} + \dfrac{1}{20} = \dfrac{1}{15}$ [Substitute the known values]

$\Rightarrow \dfrac{1}{x} = \dfrac{1}{15} - \dfrac{1}{20}$ [Subtract 1/20 from both sides]

$\Rightarrow \dfrac{1}{x} = \dfrac{4}{60} - \dfrac{3}{60}$ [Scale-up the fractions to their LCD, which is 60]

$\Rightarrow \dfrac{1}{x} = \dfrac{1}{60}$ [Combine like-terms]

$\Rightarrow x = 60$ minutes [Cross-multiply]

Therefore, if tap-1 is open and tap-2 is closed, it will take 60 minutes or 1 hour to completely drain the tank.

Inlet and Outlet Problems: Some tank problems involve an inlet pipe, which fills the tank, and an outlet pipe, which drains the tank. The rate of the inlet pipe is usually greater than the rate of outlet pipe so that there is a net gain. Such problems are solved just like other work related problems by modifying the work formula. The only difference is that instead of adding, we subtract the two fractions since one inlet pipe is adding water and the other outlet pipe is subtracting water. In this case, the outlet pipe is not helping the inlet pipe but is working against it.

Example #7: A swimming pool can be filled by an inlet pipe in 2 hours. It can be drained by an outlet pipe in 10 hours. By mistake, both pipes are opened at the same time. If the pool is empty, in how many hours will it be filled?

Solution: We can use the same formula to solve this problem. The only difference is that instead of adding, we subtract the two fractions since one inlet pipe is adding water and the other outlet pipe is subtracting water. In this case, the outlet pipe is not helping the inlet pipe but is working against it.

The No. of hours in which the inlet pipe can fill the pool $\Rightarrow x = 2$

The No. of hours in which the outlet pipe can drain the pool $\Rightarrow y = 10$

Let, the No. of hours in which the pool will be filled = z

$\Rightarrow \dfrac{1}{x} - \dfrac{1}{y} = \dfrac{1}{z}$ [Write the appropriate formula]

$\Rightarrow \dfrac{1}{2} - \dfrac{1}{10} = \dfrac{1}{z}$ [Substitute the known values]

$\Rightarrow \dfrac{5}{10} - \dfrac{1}{10} = \dfrac{1}{z}$ [Scale-up the fractions to their LCD, which is 10]

$\Rightarrow \dfrac{1}{z} = \dfrac{4}{10} = \dfrac{2}{5}$ [Combine like-terms]

$\Rightarrow 2z = 5$ [Cross multiply]

$\Rightarrow z = \dfrac{5}{2} = 2.5$ hours [Divide both sides by 2]

Therefore, it will take 2.5 hours to completely fill the pool.

PRACTICE EXERCISE – QUESTIONS AND ANSWERS WITH EXPLANATIONS: WORK PROBLEMS:

Question #1: If 155 pages have 7,750 words, what is the number of words per page?
Solution: Pages ⇒ 155 pages
Words ⇒ 7,750 words

Rate of words per page ⇒ $\dfrac{Words}{Page} = \dfrac{7,750\,Words}{155\,Page}$ = 50 words per page

Question #2: If 95 pages have 7,600 words, what is the number of words per page?
Solution: Pages ⇒ 95 pages
Words ⇒ 7,600 words

Rate of words per page ⇒ $\dfrac{Words}{Pages} = \dfrac{7,600\,Words}{95\,Page}$ = 80 words per page

Question #3: If a man can type 9,750 words in 2½ hours, what is his rate in words per minute?
Solution: Time ⇒ 2.5 hours = 150 minutes
Words ⇒ 9,750 words

Rate of words per minute ⇒ $\dfrac{Words}{Minutes} = \dfrac{9,750\,Words}{150\,Minutes}$ = 65 words per minute

Question #4: If a man types first 10,000 words in 1¼ hours and the remaining 6,200 words in 1 hour, what is his average rate of words per minute for the entire project?
Solution: Total Words ⇒ 10,000 + 6,200 = 16,200
Total Time ⇒ 1¼ + 1 = 2.25 hours = 2.25 × 60 = 135 minutes

Average Rate of words per minute ⇒ $\dfrac{Total\,Words}{Total\,Minutes} = \dfrac{16,200}{135}$ = 120 words per minute

Question #5: If the first 80 pages have an average of 100 words per page, and the remaining 20 pages have an average of 500 words per page, what is the average number of words per page for the entire 100 pages?
Solution: Total Pages ⇒ 80 + 20 = 100
Total Words ⇒ (80 × 100) + (20 × 500) = 8,000 + 10,000 = 18,000

Average words per page ⇒ $\dfrac{Total\,Words}{Total\,Page} = \dfrac{18,000}{100}$ = 180 words per page

Question #6: If the first 90 pages have an average of 200 words per page, and the remaining 10 pages have an average of 600 words per page, what is the average number of words per page for the entire 100 pages?
Solution: Total Pages ⇒ 90 + 10 = 100
Total Words ⇒ (90 × 200) + (10 × 600) = 18,000 + 6,000 = 24,000

Average words per page ⇒ $\dfrac{Total\,Words}{Total\,Pages} = \dfrac{24,000}{100}$ = 240 words per page

Question #7: If John can mow two-fifths of his lawn in one hour, how many minutes will it take John to mow his entire lawn?
Solution: Amount of time it takes John to mow $\dfrac{2}{5}$ of his lawn ⇒ 60 minutes

Amount of time it takes John to mow his entire lawn ⇒ $60 \times \dfrac{5}{2}$ = 150 minutes

Question #8: If John can mow two-fifths of his lawn in one hour, how many minutes will it take John to mow the rest of his lawn?

Solution:

Amount of time it takes John to mow $\frac{2}{5}$ of his lawn	$\Rightarrow$ 60 minutes
Amount of time it takes John to mow his entire lawn	$\Rightarrow 60 \times \frac{5}{2} = 150$ minutes
Amount of time it takes John to mow $\frac{3}{5}$ of his lawn	$\Rightarrow 150 \times \frac{3}{5} = 90$ or $(150 - 60) = 90$ minutes

Question #9: If John can mow two-fifths of his lawn in 9 hours, how many hours will it take John to mow his entire lawn?

Solution:

Amount of time it takes John to mow $\frac{2}{5}$ of his lawn	$\Rightarrow$ 9 hours
Amount of time it takes John to mow his entire lawn	$\Rightarrow 9 \times \frac{5}{2} = 22\frac{1}{2}$ hours

Question #10: If John can mow two-fifths of his lawn in 9 hours, how many hours will it take John to mow the rest of his lawn?

Solution:

Amount of time it takes John to mow $\frac{2}{5}$ of his lawn	$\Rightarrow$ 9 hours
Amount of time it takes John to mow his entire lawn	$\Rightarrow 9 \times \frac{5}{2} = 22\frac{1}{2}$ hours
Amount of time it takes John to mow $\frac{3}{5}$ of his lawn	$\Rightarrow 22\frac{1}{2} \times \frac{3}{5} = 13\frac{1}{2}$ or $(22\frac{1}{2} - 9) = 13\frac{1}{2}$ hours

Question #11: John can make marshmallows twice as fast as George can. George can make 72 marshmallows in 16 minutes. If both, John and George makes marshmallows at a constant rate, how many marshmallows can John make in 18 minutes?

Solution: Amount of time it takes George to make 72 marshmallows $\Rightarrow$ 16 minutes.
Amount of time it takes John to make 72 marshmallows $\Rightarrow$ 8 minutes
Since John is twice as fast as George $\Rightarrow$ John can do the same job in half the time it takes George
John's rate of works $\Rightarrow 72 \div 8 = 9$ marshmallows per minute
No. of marshmallows that John can make in 1 minute $\Rightarrow$ 9
No. of marshmallows that John can make in 18 minute $\Rightarrow 9 \times 18 = 162$

Question #12: A man is paid $200 for the first 40 hours of his work in a week, and is then paid 1½ times his regular hourly rate for any additional hours for overtime. How many hours must he work to make $290 in a week?

Solution: Regular Wages for 40 hours $\Rightarrow$ $200
Regular Hourly Rate $\Rightarrow$ $200 $\div$ 40 = $5 per hour
Overtime Hourly Rate $\Rightarrow$ 1.5 × Regular Hourly Wages = 1.5 × $5 = $7.50
Total Required Wages $\Rightarrow$ Wages for 40 Regular Hours + Wages for Overtime Hours = $290
$\Rightarrow$ $200 + Wages for Overtime Hours = $290
Wages for Overtime Hours $\Rightarrow$ Total Required Wages – Regular Wages = $290 – $200 = $90
No. of Overtime Hours $\Rightarrow$ Overtime Wages $\div$ Overtime Hourly Rate = $90 $\div$ 7.5 = 12
Total No. of Hours to make $290 $\Rightarrow$ 40 Regular Hours + 12 Overtime Hours = 52 total hours

Question #13: John finds out that 2¼ ink of cartridges are just enough to print one-third of his project report. How many additional cartridges of ink will he need to print two copies of his project report?

Solution:

To Print One-Third of Project Report, No. of Cartridges Required	$\Rightarrow 2\frac{1}{4}$
To Print the Whole Project Report, No. of Cartridges Required	$\Rightarrow 3 \times 2\frac{1}{4} = 6\frac{3}{4}$
To Print 2 Whole Project Report, No. of Cartridges Required	$\Rightarrow 6\frac{3}{4} \times 2 = 13\frac{1}{2}$
To Print 2 Whole Project Report, No. of Additional Cartridges of Ink Required	$\Rightarrow 13\frac{1}{2} - 2\frac{1}{4} = 11\frac{1}{4}$

Question #14: Working at a uniform rate, 8 identical machines can make 176 identical moldings per minute. At the same rate, how many moldings could 10 such machines make in 5.5 minutes?

Solution:
No. of moldings 8 machines can make in 1 minute $\Rightarrow$ 176
No. of moldings 1 machine can make in 1 minute $\Rightarrow$ 176 ÷ 8 = 22
No. of moldings 10 machines can make in 1 minute $\Rightarrow$ 22 × 10 = 220
No. of moldings 10 machines can make in 5.5 minutes $\Rightarrow$ 220 × 5.5 = 1,210

Question #15: A handyman charges $11 an hour, while his assistant charges $7 an hour. If the handyman and his assistant worked the same amount of time together on a job, how many hours did each of them work if the combined charge for their labor was $162?

Solution:
Hourly Rate for Handyman $\Rightarrow$ $11
Hourly Rate for Assistant $\Rightarrow$ $7
Hourly Rate for Handyman & Assistant Working Together $\Rightarrow$ $11 + $7 = $18
Total Combined Charges for Labor $\Rightarrow$ $18 × No. of Hours = $162
No. of Hours Each Worked $\Rightarrow$ $162 ÷ $18 = 9

Question #16: If Monika can clean a room in 2 hours, and Tiffany can clean the same room in 4 hours, how many hours will it take Monika and Tiffany to clean the same room if they work together at these rates?

Solution:
The No. of hours it takes Monika alone to clean the room $\Rightarrow x = 2$
The No. of hours it takes Tiffany alone to clean the room $\Rightarrow y = 4$
Let, the No. of hours it takes Monika and Tiffany together to clean the room = z

$\Rightarrow \dfrac{1}{x} + \dfrac{1}{y} = \dfrac{1}{z}$ [Write the appropriate formula]

$\Rightarrow \dfrac{1}{2} + \dfrac{1}{4} = \dfrac{1}{z}$ [Substitute the known values]

$\Rightarrow \dfrac{2}{4} + \dfrac{1}{4} = \dfrac{1}{z}$ [Scale-up the fractions to their LCD, which is 4]

$\Rightarrow \dfrac{3}{4} = \dfrac{1}{z}$ [Combine like-terms]

$\Rightarrow 3z = 4$ [Cross-multiply]

$\Rightarrow z = \dfrac{4}{3} = 1\dfrac{1}{3}$ hours   [Divide both sides by 3]

Therefore, it will take Monika & Tiffany $1\dfrac{1}{3}$ hours to clean the room working together.

Question #17: If Machine-A can print a job in 5 hours, and Machine-B can print the same job in 6 hours, how many hours will it take Machine-A and Machine-B to print the same job if they operate together at these rates?

Solution:
The No. of hours it takes Machine-A alone to print a job $\Rightarrow x = 5$
The No. of hours it takes Machine-B alone to print a job $\Rightarrow y = 6$
Let, the No. of hours it takes Machine-A and Machine-B together to print a job = z

$\Rightarrow \dfrac{1}{x} + \dfrac{1}{y} = \dfrac{1}{z}$ [Write the appropriate formula]

$\Rightarrow \dfrac{1}{5} + \dfrac{1}{6} = \dfrac{1}{z}$ [Substitute the known values]

$\Rightarrow \dfrac{6}{30} + \dfrac{5}{30} = \dfrac{1}{z}$ [Scale-up the fractions to their LCD, which is 30]

$\Rightarrow \dfrac{11}{30} = \dfrac{1}{z}$ [Combine like-terms]

$\Rightarrow 11z = 30$ [Cross-multiply]

$\Rightarrow z = \dfrac{30}{11} = 2\dfrac{8}{11}$ [Divide both sides by 11]

Therefore, it will take Machine-A & Machine-B, $2\frac{8}{11}$ hours to print the job working together.

Question #18: If Ricky can mow his lawn in 12 hours working alone, and with his little brother's help, he can finish the same job in 8 hours, how many hours will it take the little brother to mow the entire lawn alone?

Solution: The No. of hours it takes Ricky alone to mow the lawn $\Rightarrow x = 12$
The No. of hours it takes Ricky and Brother together to mow the lawn $\Rightarrow z = 12$
Let, the No. of hours it takes the Brother alone to mow the lawn $= y$

$\Rightarrow \dfrac{1}{x} + \dfrac{1}{y} = \dfrac{1}{z}$ [Write the appropriate formula]

$\Rightarrow \dfrac{1}{12} + \dfrac{1}{y} = \dfrac{1}{8}$ [Substitute the known values]

$\Rightarrow \dfrac{1}{y} = \dfrac{1}{8} - \dfrac{1}{12}$ [Subtract both sides by 1/12]

$\Rightarrow \dfrac{1}{y} = \dfrac{3}{24} - \dfrac{2}{24}$ [Scale-up the fractions to their LCD, which is 24]

$\Rightarrow \dfrac{1}{y} = \dfrac{1}{24}$ [Combine like-terms]

$\Rightarrow y = 24$ hours   [Cross-multiply]

Therefore, it will take the little brother 24 hours to mow the lawn working alone.

Question #19: If John can type 25 pages in 10 hours working alone, and with his secretary's help, he can finish the same job in 6 hours, how many hours will it take the secretary to type the same 25 pages alone?

Solution: The No. of hours it takes John alone to type 25 pages $\Rightarrow x = 10$
The No. of hours it takes John and the Secretary together to type 25 pages $\Rightarrow z = 6$
Let, the No. of hours it takes the Secretary alone to type 25 pages $= y$

$\Rightarrow \dfrac{1}{x} + \dfrac{1}{y} = \dfrac{1}{z}$ [Write the appropriate formula]

$\Rightarrow \dfrac{1}{10} + \dfrac{1}{y} = \dfrac{1}{6}$ [Substitute the known values]

$\Rightarrow \dfrac{1}{y} = \dfrac{1}{6} - \dfrac{1}{10}$ [Subtract both sides by 1/10]

$\Rightarrow \dfrac{1}{y} = \dfrac{10}{60} - \dfrac{6}{60}$ [Scale-up the fractions to their LCD, which is 60]

$\Rightarrow \dfrac{1}{y} = \dfrac{4}{60}$ [Combine like-terms]

$\Rightarrow 4y = 60$ [Cross-multiply]

$\Rightarrow y = \dfrac{60}{4} = 15$ [Divide both sides by 4]

Therefore, it will take the secretary 15 hours to type 25 pages working alone.

Question #20: If a man can fence his yard in 10 hours, his wife can do it in 25 hours, and his son can do it in 50 hours, how many hours will it take the man, his wife, and son working together to fence the yard at these rates?

Solution: The No. of hours it takes the Man alone to fence the yard $\Rightarrow a = 10$
The No. of hours it takes the Wife alone to fence the yard $\Rightarrow b = 25$
The No. of hours it takes the Son alone to fence the yard $\Rightarrow c = 50$
Let, the No. of hours it takes the Man, Wife, and Son together to fence the yard $= z$

$\Rightarrow \dfrac{1}{a} + \dfrac{1}{b} + \dfrac{1}{c} = \dfrac{1}{z}$ [Write the appropriate formula]

$\Rightarrow \dfrac{1}{10} + \dfrac{1}{25} + \dfrac{1}{50} = \dfrac{1}{z}$ [Substitute the known values]

$\Rightarrow \dfrac{5}{50} + \dfrac{2}{50} + \dfrac{1}{50} = \dfrac{1}{z}$ [Scale-up the fractions to their LCD, which is 50]

$\Rightarrow \dfrac{8}{50} = \dfrac{1}{z}$ [Combine like-terms]

$\Rightarrow 8z = 50$ [Cross-multiply]

$\Rightarrow z = \dfrac{50}{8} = 6\dfrac{1}{4}$ [Divide both sides by 8]

Therefore, it will take the man, his wife and son $6\dfrac{1}{4}$ hours to fence the yard working jointly.

Question #21: First pipe can fill a tank in 2 hours, a second pipe can fill the tank in 8 hours, and a third pipe can fill the tank in 16 hours. At these rates, how long will it take the three pipes together to fill the tank?

Solution: We can use the same work formula to solve this problem. The only difference is that instead of machines or people, it's the pipes that are doing the work, which is filling the tank.
The No. of hours it takes the First Pipe alone to fill the tank $\Rightarrow a = 2$
The No. of hours it takes the Second Pipe alone to fill the tank $\Rightarrow b = 8$
The No. of hours it takes the Third Pipe alone to fill the tank $\Rightarrow c = 16$
Let the No. of hours it takes all Three Pipes together to fill the tank = z

$\Rightarrow \dfrac{1}{a} + \dfrac{1}{b} + \dfrac{1}{c} = \dfrac{1}{z}$ [Write the appropriate formula]

$\Rightarrow \dfrac{1}{2} + \dfrac{1}{8} + \dfrac{1}{16} = \dfrac{1}{z}$ [Substitute the known values]

$\Rightarrow \dfrac{8}{16} + \dfrac{2}{16} + \dfrac{1}{16} = \dfrac{1}{z}$ [Scale-up the fractions to their LCD, which is 16]

$\Rightarrow \dfrac{11}{16} = \dfrac{1}{z}$ [Combine like-terms]

$\Rightarrow 11z = 16$ [Cross-multiply]

$\Rightarrow z = \dfrac{16}{11} = 1\dfrac{5}{11}$ [Divide both sides by 11]

Therefore, it will take all three pipes $1\dfrac{5}{11}$ hours to fill the tank.

Question #22: First pipe can fill a tank in 5 hours, a second pipe can fill the tank in 10 hours, and a third pipe can fill the tank in 15 hours. At these rates, how many hours will it take the three pipes together to fill the tank?

Solution: The No. of hours it takes the First Pipe alone to fill the tank $\Rightarrow a = 5$
The No. of hours it takes the Second Pipe alone to fill the tank $\Rightarrow b = 10$
The No. of hours it takes the Third Pipe alone to fill the tank $\Rightarrow c = 15$
Let the No. of hours it takes all Three Pipes together to fill the tank = z

$\Rightarrow \dfrac{1}{a} + \dfrac{1}{b} + \dfrac{1}{c} = \dfrac{1}{z}$ [Write the appropriate formula]

$\Rightarrow \dfrac{1}{5} + \dfrac{1}{10} + \dfrac{1}{15} = \dfrac{1}{z}$ [Substitute the known values]

$\Rightarrow \dfrac{6}{30} + \dfrac{3}{30} + \dfrac{2}{30} = \dfrac{1}{z}$ [Scale-up the fractions to their LCD, which is 30]

$\Rightarrow \dfrac{11}{30} = \dfrac{1}{z}$ [Combine like-terms]

$\Rightarrow 11z = 30$ [Cross-multiply]

$\Rightarrow z = \dfrac{30}{11} = 2\dfrac{8}{11}$ [Divide both sides by 11]

Therefore, it will take all three pipes $2\frac{8}{11}$ hours to fill the tank.

Question #23: There are two taps, tap-1 and tap-2, in a tank. If both taps are opened, the tank is completely drained in 20 minutes. If tap-1 is closed and tap-2 is open, the tank will be completely drained in 30 minutes. If tap-1 is open and tap-2 is closed, how many minutes will it take to completely drain the tank?

Solution: We can use the same work formula to solve this problem. The only difference is that instead of machines or people, it's the taps that are doing the work, which is draining the tank.

The No. of minutes it takes Tap-2 alone to drain the tank $\Rightarrow y = 30$
The No. of minutes it takes Tap-1 and Tap-2 together to drain the tank $\Rightarrow z = 20$
Let, the No. of minutes it takes Tap-1 alone to drain the tank $= y$

$\Rightarrow \dfrac{1}{x} + \dfrac{1}{y} = \dfrac{1}{z}$ [Write the appropriate formula]

$\Rightarrow \dfrac{1}{x} + \dfrac{1}{30} = \dfrac{1}{20}$ [Substitute the known values]

$\Rightarrow \dfrac{1}{x} = \dfrac{1}{20} - \dfrac{1}{30}$ [Subtract both sides by 1/30]

$\Rightarrow \dfrac{1}{x} = \dfrac{3}{60} - \dfrac{2}{60}$ [Scale-up the fractions to their LCD, which is 60]

$\Rightarrow \dfrac{1}{x} = \dfrac{1}{60}$ [Combine like-terms]

$\Rightarrow x = 60$ [Cross-multiply]

Therefore, if tap-1 is open and tap-2 is closed, it will take 60 minutes or 1 hour to completely drain the tank.

Question #24: A swimming pool can be filled by an inlet pipe in 3 hours. It can be drained by a outlet pipe in 6 hours. By mistake, both pipes are opened at the same time. If the pool is empty, in how many hours will it be filled?

Solution: We can use the same work formula to solve this problem. The only difference is that instead of adding, we subtract the two fractions since one inlet pipe is adding water and the other outlet pipe is subtracting water. In this case, the outlet pipe is not helping the inlet pipe but is working against it.

The No. of hours in which the inlet pipe can fill the pool $\Rightarrow x = 3$
The No. of hours in which the outlet pipe can drain the pool $\Rightarrow y = 6$
Let, the No. of hours in which the pool will be filled $= z$

$\Rightarrow \dfrac{1}{x} - \dfrac{1}{y} = \dfrac{1}{z}$ [Write the appropriate formula]

$\Rightarrow \dfrac{1}{3} - \dfrac{1}{6} = \dfrac{1}{z}$ [Substitute the known values]

$\Rightarrow \dfrac{2}{6} - \dfrac{1}{6} = \dfrac{1}{z}$ [Scale-up the fractions to their LCD, which is 6]

$\Rightarrow \dfrac{1}{6} = \dfrac{1}{z}$ [Combine like-terms]

$\Rightarrow z = 6$ [Cross-multiply]

Therefore, it will take 6 hours to completely fill the pool.

Question #25: A swimming pool can be filled by an inlet pipe in 5 hours. It can be drained by a outlet pipe in 15 hours. By mistake, both pipes are opened at the same time. If the pool is empty, in how many hours will it be filled?

Solution: We can use the same work formula to solve this problem. The only difference is that instead of adding, we subtract the two fractions since one inlet pipe is adding water and the other outlet pipe is subtracting water. In this case, the outlet pipe is not helping the inlet pipe but is working against it.

The No. of hours in which the inlet pipe can fill the pool $\Rightarrow x = 5$
The No. of hours in which the outlet pipe can drain the pool $\Rightarrow y = 15$
Let, the No. of hours in which the pool will be filled $= z$

$\Rightarrow \dfrac{1}{x} - \dfrac{1}{y} = \dfrac{1}{z}$ [Write the appropriate formula]

$\Rightarrow \dfrac{1}{5} - \dfrac{1}{15} = \dfrac{1}{z}$ [Substitute the known values]

$\Rightarrow \dfrac{3}{15} - \dfrac{1}{15} = \dfrac{1}{z}$ [Scale-up the fractions to their LCD, which is 15]

$\Rightarrow \dfrac{1}{z} = \dfrac{2}{15}$ [Combine like-terms]

$\Rightarrow 2z = 15$ [Cross-multiply]

$\Rightarrow z = 15 \div 2 = 7.5$ [Divide both sides by 2]

Therefore, it will take 7.5 hours to completely fill the pool.

THIS PAGE HAS BEEN INTENTIONALLY LEFT BLANK

PART 7.0: MOTION PROBLEMS:

TABLE OF CONTENTS:

PART 7.0: MOTION PROBLEMS: **111**

   7.1: Basics About Motion Problems: 112

   7.2: Different Types of Motion Problems: 115

   Practice Exercise – Questions and Answers With Explanations: Motion Problems: 123

7.1: BASICS ABOUT MOTION PROBLEMS:

RATE-TIME-DISTANCE (R-T-D) RELATED WORD PROBLEMS:
One of the most common word problems involves rates. A rate is simply a ratio that relates two different quantities that are measured in different units. Some of the most common types of rate problems include motion (speed, which is expressed as a ratio of distance and time, and can be measured in miles per hour, meters per second, etc.), and work (which is expressed as a ratio of job done and time, and can be measured in work done per hour, minute, etc.). All Motion Word Problems involve three primary components, rate, time, and distance, which are related by the equation Rate × Time = Distance. They usually have one or more of the information given and they ask for the missing information.

EZ SPOT: Motion problems are easy to spot. Any problem that mentions planes, trains, cars, bicycles, running, trip, distance, miles, rate, miles per hour, or any other travel related terminology is most likely a motion (distance, rate, and time) problem. All these problems require you to have the knowledge of the rate formula and how to apply it in different variations and under different circumstances.

RATE-TIME-DISTANCE FORMULA   ⇒ DISTANCE = RATE × TIME
All motion (rate/time/distance) word problems revolve around the same fundamental relationship that involves one of the three variations of the same formula:

(A) The total distance that an object travels is equal to the product of the average rate at which it travels and the total amount of time it takes to travel that distance.
⇒ **Distance = Rate × Time**   ⇒ **D = RT**

(B) The average rate at which an object travels is equal to the quotient of the total distance it travels and the total amount of time it takes to travel that distance.
$$\Rightarrow \textbf{\textit{Rate}} = \frac{\textbf{\textit{Dist.}}}{\textbf{\textit{Time}}} \qquad\qquad \Rightarrow R = \frac{D}{T}$$

(C) The total amount of time it takes an object to travel a distance is equal to the quotient of the total distance it travels and the average rate at which it travels that distance.
$$\Rightarrow \textbf{\textit{Time}} = \frac{\textbf{\textit{Dist.}}}{\textbf{\textit{Rate}}} \qquad\qquad \Rightarrow T = \frac{D}{R}$$

Where: D = distance, which is usually in "Miles".
           R = rate, which is usually in "Miles per Hour" or "mph".
           T = time, which is usually in "Hours", (if given in minutes, first convert it into hours).
Be careful of the units used. If the distance is in miles, and time is in hours, then the rate should be in miles per hour.

EZ HINT: The formula given above is very important and you should make it a point to memorize it. Actually, the easiest way to memorize is if you can relate it to a common everyday situation of driving a car. The distance traveled (in miles) = the speed of the car (in miles per hour) × time driving at that speed (in hours). For instance, let's assume that you are driving at 25 miles per hour for 2 hours, obviously just by common sense you know, you would have traveled 50 miles. The distance traveled is 25 miles per hour × 2 hours = 50 miles. Notice that we just derived the formula. The rate is 25 miles per hour. The time is 2 hours. The distance is 50 miles. Therefore, this formula is easy to reconstruct if you ever forget it; just think of a real life situation. (Notice how the unit "hours" cancels out when you multiply).

The rate formula simply means that the distance you traveled equals the rate you were going at multiplied by the time it took you to get there.

EZ REFERENCE: For more in-depth knowledge about rate, refer to our Algebraic Applications Module.

MATCHING UNITS:

It is critical that all the units match up with one another. The two units in the rate (such as miles per hour) should match up with the unit of time (such as hours) and the unit of distance (such as miles). Make sure to convert the units of each measure to the appropriate units to match-up before you substitute the values into the formula.

For instance, if a problem asks for the rate in meters per minute, and the distance is given in kilometers and time is given in hours, you must first convert the distance from kilometers to meters and time from hours to minutes before you apply the rate formula. Likewise, if a problem asks for the time in hours, and the rate is given in kilometers per hour and distance is given in meters, you must first convert the distance from meters to kilometers before applying the time formula.

CONSTANT OR DIFFERENT RATES: The speed in the rate formula is assumed to be constant over a period of time. If you know that there are different speeds for different lengths of time, then you must use the formula more than once to get the average speed, as explained in some of the examples given in the next section. In more difficult rate problems, the rate is usually not constant over the entire period in the question.

BASIC MOTION PROBLEMS:
Following are some of the most basic and straightforward motion problems:

Example #1:   If it takes a vehicle 2.5 hours from Washington DC to New York at an average speed of 80 miles per hour, what is the distance between Washington DC and New York?

Solution: *Distance* $\Rightarrow$ *Rate × Time*
$\Rightarrow 80 \times 2.5$
$\Rightarrow 200$ miles

Example #2:   If it takes a vehicle 2.5 hours to travel 200 miles from Washington DC to New York, what should be the average speed?

Solution: *Rate* $\Rightarrow \dfrac{Dist}{Time}$
$\Rightarrow 200 \div 2.5$
$\Rightarrow 80$ miles per hour

Example #3:   If the distance between Washington DC and New York is 200 miles and a vehicle is traveling at an average speed of 80 miles/hour, how long will it take to cover the whole distance?

Solution: *Time* $\Rightarrow \dfrac{Dist}{Rate}$
$\Rightarrow 200 \div 80$
$\Rightarrow 2.5$ hours

ADVANCED MOTION PROBLEMS:
The more difficult or complex motion problems involve more than one set of concurrent rate, time, and distance. The one thing that is common to all advanced motion problems is that they all require you to find a relationship between two different rates, times, or distances.

First, formulate a grid: To solve any type of motion problem, it is helpful to organize the information in a chart or a table. Use columns for rate, time, and distance. A separate row or line should be used for each moving object.

Next, draw a sketch of the motion: The next thing you should do is draw a diagram and put down everything that's given in the problem.

Finally: Decide what you need to do in order to make a connection and find what is being asked in the question.

ASSIGNING VARIABLES IN ADVANCED MOTION PROBLEMS:
Finding the relationship alone does not necessarily mean finding the exact value. You also need to become proficient at writing down relationships by using different variables. In fact, the trickiest part of solving these problems is being able to assign variables correctly.

Use the following guidelines to assign variables in advanced motion problems:

FOR RATE RELATIONS:

While assigning variables for rate, determine which person or object is traveling at a greater rate and which one is traveling at a slower rate.

For instance: If Object-A is traveling at a certain rate and the Object-B is traveling at double that rate ⇒ then the rate for Object-A is r, and the rate for Object-B is $2r$; or the rate of Object-B is r and the rate of Object-A is $\frac{1}{2} r$.

For instance: If Object-A is traveling at a constant rate, and Object-B simultaneously follows the first one at a constant rate that is 10 miles per hour slower ⇒ then the rate for Object-A is (r) mph, and the rate for Object-B is $(r - 10)$ mph; or the rate of Object-B is (r) mph and the rate of Object-A is $(r + 10)$ mph.

FOR TIME RELATIONS:

While assigning variables for time, determine which person or object is traveling for a longer time and which one is traveling for a shorter time. The person or the object that is traveling for a longer time should get a variable plus a value or the person or the object that is traveling for a shorter time should get a variable minus a value.

For instance: If Object-A leaves 10 minutes after Object-B ⇒ then Object-A's time is (t) and Object-B's time is $(t + 10)$ minutes; or Object-B's time is (t) minutes and Object-A's time is $(t - 10)$ minutes. Remember that Object-B is traveling for a longer time, so it gets a variable plus a value; and that Object-A is traveling for a shorter time, so it gets a variable minus a value. However, don't make the mistake of assigning $(t + 10)$ for Object-B and $(t - 10)$ for Object-A, because, in that case, there will be a 20 minute difference.

FOR DISTANCE RELATIONS:

While assigning variables for distance, determine whether the two people or objects are moving towards each other or, away from each other in opposite or perpendicular direction, or along the same path.

For instance: If two objects are moving toward each other, and if they are 100 miles apart ⇒ then the distance the first object travels is d miles while the distance the other object ravels is $(100 - d)$ miles.

For instance: If a person can either take a train or a bus to travel from point A to point B ⇒ then in both cases the distance will be a constant d.

EZ TIP: Be careful while assigning variables in advanced motion problems. Sometimes, the key to solving the problem lies in being able to identify the variable that is either the same for both columns in the grid or at least share a relationship.

7.2: DIFFERENT TYPES OF MOTION PROBLEMS:

TYPE #1: TWO RELATED PARTS OF SAME TRIP:
These types of problems involve a trip, in which different parts of the trip are related to each other. The key to answering such questions is to keep finding missing information; one information will often lead to the other and eventually to the answer to the question.

Example #1: If a man drove a 100-mile road trip in 18 hours, and he averaged a 10 miles per hour rate for the first 20 miles, what speed did he average, in miles per hour, for the last 80 miles of the trip?

Solution: Organize all the given information in the following grid:

First Part of Trip	Second Part of Trip
$D_1 \Rightarrow$ 20 miles	$D_2 \Rightarrow$ 80 miles
$R_1 \Rightarrow$ 10 mph	$T_2 \Rightarrow 18 - 2 = 16$ hours
$T_1 \Rightarrow$ 2 hours	$R_2 \Rightarrow 80 \div 16 = 5$ mph

Therefore, the man averages a rate of 5 mph for the last 80 miles of the trip.

Example #2: A man drove 90 miles in one and one half hours. After one hour, he had driven 55 miles. What was his average speed for the rest of the trip?

Solution: Organize all the given information in the following grid:

First Part of Trip	Second Part of Trip
$D_1 \Rightarrow$ 55 miles	$D_2 \Rightarrow$ 35 miles
$T_1 \Rightarrow$ 1 hour	$T_2 \Rightarrow 1.5 - 1 = 0.5$ hour
$R_1 \Rightarrow 55 \div 1 = 55$ mph	$R_2 \Rightarrow 35 \div 0.5 = 70$ mph

Therefore, the man averages a rate of 70 mph for the rest of the trip

Example #3: A man and a woman traveled the same 120-mile distance. If the man took 2 hours and the woman traveled at an average rate that was 1.5 times faster than the average speed of the man, how many minutes did it take the woman to travel the same distance?

Solution: Organize all the given information in the following grid:

Man's Trip	Woman's Trip
$D_1 \Rightarrow$ 120 m	$D_2 \Rightarrow$ 120 m
$T_1 \Rightarrow$ 2 hrs	$R_2 \Rightarrow 60 \times 1.5 = 90$ mph
$R_1 \Rightarrow 120 \div 2 = 60$ mph	$T_2 \Rightarrow 120 \div 90 = 4/3$ hrs = 80 minutes

Therefore, if took the woman 80 minutes to travel the route.

Example #4: A train travels at an average speed of 60 miles per hour for 2.5 hours and then travels at a speed of 80 miles per hour for 7.5 hours. How far did the train travel in the entire 10 hours?

Solution: Organize all the given information in the following grid:

First Part of Trip	Second Part of Trip
$R_1 \Rightarrow$ 60 mph	$R_2 \Rightarrow$ 80 mph
$T_1 \Rightarrow$ 2.5 hrs	$T_2 \Rightarrow$ 7.5 hrs
$D_1 \Rightarrow 60 \times 2.5 = 150$ m	$D_2 \Rightarrow 80 \times 7.5 = 600$ m

Total Distance $\Rightarrow D_1 + D_2 = 150$ m + 600 m = 750 miles

Example #5: How many minutes did Juliet take, driving at 24 miles per hour, to cover the same distance that Romeo took 15 minutes driving at 80 miles per hour?

Solution: Organize all the given information in the following grid:

Romeo's Trip	Juliet's Trip
$R_1 \Rightarrow$ 80 miles per hour	$R_2 \Rightarrow$ 24 miles per hour
$T_1 \Rightarrow$ 15 minutes = 0.25 hours	$D_2 \Rightarrow$ 20 miles
$D_1 \Rightarrow 80 \times 0.25 = 20$ miles	$T_2 \Rightarrow 20 \div 24 = 5/6$ hours = 50 minutes

Therefore, it will take Juliet 50 minutes, driving at 24 miles per hour, to cover the same distance that Romeo took 15 minutes driving at 80 miles per hour.

Question #6: A car traveling at an average rate of 55 miles per hour made a trip in 10 hours. If it had traveled at an average rate of 50 miles per hour, the trip would have taken how many minutes longer?

Solution:

Original Situation	New Situation
$R_1 \Rightarrow$ 55 mph	$D_2 \Rightarrow$ 550 m
$T_1 \Rightarrow$ 10 hrs	$R_2 \Rightarrow$ 50 mph
$D_1 \Rightarrow R_1 \times T_1 = 55 \times 10 = 550$ m	$T_2 \Rightarrow D_2 \div R_2 = 550 \div 50 = 11$ hrs

Time Difference $\Rightarrow T_2 - T_1 = 11$ hrs $- 10$ hrs $= 1$ hour or 60 minutes

Example #7: If Simon traveled 10 miles in 2 hours and Jason traveled twice as far in half the time, what was the difference between their average speeds, in miles per hour?

Solution: Organize all the given information in the following grid:

Simon's Trip	Jason's Trip
$D_1 \Rightarrow$ 10 miles	$D_2 \Rightarrow 10 \times 2 = 20$ miles
$T_1 \Rightarrow$ 2 hours	$T_2 \Rightarrow \frac{1}{2} \times 2 = 1$ hour
$R_1 \Rightarrow 10 \div 2 = 5$ miles per hour	$R_2 \Rightarrow 20 \div 1 = 20$ miles per hour

Difference between their average speed $\Rightarrow R_2 - R_1 = 20 - 5 = 15$ miles per hour

TYPE #2: AVERAGE SPEED:

Average Speed of an Object Moving at Same/Different Rates for Same/Different Parts of the Same Trip: These types of problems involve a trip, in which the object is moving at different rates for different parts of the same trip. In such problems, the rate, time, and distance are different for different parts of the trip. The key to solving such problems is to deal with the total distance, time, and rate. Therefore, in order to find the average rate, you must first find the total combined distance for the trips and the total combined time for the trips; and then use these totals to calculate the overall average rate.

Example #1: On a road trip, if the first half of the trip is traveled at 40 miles per hour and the second half at 60 miles per hour, what will be the average speed for the entire trip?

Solution: Sketch the following diagram and put down everything that's given in the problem:
Let each half of the trip be 120 miles long. (note, 120 is a multiple of both rates, 40 as well as 60)

1st Part $\Rightarrow d = 120$ m, $r = 40$ mph   2nd Part $\Rightarrow d = 120$ m, $r = 60$ mph

Start   End

$d = 240$ m

Organize all the given information in the following grid:

First Half of Trip	Second Half of Trip
$D_1 \Rightarrow$ 120 m	$D_2 \Rightarrow$ 120 m
$R_1 \Rightarrow$ 40 mph	$R_2 \Rightarrow$ 60 mph
$T_1 \Rightarrow \dfrac{D}{T} = \dfrac{120}{40} = 3$ hours	$T_2 \Rightarrow \dfrac{D}{T} = \dfrac{120}{60} = 2$ hours

Total Trip

Total time	$\Rightarrow T_1 + T_2 = 3 + 2 = 5$ hours	[Add the total time]
Total Distance	$\Rightarrow D_1 + D_2 = 120 + 120 = 240$ m	[Add the total distance]
Average Rate	$\Rightarrow \dfrac{Total\ Distance}{Total\ Time} = \dfrac{240}{5} = 48$ mph	[Find the total average rate]

Therefore, the average speed for the entire trip is 48 mph.

EZ TRAP: To find an average rate, you can't just average the individual rates. In this question, you may get tempted to simply add 40 and 60 and divide by two, which gives you 50. This answer is too easy to be true, and is wrong. Now, you must be wondering why the average speed is not 50. It is primarily because the car spent different times traveling at different rates. Notice that the person spent slightly more time traveling at 40 mph than 60 mph; therefore, the average speed is slightly closer to 40 mph. Even if each leg of the trip were of the different distance, even then, we would have to adopt the same approach, because, then, each leg would have been covered at different rates, which would take different times. The next example is of this type.

Example #2: On a 100 mile road trip, if the first 60 miles of the trip is traveled at 10 miles per hour and the other 40 miles of the trip is traveled at 20 miles per hour, what is be the average speed for the entire trip?

Solution: Organize all the given information in the following grid:

First Half of Trip	Second Half of Trip
$D_1 \Rightarrow$ 60 m	$D_2 \Rightarrow$ 40 m

$$R_1 \Rightarrow 10 \text{ mph} \qquad\qquad\qquad\qquad R_2 \Rightarrow 20 \text{ mph}$$

$$T_1 \Rightarrow \frac{D}{T} = \frac{60}{10} = 6 \text{ hours} \qquad\qquad T_2 \Rightarrow \frac{D}{T} = \frac{40}{20} = 2 \text{ hours}$$

Total Trip

Total time	$\Rightarrow T_1 + T_2 = 6 + 2 = 8$ hours	[Add the total time]
Total Distance	$\Rightarrow D_1 + D_2 = 60 + 40 = 100$ m	[Add the total distance]
Average Rate	$\Rightarrow \dfrac{Total\,Dis\tan ce}{Total\,Time} = \dfrac{100}{8} = 12.5$ mph	[Find the total average rate]

Therefore, the average speed for the entire trip is 12.5 mph.

TYPE #3: ROUND TRIP – OUTBOUND/INBOUND TRIPS:

Distance Covered by an Object or a Person Moving at Different Rates for Outbound and Inbound Trip: These types of problems involve a round trip, that is, an outbound (going) trip from point A to point B, and an inbound (returning) trip back from point B to point A, following the same path. In such problems, the rates are different for outbound and inbound trips. The times are also different for outbound and inbound trips. However, if we go somewhere and then return to the starting point, the distances must be equal. So, the distances are the same for both outbound and inbound trips.

Example #1: A man drives from home to work at the rate of 60 miles per hour. While returning back following the same route, due to rush hour traffic, he could only drive at the rate of 40 miles per hour. If the return trip took one hour longer, how many miles did he drive each way?

Solution: Sketch the following diagram and put down everything that's given in the problem:

Organize all the given information in the following grid:

Outbound Trip	**Inbound Trip**
$R_1 \Rightarrow 60$ mph	$R_2 \Rightarrow 40$ mph
$T_1 \Rightarrow t$	$T_2 \Rightarrow t + 1$
$D_1 \Rightarrow 60t$	$D_2 \Rightarrow 40(t + 1)$

EZ Problem Set-Up $\Rightarrow$ Distance of Outbound Trip (D_1) = Distance of Inbound Trip (D_2)

$\Rightarrow 60t = 40(t+1)$	[Set up the equation]
$\Rightarrow 60t = 40t + 40$	[Apply distributive property]
$\Rightarrow 20t = 40$	[Subtract $40t$ from both sides]
$\Rightarrow t = 2$	[Divide both sides by 20]

Distance for Outbound Trip $\Rightarrow D_1 = 60t = 60 \times 2 = 120$
Distance for Inbound Trip $\Rightarrow D_2 = 40(t + 1) = 40(2 + 1) = 40 \times 3 = 120$
Total distance $\Rightarrow D_1 + D_2 = 120 + 120 = 240$ miles

Example #2: It took a man 12 hours to travel by train from Washington DC to Toledo, OH at an average speed of 75 miles per hour. On the return trip from Toledo, OH to Washington, DC, he traveled by bus and averaged 50 miles per hour. How many hours did the return trip take?

Solution: Organize all the given information in the following grid:

DC to OH Trip	**OH to DC Trip**
$R_1 \Rightarrow 75$ mph	$R_2 \Rightarrow 50$ mph
$T_1 \Rightarrow 12$ hours	$D_2 \Rightarrow 900$ miles
$D_1 \Rightarrow 900$ miles	$T_2 \Rightarrow 900 \div 50 = 18$ hours

Therefore, it took him 18 hours for the return trip.

TYPE #4: MOTION IN OPPOSITE DIRECTIONS:

Two Objects or People Moving Away From Each Other in Opposite Directions: These types of problems involve motion in opposite directions, that is, two objects, starting at the same point, and moving away from each other, in the opposite directions. In such problems, usually two objects leave the same place at same times but at different rates. The rates are usually different for both objects. The times are usually same for both objects. The distances covered are different. The key fact to realize in such problem is that the distance covered by the first object plus the distance covered by the second object is equal to the total distance covered by both objects.

Example #1: If a man leaves Point-*X* traveling West at the speed of 55 miles per hour and at the same time a woman leaves Point-*X* traveling East at the speed of 25 miles per hour, after 2 hours, how far apart will they be from each other?

Solution: Sketch the following diagram and put down everything that's given in the problem:

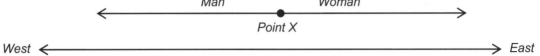

Organize all the given information in the following grid:

Man's Trip
$R_M \Rightarrow$ 55 mph
$T_M \Rightarrow$ 2 hrs
$D_M \Rightarrow$ 55 mph × 2 hrs = 110 m
   (Distance between Man & Pt-*X*)

Woman's Trip
$R_W \Rightarrow$ 25 mph
$T_M \Rightarrow$ 2 hrs
$D_W \Rightarrow$ 25 mph × 2 hrs = 50 m
   (Distance between Woman & Pt-*X*)

EZ Problem Set-Up $\Rightarrow$ Total Distance between Man and Woman (D_T) = Distance between Man & Point-*X* (D_M) + Distance between Woman & Point-*X* (D_W)
   $\Rightarrow$ 110 miles + 50 miles   [Set up the equation]
   $\Rightarrow$ 160 miles   [Do the addition]
Therefore, after 2 hours, they will be 160 miles apart from each other.

Example #2: If a man leaves Point-*X* traveling West at the speed of 55 miles per hour and at the same time a woman leaves Point-*X* traveling East at the speed of 25 miles per hour, at what time will be they be 160 miles apart from each other?

Solution: Sketch the following diagram and put down everything that's given in the problem:

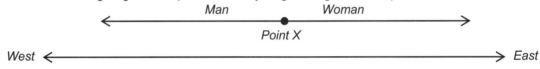

Organize all the given information in the following grid:

Man's Trip
$R_M \Rightarrow$ 55 mph
$T_M \Rightarrow t$
$D_M \Rightarrow R_M \times t$ = 55 mph × t = 55t
   (Distance between Man & Pt-*X*)

Woman's Trip
$R_W \Rightarrow$ 25 mph
$T_M \Rightarrow t$
$D_W \Rightarrow R_W \times t$ = 25 mph × t = 25t
   (Distance between Woman & Pt-*X*)

Total Distance between the Man & Woman = 160 miles
EZ Problem Set-Up $\Rightarrow$ Total Distance between Man and Woman (D_T) = Distance between Man & Point-*X* (D_M) + Distance between Woman & Point-*X* (D_W)
   $\Rightarrow$ 160 = 55t + 25t [Set up the equation]
   $\Rightarrow$ 160 = 80t [Combine like-terms]
   $\Rightarrow t$ = 2 hours   [Divide both sides by 80]
Therefore, they will be 160 miles apart in 2 hours.

Example #3: A man leaves Point-*X* traveling west and at the same time a woman leaves Point-*X* traveling east. The woman is traveling five times as fast as the man. After two hours of traveling in opposite directions, the man and the woman are 1,800 miles apart. How fast is the woman traveling?

Solution: Sketch the following diagram and put down everything that's given in the problem:

Organize all the given information in the following grid:
Man's Trip   **Woman's Trip**

$R_M \Rightarrow r$ mph

$T_M \Rightarrow 2$

$D_M \Rightarrow r$ mph $\times 2 = 2r$

    (Distance between Man & Pt-X)

$R_W \Rightarrow 5r$ mph

$T_M \Rightarrow 2$

$D_W \Rightarrow 5r$ mph $\times 2 = 10r$

    (Distance between Woman & Pt-X)

D_{Total} = Total Distance between the Man & Woman = 1,800 miles

EZ Problem Set-Up $\Rightarrow$ Total Distance between Man and Woman (D_T) = Distance between Man & Point-X (D_M) + Distance between Woman & Point-X (D_W)

$\Rightarrow 1,800 = 2r + 10r$ [Set up the equation]

$\Rightarrow 1,800 = 12r$ [Combine like-terms]

$\Rightarrow r = 150$ mph   [Divide both sides by 12]

Speed of Man $\Rightarrow 150$ mph

Speed of Woman $\Rightarrow 150 \times 5 = 750$ mph

TYPE #5: MOTION IN PERPENDICULAR DIRECTIONS:

Two Objects or People Moving Away From Each Other in Perpendicular Directions: These types of problems involve motion in perpendicular directions, that is, two objects, starting at the same point, and moving away from each other, in the perpendicular directions. In such problems, usually two objects leave the same place at same times but at different rates. The rates are usually different for both objects. The times are usually same for both objects. The distances covered are different. The key fact to realize in such problem is that path of both objects forms a right triangle in which you can use the Pythagorean Theorem. The square of the distance covered by the first object plus the square of the distance covered by the second is equal to the square of the total distance between them. This is nothing but the Pythagorean Theorem, which is often used in right triangles.

Example #1: If a man leaves Point-X traveling North at the speed of 15 miles per hour and at the same time a woman leaves Point-X traveling West at the speed of 20 miles per hour, how many miles apart from each other will they be after 2 hours?

Solution: Sketch the following diagram and put down everything that's given in the problem:

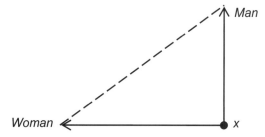

Organize all the given information in the following grid:

Man' Trip

$R_M \Rightarrow 15$ mph

$T_M \Rightarrow 2$ hrs

$D_M \Rightarrow 15 \times 2 = 30$ m

Woman's Trip

$R_W \Rightarrow 20$ mph

$T_W \Rightarrow 2$ hrs

$D_W \Rightarrow 20 \times 2 = 40$ m

EZ Problem Set-Up $\Rightarrow$ (Distance between Man & Woman)^2 = (D_M)^2 + (D_W)^2 (Pythagorean Theorem)

$\Rightarrow d^2 = 30^2 + 40^2$ [Set up the equation]

$\Rightarrow d^2 = 900 + 1600$ [Solve the exponents]

$\Rightarrow d^2 = 2,500$ [Combine like-terms]

$\Rightarrow d = 50$ [Square root both sides]

Therefore, the man and the woman will be 50 miles apart.

TYPE #6: MOTION IN SAME DIRECTION – TOWARDS EACH OTHER:

Two Objects or People Moving Towards Each Other in Same Direction: These types of problems involve motion in the same direction, that is, two objects, start at a given distance apart, starting at different points, and moving towards each other, in the same direction. In such problems, usually two objects leave the different place at same times but at different rates. The rates are usually different for both objects. The times are usually same for both objects. The distances covered are different. The key fact to realize in such problems is that the distance covered by the first object plus the distance covered by the second object is equal to the total distance covered by both objects.

Example #1: Two towns are 660 miles apart. A car leaves the first town traveling toward the second town at 55 mph. At the same time, another car leaves the second town and heads toward the first town at 65 mph. How long will it take for the two cars to meet?

Solution: Sketch the following diagram and put down everything that's given in the problem:

Organize all the given information in the following grid:

Car A
$R_1 \Rightarrow 55$ mph
$T_1 \Rightarrow t$
$D_1 \Rightarrow 55t$

Car B
$R_2 \Rightarrow 65$ mph
$T_2 \Rightarrow t$
$D_2 \Rightarrow 65t$

EZ Problem Set-Up $\Rightarrow$ Distance of First Car (D_1) + Distance of Second Car (D_2) = Total Distance
$\Rightarrow 55t + 65t = 660$ [Set up the equation]
$\Rightarrow 120t = 660$ [Combine like-terms]
$\Rightarrow t = 5.5$ hours   [Divide both sides by 120]

Therefore, it will take 5 hours & 30 minutes for the two cars to meet.

EZ ALTERNATE METHOD: In each hour of travel toward each other, the cars will cut down a distance equal to the sum of their speeds, which is, 55 + 65 = 120 mph. To meet, they must cut down 660 miles, and at 120 miles per hour this would be: Time = D/R = 660 ÷ 120 = 5.5 hours

Example #2: Two towns are 120 miles apart. Car A leaves the first town toward the second town traveling at a constant rate, completing the 120-mile trip in 2 hours. At the same time, car B leaves the second town and heads toward the first town traveling at a constant rate, completing the 120-mile trip in 8 hours. How many miles had car A traveled when it met car B?

Solution: Sketch the following diagram and put down everything that's given in the problem:

Organize all the given information in the following grid:

Car A
$T_1 \Rightarrow 2$ hours
$D_1 \Rightarrow 120$ miles
$R_1 \Rightarrow 120 ÷ 2 = 60$ mph

Car B
$T_2 \Rightarrow 8$ hours
$D_2 \Rightarrow 120$ miles
$R_2 \Rightarrow 120 ÷ 8 = 15$ mph

Let the No. of hours the cars take to meet = t
When the two cars meet, Car A must have traveled a distance of $60t$ miles and Car B must have traveled a distance of $15t$ miles.

EZ Problem Set-Up $\Rightarrow$ Distance of First Car (D_1) + Distance of Second Car (D_2) = Total Distance
$\Rightarrow 60t + 15t = 120$ [Set up the equation]
$\Rightarrow 75t = 120$ [Combine like-terms]
$\Rightarrow t = 1.6$ hours   [Divide both sides by 75]

Therefore, Car A must have traveled $60t$ miles or 60(1.6) = 96 miles

EZ ALTERNATE METHOD: In each hour of travel toward each other, the cars will cut down a distance equal to the sum of their speeds, which is, 60 + 15 = 75 mph. To meet, they must cut down 120 miles, and at 75 miles per hour, this would be: Time = D/R = 120 ÷ 75 = 1.6 hours. When the two cars meet, Car A must have traveled 60 × 1.6, or 96 miles.

TYPE #7: MOTION IN SAME DIRECTION – "OVERTAKE" OR "CATCH UP":
Time and Distance it Takes to Overtake or Catch Up When Two Objects or People Move in the Same Direction at Different Times: These types of problems involve motion in same direction, that is, two objects moving in the same direction, following the same path. These types of problems are sometimes referred to as "overtake" or "catch up" problems. Usually two objects leave the same place at different times and at different rates, but one that leaves later "overtakes" or "catches up" the one that leaves earlier. In such problems, the rates are different for both objects. The times are also different for both objects. However, if both objects start from the starting point, and one catches up with the other one, the distances must be equal. So, the two distances must be the same for both objects.

Example #1: Two motorists start driving from a certain point at different times. The second motorist, whose speed is 25 miles per hour, starts 2 hours after the first motorist, whose speed is 5 miles per hour. Determine the amount of time and distance that will be elapsed before the second motorist catches up with the first one.

Solution: Organize all the given information in the following grid:

First Motorist
$R_1 \Rightarrow 5$ mph
$T_1 \Rightarrow t$
$D_1 \Rightarrow 5t$

Second Motorist
$R_2 \Rightarrow 25$ mph
$T_2 \Rightarrow t - 2$
$D_2 \Rightarrow 25(t - 2) = 25t - 50$

EZ Problem Set-Up $\Rightarrow$ Distance of First Motorist (D_1) = Distance of Second Motorist (D_2)
$\Rightarrow 5t = 25t - 50$ [Set up the equation]
$\Rightarrow -20t = -50$ [Subtract 25t from both sides]
$\Rightarrow t = 2.5$ [Divide both sides by –20]

Therefore, the First Motorist has already traveled for 2.5 hours when the Second Motorist catches up to him. Since Second Motorist started 2 hours later than the First Motorist, he must have traveled for 2.5 – 2 = 0.5 hours.

First Motorist
$R_1 \Rightarrow 5$ mph
$T_1 \Rightarrow t = 2.5$ hrs
$D_1 \Rightarrow 5t = 5 \times 2.5 = 12.5$ m

Second Motorist
$R_2 \Rightarrow 25$ mph
$T_2 \Rightarrow t - 2 = 2.5 - 2 = 0.5$
$D_2 \Rightarrow 25 \times 0.5 = 12.5$ m

Therefore, First Motorist traveled for 2.5 hours at 5 mph to cover 12.5 miles
And, Second Motorist traveled for 0.5 hours at 25 mph to cover the same 12.5 miles.

EZ ALTERNATE METHOD: Since the First Motorist has a 2-hour lead and is driving at the rate of 5 mph – he is 10 miles from that certain point when the Second Motorist starts. ($d = rt$). Subtracting 5 mph from 25 mph gives us 20 mph, or the difference in the rates of speed of the two motorists. In other words, the second motorist gains 20 mile on the first motorist every hour. Since there is a 10 mile difference to cut down and it is cut down 20 mile every hour, it is clear that the second motorist will need 0.5 hours to overtake the first motorist. In this time, he must have traveled 25 × 0.5 = 12.5 miles. The first motorist must have been driving 2.5 hours, since he had a 2-hour lead, 5 × 2.5 = 12.5 miles.

TYPE #8: HOW CHANGE IN SPEED OF AN OBJECT OR PERSON AFFECTS TIME TAKEN:
These types of problems demonstrate the fact that how a change in speed of an object affects the time taken.

Example #1: A man drove 100 miles to go somewhere. If he had driven 10 miles per hour faster, he would have reached that place in 5/6 of the time he actually took. How many minutes did the whole trip take and what was the speed?

Solution: Organize all the given information in the following grid:

Original Situation
$T_1 \Rightarrow t$
$R_1 \Rightarrow r$
$D_1 \Rightarrow rt = 100$

New Situation
$T_2 \Rightarrow \frac{5}{6}t$
$R_2 \Rightarrow r + 10$
$D_2 \Rightarrow (r + 10) \times \frac{5}{6}t = 100$

EZ Problem Set-Up $\Rightarrow$ Distance in the Original Situation (D_1) = Distance in the New Situation (D_2)

$\Rightarrow rt = (r + 10) \times \frac{5}{6}t$ [Set up the equation]

$\Rightarrow rt = \frac{5}{6}rt + \frac{50}{6}t$ [Apply distributive property]

$\Rightarrow rt = \frac{5rt + 50t}{6}$ [Combine like-fractions]

$\Rightarrow 100 = \frac{5 \times 100 + 50t}{6}$ [Substitute rt = 100]

$\Rightarrow 100 = \frac{500 + 50t}{6}$ [Combine like-terms]

$\Rightarrow 600 = 500 + 50t$	[Cross multiply]
$\Rightarrow 100 = 50t$	[Subtract 500 from both sides]
$\Rightarrow t = 100 \div 50 = 2$ hours	[Divide both sides by 50]

Solve for r

$\Rightarrow rt = 100$	[Given]
$\Rightarrow r \times 2 = 100$	[Substitute $t = 2$]
$\Rightarrow r = 100 \div 2 = 50$ mph	[Divide both sides by 2]

Therefore, the whole trip took 2 hours or 120 minutes at the rate of 50 miles per hour.

EZ ALTERNATIVE METHOD:

Let, t = time (in hours) and r = rate (in miles per hour). Then, $t = d \div r = 100 \div r$

EZ Problem Set-Up $\Rightarrow$ If the man had driven 10 mph faster, he would have reached that place in 5/6 of the time.

$$\Rightarrow \frac{5}{6}t = \frac{100}{r+10}t \qquad \text{[Set up the equation]}$$

$$\Rightarrow \frac{6}{5}\left(\frac{5}{6}t\right) = \frac{6}{5}\left(\frac{100}{r+10}\right) \qquad \text{[Multiply both sides by 6/5]}$$

$$\Rightarrow t = \frac{600}{5r+50} \qquad \text{[Apply distributive property]}$$

$$\Rightarrow \frac{100}{r} = \frac{600}{5r+50} \qquad \text{[Substituting } t = 100/r \text{]}$$

$\Rightarrow 500r + 5000 = 600r$	[Cross multiply]
$\Rightarrow 100r = 5000$	[Subtract 500r from both sides]
$\Rightarrow r = 50$ mph	[Divide both sides by 100]

Now, $r = 50$ mph; $d = 100$ miles and $t = d \div r = 100 \div 50 = 2$ hours $= 2 \times 60 = 120$ minutes.

Therefore, the man drove at 50 mph and the trip took 120 minutes.

PRACTICE EXERCISE – QUESTIONS AND ANSWERS WITH EXPLANATIONS: MOTION PROBLEMS:

Question #1: If it takes a vehicle 8 hours from Point-A to Point-B at an average speed of 65 miles per hour, what is the distance in miles between Point-A and Point-B?

Solution: Distance $\Rightarrow$ Rate × Time
                        $\Rightarrow$ 65 × 8
                        $\Rightarrow$ 520 miles

Question #2: If it takes a vehicle 9 hours to travel 522 miles from Point-A to Point-B, what should be the average speed in miles per hour?

Solution: Rate $\Rightarrow$ Distance ÷ Time
                        $\Rightarrow$ 522 ÷ 9
                        $\Rightarrow$ 58 miles per hour

Question #3: If the distance between Point-A and Point-B is 546 miles and a vehicle is traveling at an average speed of 78 miles per hour, how many hours will it take to cover the whole distance?

Solution: Time $\Rightarrow$ Distance ÷ Rate
                        $\Rightarrow$ 546 ÷ 78
                        $\Rightarrow$ 7 hours

Question #4: A bus travels from Washington DC to Omaha, NE, which is a distance of 1,125 miles, at an average rate of 75 miles per hour and arrives in Omaha at 9:00 PM in the evening, local time. At what hour in the morning, Washington time, did the bus depart from Washington for Omaha? (Note: Omaha time is one hour behind Washington time.)

Solution: Time $\Rightarrow$ Distance ÷ Rate
                   $\Rightarrow$ 1125 ÷ 75
                   $\Rightarrow$ 15
The bus arrives in Omaha at 9:00 PM, which means it left Washington 15 hours ago, which is 6:00 AM Omaha time, which in turn is 7:00 AM Washington time, since Washington time is 1 hour ahead of Omaha time.

Question #5: A man travels 50 miles in 2 hours. If he travels at the same rate for another 5 hours, how many more miles will he travel?

Solution: Distance = Rate × Time
$\Rightarrow$ 50 miles = Rate × 2 hour
$\Rightarrow$ Rate = 25 miles per hour
If the man travels for 5 hours at 25 mph, he will travel $\Rightarrow$ $D = RT$ = 25 mph × 5 hours = 125 miles

Question #6: A person drives 900 miles on a trip in 12 hours. If the vehicle averaged 15 miles per gallon of gasoline and gasoline cost an average of $2.75 per gallon, how much was the total cost of gasoline for the entire trip?

Solution: Distance of Trip $\Rightarrow$ 900 miles
Consumption $\Rightarrow$ 15 miles per gallon (note: the travel time is irrelevant in this case)
No. of gallons of gasoline needed to drive 15 miles $\Rightarrow$ 1

No. of gallons of gasoline needed to drive 1 mile $\Rightarrow \dfrac{1}{15}$

No. of gallons of gasoline needed to drive 900 mile $\Rightarrow \dfrac{1}{15} \times 900 = 60$

Cost of 1 gallon of gasoline $\Rightarrow$ $2.75
Cost of 60 gallons of gasoline $\Rightarrow$ $2.75 × 60 = $165

Question #7: A car traveling at an average rate of 75 miles per hour made a trip in 10 hours. If it had traveled at an average rate of 50 miles per hour, the trip would have taken how many hours/ minutes longer?

Solution: Organize all the given information in the following grid:

Original Situation
$R_1 \Rightarrow 75$ mph
$T_1 \Rightarrow 10$ hrs
$D_1 \Rightarrow R_1 \times T_1 = 75 \times 10 = 750$ m

New Situation
$D_2 \Rightarrow 750$ m
$R_2 \Rightarrow 50$ mph
$T_2 \Rightarrow D_2 \div R_2 = 750 \div 50 = 15$ hrs

Time Difference $\Rightarrow T_2 - T_1 = 15$ hrs $- 10$ hrs $= 5$ hour or 300 minutes

Question #8: A man drove 500 miles in 10 hours nonstop. If he had driven an average of 10 miles per hour faster, how many minutes would he have saved?

Solution: Organize all the given information in the following grid:

Original Trip
$D_1 \Rightarrow 500$ m
$T_1 \Rightarrow 10$ hrs
$R_1 \Rightarrow 500 \div 10 = 50$ mph

Modified Trip
$D_2 \Rightarrow 500$ m
$R_2 \Rightarrow 50 + 10 = 60$ mph
$T_2 \Rightarrow 500 \div 60 = 8\ 1/3$ hrs

Time Difference $\Rightarrow T_2 - T_1 = 10$ hrs $- 8\ 1/3$ hrs $= 600$ minutes $- 500$ minutes $= 100$ minutes
Therefore, if the man had driven 10 miles per hour faster, he would have saved 100 minutes.

Question #9: A train travels at an average speed of 70 miles per hour for 2.5 hours and then travels at a speed of 90 miles per hour for 7.5 hours. How far did the train travel in the entire 10 hours?

Solution: Organize all the given information in the following grid:

First Part of Trip
$R_1 \Rightarrow 70$ mph
$T_1 \Rightarrow 2.5$ hrs
$D_1 \Rightarrow 70 \times 2.5 = 175$ m

Second Part of Trip
$R_2 \Rightarrow 90$ mph
$T_2 \Rightarrow 7.5$ hrs
$D_2 \Rightarrow 90 \times 7.5 = 675$ m

Total Distance $\Rightarrow D_1 + D_2 = 175$ m $+ 675$ m $= 850$ miles

Question #10: A man drove 650 miles at an average speed of 50 miles per hour. How many miles per hour faster would he have to drive in order for the trip to have taken 3 hours less?

Solution: Organize all the given information in the following grid:

Original Trip
$D_1 \Rightarrow 650$ m
$R_1 \Rightarrow 50$ mph
$T_1 \Rightarrow 650 \div 50 = 13$ hrs

Modified Trip
$D_2 \Rightarrow 650$ m
$T_2 \Rightarrow 13 - 3 = 10$ hrs
$R_2 \Rightarrow 650 \div 10 = 65$ mph

Rate Difference $\Rightarrow R_2 - R_1 = 65$ mph $- 50$ mph $= 15$ mph
Therefore, in order to cover the same trip in 3 hours less, the man will have to drive 15 mph faster.

Question #11: If a man drove a 100-mile road trip in 12 hours, and he averaged a 10 miles per hour rate for the first 20 miles, what speed did he average, in miles per hour, for the last 80 miles of the trip?

Solution: Organize all the given information in the following grid:

First Part of Trip
$D_1 \Rightarrow 20$ miles
$R_1 \Rightarrow 10$ mph
$T_1 \Rightarrow 2$ hours

Second Part of Trip
$D_2 \Rightarrow 80$ miles
$T_2 \Rightarrow 12 - 2 = 10$ hours
$R_2 \Rightarrow 80 \div 10 = 8$ mph

Therefore, he averages a rate of 8 mph for the last 80 miles of the trip.

Question #12: A man drove 180 miles in one and one half hours. After one hour, he had driven 110 miles. What was his average speed for the rest of the trip?

Solution: Organize all the given information in the following grid:

First Part of Trip
$D_1 \Rightarrow 110$ miles
$T_1 \Rightarrow 1$ hour
$R_1 \Rightarrow 110 \div 1 = 110$ mph

Second Part of Trip
$D_2 \Rightarrow 70$ miles
$T_2 \Rightarrow 1.5 - 1 = 0.5$ hour
$R_2 \Rightarrow 70 \div 0.5 = 140$ mph

Therefore, he averages a rate of 140 mph for the rest of the trip.

Question #13: Two cars travel away from each other in opposite directions at 24 miles per hour and 55 miles per hour respectively. If the first car travels for 20 minutes and the second car for 12 minutes, how many miles apart will they be at the end of their trips?

Solution: Organize all the given information in the following grid:

First Car
$R_1 \Rightarrow$ 24 mph
$T_1 \Rightarrow$ 20 min = 1/3 hr
$D_1 \Rightarrow RT = 24 \times 1/3 = 8$ m

Second Car
$R_2 \Rightarrow$ 55 mph
$T_2 \Rightarrow$ 12 min = 1/5 hr
$D_2 \Rightarrow RT = 55 \times 1/5 = 11$ m

Total Distance between the two cars $\Rightarrow D_1 + D_2 = 8$ m + 11 m = 19 miles
Therefore, the two cars will be 19 miles apart at the end of their trips.

Question #14: On a 200-mile road trip, if the first half of the trip is driven at 50 miles per hour and the second half of the trip is driven at 25 miles per hour, what should be the average speed for the entire trip in miles per hour?

Solution: Organize all the given information in the following grid:

First Half of Trip
$D_1 \Rightarrow$ 100 m
$R_1 \Rightarrow$ 50 mph
$T_1 \Rightarrow \dfrac{D}{T}$ = 100/50 = 2 hours

Second Half of Trip
$D_2 \Rightarrow$ 100 m
$R_2 \Rightarrow$ 25 mph
$T_2 \Rightarrow \dfrac{D}{T}$ = 100/25 = 4 hours

Total Trip

Total Time	$\Rightarrow T_1 + T_2 = 2 + 4 = 6$ hours	[Add the total time]
Total Distance	$\Rightarrow D_1 + D_2 = 200$ m	[Add the total distance]
Average Rate	$\Rightarrow \dfrac{Distance}{Time} = \dfrac{200}{6} = 33.33$ mph	[Find the average rate]

Therefore, the average speed for the entire trip is 33.33 mph or $33\dfrac{1}{3}$ mph.

Question #15: On a 500-mile road trip, if the first half of the trip is driven at 50 miles per hour and the second half of the trip is driven at 62.5 miles per hour, what should be the average speed for the entire trip in miles per hour?

Solution: Organize all the given information in the following grid:

First Half of Trip
$D_1 \Rightarrow$ 250 m
$R_1 \Rightarrow$ 50 mph
$T_1 \Rightarrow \dfrac{D}{T}$ = 250/50 = 5 hours

Second Half of Trip
$D_2 \Rightarrow$ 250 m
$R_2 \Rightarrow$ 62.5 mph
$T_2 \Rightarrow \dfrac{D}{T}$ = 250/62.5 = 4 hours

Total Trip

Total Time	$\Rightarrow T_1 + T_2 = 5 + 4 = 9$ hours	[Add the total time]
Total Distance	$\Rightarrow D_1 + D_2 = 500$ m	[Add the total distance]
Average Rate	$\Rightarrow \dfrac{Distance}{Time} = \dfrac{500}{9} = 55.55$ mph	[Find the average rate]

Therefore, the average speed for the entire trip is 55.55 mph.

Question #16: A man drives from Washington DC to NYC at the rate of 70 miles per hour. While returning back following the same route, due to rush hour traffic, he could only drive at the rate of 50 miles per hour. If the return trip took one hour longer, how many miles did he drive each way?

Solution: Organize all the given information in the following grid:

Outbound Trip
$R_1 \Rightarrow$ 70 mph
$T_1 \Rightarrow t$
$D_1 \Rightarrow 70t$

Inbound Trip
$R_2 \Rightarrow$ 50 mph
$T_2 \Rightarrow t + 1$
$D_2 \Rightarrow 50(t + 1)$

EZ Problem Set-Up	$\Rightarrow$ Distance of Outbound Trip (D_1) = Distance of Inbound Trip (D_2)	
	$\Rightarrow 70t = 50(t + 1)$	[Set up the equation]
	$\Rightarrow 70t = 50t + 50$	[Apply distributive property]
	$\Rightarrow 20t = 50$	[Subtract 50t from both sides]
	$\Rightarrow t = 2.5$	[Divide both sides by 20]
Outbound Trip	$\Rightarrow D_1 = 70t = 70 \times 2.5 = 175$	
Inbound Trip	$\Rightarrow D_2 = 50(t + 1) = 50(2.5 + 1) = 50 \times 3.5 = 175$	
Total distance	$\Rightarrow D_1 + D_2 = 175 \times 2 = 350$ miles	

Question #17: A man drives from Miami, FL to Boston, MA at the rate of 90 miles per hour. While returning back following the same route, due to rush hour traffic, he could only drive at the rate of 70 miles per hour. If the return trip took 2 hours longer, how many miles did he drive both way?

Solution: Organize all the given information in the following grid:

Outbound Trip	**Inbound Trip**
$R_1 \Rightarrow$ 90 mph	$R_2 \Rightarrow$ 70 mph
$T_1 \Rightarrow t$	$T_2 \Rightarrow t + 2$
$D_1 \Rightarrow 90t$	$D_2 \Rightarrow 70(t + 2)$

EZ Problem Set-Up $\Rightarrow$ Distance of Outbound Trip (D_1) = Distance of Inbound Trip (D_2)

$\Rightarrow 90t = 70(t + 2)$ [Set up the equation]
$\Rightarrow 90t = 70t + 140$ [Apply distributive property]
$\Rightarrow 20t = 140$ [Subtract $70t$ from both sides]
$\Rightarrow t = 7$ [Divide both sides by 20]

Outbound Trip $\Rightarrow D_1 = 90t = 90 \times 7 = 630$
Inbound Trip $\Rightarrow D_2 = 70(t+2) = 70(7 + 2) = 70 \times 9 = 630$
Total distance $\Rightarrow D_1 + D_2 = 630 \times 2 = 1{,}260$ miles

Question #18: John and Tom drove to a meeting 140 miles away in the same car. John drove to the meeting and Tom drove back along the same route. If John drove at 70 miles per hour and Tom drove back 50 miles per hour, how much longer, in minutes, did it take Tom to travel the distance than it did John?

Solution: Organize all the given information in the following grid:

Outbound Trip	**Inbound Trip**
$D_1 \Rightarrow$ 140 m	$D_2 \Rightarrow$ 140 m
$R_1 \Rightarrow$ 70 mph	$R_2 \Rightarrow$ 50 mph
$T_1 \Rightarrow 140 \div 70 = 2$ hrs = 120 min	$T_2 \Rightarrow 140 \div 50 = 2.8$ hr = 168 min

Time Difference $\Rightarrow T_2 - T_1 = 168$ min $-$ 120 min = 48 minutes

Question #19: It took a man 12 hours to travel by train from Washington DC to Toledo, OH at an average speed of 65 miles per hour. On the return trip from Toledo, OH to Washington, DC, he traveled by bus and averaged 60 miles per hour. How many hours did the return trip take?

Solution: Organize all the given information in the following grid:

Outbound Trip	**Inbound Trip**
$R_1 \Rightarrow$ 65 mph	$R_2 \Rightarrow$ 60 mph
$T_1 \Rightarrow$ 12 hours	$D_2 \Rightarrow$ 780 hours
$D_1 \Rightarrow$ 780 miles	$T_2 \Rightarrow 780 \div 60 = 13$ hours

Therefore, it took him 13 hours for the return trip.

Question #20: John and Tom drove from work to a meeting 120 miles away in the same car. John drove to the meeting and Tom drove back along the same route. If John drove at 60 miles per hour and Tom drove back 50 miles per hour, how much longer, in minutes, did it take Tom to travel the distance than it did John?

Solution: Organize all the given information in the following grid:

Work to Meeting Trip	**Meeting to Work Trip**
$D_1 \Rightarrow$ 120 m	$D_2 \Rightarrow$ 120 m
$R_1 \Rightarrow$ 60 mph	$R_2 \Rightarrow$ 50 mph
$T_1 \Rightarrow 120 \div 60 = 2$ hrs = 120 min	$T_2 \Rightarrow 120 \div 50 = 2.4$ hr = 144 min

Time Difference $\Rightarrow T_2 - T_1 = 144$ min $-$ 120 min = 24 minutes

Question #21: If a man leaves Point-X traveling West at the speed of 80 miles per hour and at the same time a woman leaves Point-X traveling East at the speed of 60 miles per hour, after 5 hours, how far apart from each other will they be from each other?

Solution: Organize all the given information in the following grid:

Man	**Woman**
$R_M \Rightarrow$ 80 mph	$R_W \Rightarrow$ 60 mph
$T_M \Rightarrow$ 5 hrs	$T_M \Rightarrow$ 5 hrs
$D_M \Rightarrow$ 80 mph $\times$ 5 hrs = 400 m	$D_W \Rightarrow$ 60 mph $\times$ 5 hrs = 300 hrs

(Distance between Man & Pt-X)   (Distance between Woman & Pt-X)

EZ Problem Set-Up $\Rightarrow$ Total Distance between Man and Woman (D_T) = Distance between Man & Point-X (D_M) + Distance between Woman & Point-X (D_W)

$\Rightarrow$ 400 miles + 300 miles   [Set up the equation]
$\Rightarrow$ 700 miles   [Do the addition]

Therefore, after 5 hours, they will be 700 miles apart from each other.

Question #22: If a man leaves Point-X traveling West at the speed of 80 miles per hour and at the same time a woman leaves Point-X traveling East at the speed of 60 miles per hour, in how many hours will they be 700 miles apart from each other?

Solution: Organize all the given information in the following grid:

Man	**Woman**
$R_M \Rightarrow$ 80 mph	$R_W \Rightarrow$ 60 mph
$T_M \Rightarrow t$	$T_W \Rightarrow t$
$D_M \Rightarrow$ Distance between Man & Pt-X	$D_W \Rightarrow$ Distance between Woman & Pt-X
$\Rightarrow R_M \times T$ = 80 mph $\times t$ = 80t	$\Rightarrow R_W \times T$ = 60 mph $\times t$ = 60t

Total Distance between the Man & Woman = 700 miles

EZ Problem Set-Up $\Rightarrow$ Total Distance between Man and Woman (D_T) = Distance between Man & Point-X (D_M) + Distance between Woman & Point-X (D_W)

$\Rightarrow$ 700 = 80t + 60t [Set up the equation]
$\Rightarrow$ 700 = 140t [Combine like-terms]
$\Rightarrow t$ = 5 hours   [Divide both sides by 140]

Therefore, they will be 700 miles apart in 5 hours.

Question #23: If a man leaves Point-X traveling West at the speed of 90 miles per hour and at the same time a woman leaves Point-X traveling East at the speed of 70 miles per hour, in how many hours will they be 200 miles apart from each other?

Solution: Organize all the given information in the following grid:

Man	**Woman**
$R_M \Rightarrow$ 90 mph	$R_W \Rightarrow$ 70 mph
$T_M \Rightarrow t$	$T_W \Rightarrow t$
$D_M \Rightarrow$ Distance between Man & Pt-X	$D_W \Rightarrow$ Distance between Woman & Pt-X
$\Rightarrow R_M \times T$ = 90 mph $\times t$ = 90t	$\Rightarrow R_W \times T$ = 70 mph $\times t$ = 70t

Total Distance between the Man & Woman = 200 miles

EZ Problem Set-Up $\Rightarrow$ Total Distance between Man and Woman (D_T) = Distance between Man & Point-X (D_M) + Distance between Woman & Point-X (D_W)

$\Rightarrow$ 200 = 90t + 70t [Set up the equation]
$\Rightarrow$ 200 = 160t [Combine like-terms]
$\Rightarrow t$ = 1.25 hours   [Divide both sides by 160]

Therefore, they will be 200 miles apart in 1.25 hours.

Question #24: If a man leaves Point-X traveling North at the speed of 30 miles per hour and at the same time a woman leaves Point-X traveling West at the speed of 40 miles per hour, how many miles apart from each other will they be after 2 hours?

Solution: Organize all the given information in the following grid:

Man	**Woman**
$R_M \Rightarrow$ 30 mph	$R_W \Rightarrow$ 40 mph
$T_M \Rightarrow$ 2 hrs	$T_W \Rightarrow$ 2 hrs
$D_M \Rightarrow$ 30 × 2 = 60 m	$D_W \Rightarrow$ 40 × 2 = 80 m

EZ Problem Set-Up $\Rightarrow$ (Distance between Man & Woman)^2 = (D_M)^2 + (D_W)^2 (Pythagorean Theorem)

$\Rightarrow d^2 = 60^2 + 80^2$ [Set up the equation]
$\Rightarrow d^2 = 3600 + 6400$ [Solve the exponents]
$\Rightarrow d^2 = 10,000$ [Combine like-term]
$\Rightarrow d = 100$ [Square root both sides]

Therefore, the man and the woman will be 100 miles apart.

Question #25: Two towns are 550 miles apart. A car leaves the first town traveling toward the second town at 50 mph. At the same time, another car leaves the second town and heads toward the first town at 60 mph. How many hours will it take for the two cars to meet?

Solution: Organize all the given information in the following grid:

Car 1   **Car 2**

$R_1 \Rightarrow$ 50 mph $R_2 \Rightarrow$ 60 mph

$T_1 \Rightarrow t$ $T_2 \Rightarrow t$

$D_1 \Rightarrow 50t$ $D_2 \Rightarrow 60t$

It needs to be noted that both cars must have traveled for the same length of time when they meet one another.

EZ Problem Set-Up $\Rightarrow$ Distance of First Car (D_1) + Distance of Second Car (D_2) = Total Distance

$\Rightarrow 50t + 60t = 550$ [Set up the equation]

$\Rightarrow 110t = 550$ [Combine like-terms]

$\Rightarrow t = 5$ hours   [Divide both sides by 110]

Therefore, it will take 5 hours for the two cars to meet.

Question #26: Two towns are 900 miles apart. A car leaves the first town traveling toward the second town at 70 mph. At the same time, another car leaves the second town and heads toward the first town at 80 mph. How many hours will it take for the two cars to meet?

Solution: Organize all the given information in the following grid:

Car 1   **Car 2**

$R_1 \Rightarrow$ 70 mph $R_2 \Rightarrow$ 80 mph

$T_1 \Rightarrow t$ $T_2 \Rightarrow t$

$D_1 \Rightarrow 70t$ $D_2 \Rightarrow 80t$

It needs to be noted that both cars must have traveled for the same length of time when they meet one another.

EZ Problem Set-Up $\Rightarrow$ Distance of First Car (D_1) + Distance of Second Car (D_2) = Total Distance

$\Rightarrow 70t + 80t = 900$ [Set up the equation]

$\Rightarrow 150t = 900$ [Combine like-terms]

$\Rightarrow t = 6$ hours   [Divide both sides by 150]

Therefore, it will take 6 hours for the two cars to meet.

Question #27: Two towns are 150 miles apart. Car A leaves the first town toward the second town traveling at a constant rate, completing the 150-mile trip in 2 hours. At the same time, car B leaves the second town and heads toward the first town traveling at a constant rate, completing the 150-mile trip in 6 hours. How many miles had car A traveled when it met car B?

Solution: Organize all the given information in the following grid:

Car A   **Car B**

$T_1 \Rightarrow$ 2 hours $T_2 \Rightarrow$ 6 hours

$D_1 \Rightarrow$ 150 miles $D_2 \Rightarrow$ 150 miles

$R_1 \Rightarrow 150 \div 2 = 75$ mph $R_2 \Rightarrow 150 \div 6 = 25$ mph

Let the No. of hours the cars take to meet = t

When the two cars meet, Car A must have traveled a distance of $75t$ miles and Car B must have traveled a distance of $25t$ miles.

EZ Problem Set-Up $\Rightarrow$ Distance of First Car (D_1) + Distance of Second Car (D_2) = Total Distance

$\Rightarrow 75t + 25t = 150$ [Set up the equation]

$\Rightarrow 100t = 150$ [Combine like-terms]

$\Rightarrow t = 1.5$ hours   [Divide both sides by 100]

Therefore, Car A must have traveled $75t$ miles or $75(1.5) = 112.5$ miles

Question #28: Two motorists start driving from a certain point at different times. The second motorist, whose speed is 60 miles per hour, starts 2 hours after the first motorist, whose speed is 50 miles per hour. Determine the distance in miles that will be elapsed before the second motorist catches up with the first one.

Solution: Organize all the given information in the following grid:

First Motorist   **Second Motorist**

$R_1 \Rightarrow$ 50 mph $R_2 \Rightarrow$ 60 mph

$T_1 \Rightarrow t$ $T_2 \Rightarrow t - 2$

$D_1 \Rightarrow 50t$ $D_2 \Rightarrow 60(t - 2) = 60t - 120$

When the two motorists meet, each will have covered the same distance, therefore:

EZ Problem Set-Up $\Rightarrow$ Distance of First Motorist (D_1) = Distance of Second Motorist (D_2)

$\Rightarrow 50t = 60t - 120$ [Set up the equation]

$\Rightarrow -10t = -120$ [Subtract 60t from both sides]

$\Rightarrow t = 12$ [Divide both sides by –10]

Therefore, the First Motorist has already traveled for 12 hours when the Second Motorist catches up to him. Since Second Motorist started 2 hours later than the first motorist, he must have traveled for 12 – 2 = 10 hours.

First Motorist

$R_1 \Rightarrow 50$ mph

$T_1 \Rightarrow t = 12$ hrs

$D_1 \Rightarrow 50t = 50 \times 12 = 600$ m

Second Motorist

$R_2 \Rightarrow 60$ mph

$T_2 \Rightarrow t - 2 = 12 - 2 = 10$ hrs

$D_2 \Rightarrow 60(t - 2) = 60(10) = 600$ m

Therefore, First Motorist traveled for 12 hours at 50 mph to cover 600 miles

And, Second Motorist traveled for 10 hours at 60 mph to cover the same 600 miles.

Question #29: Two motorists start driving from a certain point at different times. The second motorist, whose speed is 80 miles per hour, starts 2 hours after the first motorist, whose speed is 70 miles per hour. Determine the distance in miles that will be elapsed before the second motorist catches up with the first one.

Solution: Organize all the given information in the following grid:

First Motorist

$R_1 \Rightarrow 70$ mph

$T_1 \Rightarrow t$

$D_1 \Rightarrow 70t$

Second Motorist

$R_2 \Rightarrow 80$ mph

$T_2 \Rightarrow t - 2$

$D_2 \Rightarrow 80(t - 2) = 80t - 160$

When the two motorists meet, each will have covered the same distance, therefore:

EZ Problem Set-Up $\Rightarrow$ Distance of First Motorist (D_1) = Distance of Second Motorist (D_2)

$\Rightarrow 70t = 80t - 160$ [Set up the equation]

$\Rightarrow -10t = -160$ [Subtract 80t from both sides]

$\Rightarrow t = 16$ [Divide both sides by –10]

Therefore, the First Motorist has already traveled for 16 hours when the Second Motorist catches up to him. Since Second Motorist started 2 hours later than the first motorist, he must have traveled for 16 – 2 = 14 hours.

First Motorist

$R_1 \Rightarrow 70$ mph

$T_1 \Rightarrow t = 16$ hrs

$D_1 \Rightarrow 70t = 70 \times 16 = 1120$ m

Second Motorist

$R_2 \Rightarrow 80$ mph

$T_2 \Rightarrow t - 2 = 16 - 2 = 14$

$D_2 \Rightarrow 80(t - 2) = 80(14) = 1120$ m

Therefore, First Motorist traveled for 16 hours at 70 mph to cover 1120 miles

And, Second Motorist traveled for 14 hours at 80 mph to cover the same 1120 miles.

Question #30: A man drove 100 miles to go somewhere. If he had driven 5 miles per hour faster, he would have reached that place in 8/9 of the time he actually took. How many minutes did the whole trip take?

Solution: Organize all the given information in the following grid:

Let, t = time (in hours) and r = rate (in miles per hour)

Original Situation

$D_1 \Rightarrow 100$ m

$T_1 \Rightarrow t$

$R_1 \Rightarrow r$

$D \Rightarrow 100 = rt$

New Situation

$D_2 \Rightarrow 100$ m

$T_2 \Rightarrow 8/9t$

$R_2 \Rightarrow r + 5$

$D \Rightarrow 100 = (r + 5) \times 8/9t$

EZ Problem Set-Up $\Rightarrow$ Distance in the Original Situation (D_1) = Distance in the New Situation (D_2)

$\Rightarrow rt = (r + 5) \times \dfrac{8}{9}t$ [Set up the equation]

$\Rightarrow rt = \dfrac{8}{9}rt + \dfrac{40}{9}t$ [Apply distributive property]

$\Rightarrow rt = \dfrac{8rt + 40t}{9}$ [Combine like-fractions]

$\Rightarrow 100 = \dfrac{8 \times 100 + 40t}{9}$ [Substitute $rt = 100$]

$\Rightarrow 100 = \dfrac{800 + 40t}{9}$ [Combine like-terms]

$\Rightarrow 900 = 800 + 40t$ [Cross multiply]

$\Rightarrow 100 = 40t$ [Subtract 800 from both sides]

$\Rightarrow t = 2.5$ hours   [Divide both sides by 40]

Solve for r $\Rightarrow rt = 100$ [Given]

$\Rightarrow r \times 2.5 = 100$ [Substitute $t = 2.5$]

$\Rightarrow r = 40$ mph   [Divide both sides by 2.5]

Therefore, the whole trip took 150 minutes at the rate of 40 miles per hour.

PART 8.0: MIXTURE PROBLEMS:

TABLE OF CONTENTS:

PART 8.0: MIXTURE PROBLEMS: 131
    8.1: Cost per Unit of Mixture: 132
    8.2: Simple Mixtures: 133
    8.3: Mixture of Weaker & Stronger Solution: 134
    8.4: Dilution/Concentration of Mixture: 135
    Practice Exercise – Questions and Answers With Explanations: Mixture Problems: 136

In mixture problems, substances with different characteristics are combined, and it is required to determine the characteristics of the resulting mixture. In other words, mixture problem represents the combination of two or more different substances and asks to solve for the different parts of the resulting mixture.

8.1: COST PER UNIT OF MIXTURE:

Some mixture problems involve different types of solutions, which are priced at different rates, and ask to find the unit cost of the final mixture.

USE THE COST PER UNIT METHOD: $\Rightarrow$ Cost per unit $= \dfrac{\textit{Total Cost of Mixture}}{\textit{Total Weight of Mixture}}$

Example #1: If 2 pounds of almonds that cost $1.25 per pound are mixed with 8 pounds of pecans that cost $2.25 per pound, what is the cost per pound of the resulting mixture?

Solution:

Total cost of the mixture	$\Rightarrow 2(\$1.25) + 8(\$2.25)$	[Express the total cost of mixture]
	$\Rightarrow \$2.50 + \$18$	[Apply distributive property]
	$\Rightarrow \$20.50$	[Do the addition]
Total weight of the mixture	$\Rightarrow 2 + 8$	[Express the total weight of mixture]
	$\Rightarrow 10$ pounds	[Do the addition]
Cost per pound of the mixture	$\Rightarrow \dfrac{\textit{Total Cost of Mixture}}{\textit{Total Weight of Mixture}}$	[Write the appropriate formula]
	$\Rightarrow \dfrac{20.50}{10}$	[Substitute the values]
	$\Rightarrow \$2.05$	[Simplify the fraction]

Example #2: If 5 pounds of hazelnuts that cost $x per pound are mixed with 7 pounds of walnuts that cost $y per pound, what is the cost per pound of the resulting mixture?

Solution:

Total cost of the mixture	$\Rightarrow 5(\$x) + 7(\$y)$	[Express the total cost of mixture]
	$\Rightarrow \$5x + \$7y$	[Apply distributive property]
Total weight of the mixture	$\Rightarrow 5 + 7$	[Express the total weight of mixture]
	$\Rightarrow 12$ pounds	[Do the addition]
Cost per pound of the mixture	$\Rightarrow \dfrac{\textit{Total Cost of Mixture}}{\textit{Total Weight of Mixture}}$	[Write the appropriate formula]
	$\Rightarrow \dfrac{5x + 7y}{12}$	[Substitute the values]

8.2: SIMPLE MIXTURES:

Sometimes simple mixture problems can be solved just by using common sense and knowledge of fractions, decimals, and percents.

Example #1:   A 50-ounce solution is 20 percent alcohol. If 75 ounces of water is added to it, what percent of the new solution is alcohol?

Solution:

Original Solution	⇒ Volume of Solution	⇒ 50 oz	[Given]
	⇒ Alcohol Content	⇒ 20% of 50 oz	[Given]
		⇒ 0.50 × 50	[Convert the percent to decimal]
		⇒ 10 oz	[Simplify the expression]
New Solution	⇒ Volume of Solution	⇒ Original + New	[Find the amount of new solution]
		⇒ 50 oz + 75 oz	[Substitute the values]
		⇒ 125 oz	[Simplify the expression]
Percent of Alcohol in New Solution		⇒ $\dfrac{10}{125}$ × 100	[Calculate the percent]
		⇒ 8%	[Simplify the expression]

Example #2:   A 75-liter solution of alcohol and water is 8 percent alcohol. If 5.25 liters of alcohol and 9.75 liters of water are added to this solution, what percent of the solution produced is alcohol?

Solution:

Original Solution	⇒ Volume of Solution	⇒ 75 liters	[Given]
	⇒ Alcohol Content	⇒ 8% of 75	[Given]
		⇒ 0.08 × 75	[Convert the percent to decimal]
		⇒ 6 liters	[Simplify the expression]
New Solution	⇒ Volume of Solution	⇒ Original + New	[Find the amount of new solution]
		⇒ 75 + 5.25 + 9.75	[Substitute the values]
		⇒ 90 liters	[Simplify the expression]
	⇒ Alcohol Content	⇒ Original + New	[Find the alcohol of new solution]
		⇒ 6 + 5.25	[Substitute the values]
		⇒ 11.25 liters	[Simplify the expression]
Percent of Alcohol in New Solution		⇒ $\dfrac{11.25}{90}$ × 100	[Calculate the percent]
		⇒ 12.50%	[Simplify the expression]

8.3: MIXTURE OF WEAKER & STRONGER SOLUTION:

To determine how to combine substances with different characteristics to produce a desired mixture, or to determine the characteristics of the resulting mixture when substances with different characteristics are combined, following are the two different methods for solving such problems:

EZ METHOD #1:   **Use the (Weaker + Stronger = Desired) Method:**
$\Rightarrow$ (amount of first solution) × (percent of first solution) + (amount of second solution) × (percent of second solution)

=

(amount of first plus second solution) × (percent of desired solution)
$\Rightarrow$ **f(First Solution%) + s(Second Solution%) = (f + s) (Desired Solution%)**

EZ METHOD #2:   **Use the Balancing Method:**
Make the weaker and stronger (or cheaper and more expensive, etc.) substances balance by setting up the following equation:
$\Rightarrow$ (amount of weaker solution) × (percent/price difference between the weaker solution and the desired solution)

=

(amount of stronger solution) × (percent/price difference between the stronger solution and the desired solution)
$\Rightarrow$ **$w(D - W) = s(S - D)$**

Example #1:   How many liters of a solution that is 15 percent alcohol by volume must be added to 2 liters of a solution that is 50 percent alcohol by volume to create a solution that is 25 percent alcohol by volume?

Solution: **Method #1:** $\Rightarrow$ f(First Solution%) + s(Second Solution%) = (f + s) (Desired Solution%)
$\Rightarrow$ f(15%) + 2(50%) = (f + 2) (25%)   [Set up the equation]
$\Rightarrow$ f(0.15) + 2(0.50) = (f + 2) (0.25)   [Convert the percents into decimals]
$\Rightarrow$ 0.15f + 1 = 0.25f + 0.50   [Apply distributive property]
$\Rightarrow$ 0.10f + 0.50 = 1   [Subtract 0.15f from both sides]
$\Rightarrow$ 0.50 = 0.10f [Subtract 0.50 from both sides]
$\Rightarrow$ f = 5   [Divide both sides by 0.10]
Therefore, 5 liters of the 15 percent solution must be added.
Check: 5(15%) + 2(50%) = (5 + 2) (25%)
$\Rightarrow$ 0.75 + 1 = 7(25%)
$\Rightarrow$ 1.75 = 1.75 (since both sides balance, our answer is correct)
Note: The amount of alcohol in the 15% solution [0.15f] plus the amount of alcohol in the 50% solution [(2)(0.50)] must be equal to the amount of alcohol in the resulting 25% mixture [(0.25)(f + 2)].

Method #2: $\Rightarrow$ $w(D - W) = s(S - D)$
$\Rightarrow$ w(25 – 15) = 2(50 – 25)   [Set up the equation]
$\Rightarrow$ w(10) = 2(25)   [Solve within parentheses]
$\Rightarrow$ 10w = 50   [Apply distributive property]
$\Rightarrow$ w = 5   [Divide both sides by 10]
$\Rightarrow$ Therefore, 5 liters of the 15 percent solution must be added.

8.4: DILUTION/CONCENTRATION OF MIXTURE:

Some mixture problems involve dilution or concentration of a solution to a specific level by adding or subtracting another solution, usually water. Such problems can be solved easily by setting up simple equations.

Example #1: There are 10 liters of a solution that is 10 percent alcohol by volume. If we want to dilute the solution to 8 percent strength by adding water, how many liters of water must be added?

Solution: Amount of Alcohol in original solution ⇒ (10 liters) (10% alcohol)   [Given]
                                                  ⇒ (10) (0.10)   [Convert the percent to decimal]
                                                  ⇒ 1 liter   [Simplify the expression]

The amount of alcohol is fixed and will remain the same before and after additional water is added. Since the solution is made by adding water, the new 8 percent alcohol solution will contain more water than the old solution, but will still contain the same 1 liter of alcohol.

Let the No. of liters of water added   ⇒ x
Total Volume of new solution   ⇒ $(10 + x)$ liters.
EZ Problem Set-Up ⇒ In the new solution, 1 liter of alcohol will be 8 percent of the solution.

$$\Rightarrow \frac{1}{10 + x} = 0.08 \quad \text{[Set up the equation]}$$

⇒ 1 = 0.08(10 + x)   [Cross multiply]
⇒ 1 = 0.8 + 0.08x   [Apply distributive property]
⇒ 0.2 = 0.08x   [Subtract 0.8 from both sides]
⇒ x = 2.5   [Divide both sides by 0.08]

Therefore, 2.5 liters of water must be added to dilute the solution to 4 percent strength.

Example #2: Twenty-five pounds of fruit salad contains 50 percent strawberries. How many pounds of strawberries must be added so that the final mixture has 60 percent strawberries?

Solution: Original ⇒ Amount of Total Mixture   ⇒ 25 pounds
        ⇒ Percent of Strawberries   ⇒ 50%
        ⇒ Amount of Strawberries   ⇒ 50% of 25 pounds
                                    ⇒ 12.5 pounds
Let the amount of Strawberries Added ⇒ x pounds
New   ⇒ Amount of Total Mixture   ⇒ $(25 + x)$ pounds
      ⇒ Percent of Strawberries   ⇒ 60%
      ⇒ Amount of Strawberries   ⇒ $(12.5 + x)$ pounds OR 60% of $(25 + x)$ pounds
EZ Problem set-Up ⇒ 60% of the Total Mixture = $(12.5 + x)$ pounds of Strawberries
                  ⇒ 60% of $(25 + x)$ = 12.5 + x   [Set up the equation]
                  ⇒ 0.60(25 + x) = 12.5 + x   [Write the percent as a decimal]
                  ⇒ 15 + 0.60x = 12.5 + x   [Apply distributive property]
                  ⇒ 15 = 12.5 + 0.40x   [Subtract 0.60x from both sides]
                  ⇒ 0.40x = 2.5   [Subtract 12.5 from both sides]
                  ⇒ x = 6.25   [Divide both sides by 0.40]

PRACTICE EXERCISE – QUESTIONS AND ANSWERS WITH EXPLANATIONS: MIXTURE PROBLEMS:

Question #1: If 8 pounds of almonds that cost $1.50 per pound are mixed with 2 pounds of pecans that cost $2.50 per pound, what is the cost per pound of the resulting mixture?

Solution:

Total cost of the mixture	$\Rightarrow 8(\$1.50) + 2(\$2.50)$	[Express the total cost of mixture]
	$\Rightarrow \$12 + \$5$	[Apply distributive property]
	$\Rightarrow \$17$	[Simplify the expression]
Total weight of the mixture	$\Rightarrow 2 + 8$	[Express the total weight of mixture]
	$\Rightarrow 10$ pounds	[Simplify the expression]
Cost per pound of the mixture	$\Rightarrow \dfrac{Total\ Cost\ of\ Mixture}{Total\ Weight\ of\ Mixture}$	[Write the appropriate formula]
	$\Rightarrow \dfrac{17}{10}$	[Substitute the values]
	$\Rightarrow \$1.70$	[Simplify the expression]

Question #2: If x pounds of hazelnuts that cost $6 per pound are mixed with y pounds of walnuts that cost $8 per pound, what is the cost per pound of the resulting mixture?

Solution:

Total cost of the mixture	$\Rightarrow \$6(x) + \$8(y)$	[Express the total cost of mixture]
	$\Rightarrow \$6x + \$8y$	[Apply distributive property]
Total weight of the mixture	$\Rightarrow x + y$ pounds	[Express the total weight of mixture]
Cost per pound of the mixture	$\Rightarrow \dfrac{Total\ Cost\ Of\ Mixture}{Total\ Weight\ Of\ Mixture}$	[Write the appropriate formula]
	$\Rightarrow \dfrac{6x + 8y}{x + y}$	[Substitute the values]

Example #3: A 25-ounce solution is 20 percent alcohol. If 50 ounces of water is added to it, what percent of the new solution is alcohol?

Solution:

Original Solution	$\Rightarrow$ Volume of Solution	$\Rightarrow 25$ oz	[Given]
	$\Rightarrow$ Alcohol Content	$\Rightarrow 20\%$ of 25 oz	[Given]
		$\Rightarrow 0.20 \times 25$	[Convert the percent to decimal]
		$\Rightarrow 5$ oz	[Simplify the expression]
New Solution	$\Rightarrow$ Volume of Solution	$\Rightarrow$ Original + New	[Find the amount of new solution]
		$\Rightarrow 25$ oz + 50 oz	[Substitute the values]
		$\Rightarrow 75$ oz	[Simplify the expression]
Percent New Alcohol Content		$\Rightarrow \dfrac{5}{75} \times 100$	[Calculate the percent]
		$\Rightarrow 6.66\%$	[Simplify the expression]

Question #4: A 80-liter solution of alcohol and water is 7.5 percent alcohol. If 5.75 liters of alcohol and 8.25 liters of water are added to this solution, what percent of the solution produced is alcohol?

Solution:

Original Solution:	$\Rightarrow$ Volume of Solution	$\Rightarrow 80$ liters	[Given]
	$\Rightarrow$ Alcohol Content	$\Rightarrow 7.5\%$ of 80	[Given]
		$\Rightarrow 0.075 \times 80$	[Convert the percent to decimal]
		$\Rightarrow 6$ liters	[Simplify the expression]
New Solution:	$\Rightarrow$ Volume of Solution	$\Rightarrow$ Original + New	[Find the amount of new solution]
		$\Rightarrow 80 + 5.75 + 8.25$	[Substitute the values]
		$\Rightarrow 94$ liters	[Simplify the expression]
	$\Rightarrow$ Alcohol Content	$\Rightarrow$ Original + New	[Find the alcohol of new solution]
		$\Rightarrow 6 + 5.75$	[Substitute the values]
		$\Rightarrow 11.75$ liters	[Substitute the values]

Percent of Alcohol in New Solution: $\Rightarrow \dfrac{11.75}{94} \times 100$ [Calculate the percent]

$\Rightarrow 12.50\%$ [Simplify the expression]

Question #5: How many liters of a solution that is 15 percent alcohol by volume must be added to 2 liters of a solution that is 75 percent alcohol by volume to create a solution that is 25 percent alcohol by volume?

Solution: **Method #1:** $\Rightarrow f$(First Solution%) + s(Second Solution%) = ($f + s$) (Desired Solution%)

$\Rightarrow f(15\%) + 2(75\%) = (f + 2)\ (25\%)$ [Set up the equation]
$\Rightarrow f(0.15) + 2(0.75) = (f + 2)\ (0.25)$ [Convert the percents into decimals]
$\Rightarrow 0.15f + 1.50 = 0.25f + 0.50$ [Apply distributive property]
$\Rightarrow 0.10f + 0.50 = 1.50$ [Subtract 0.15f from both sides]
$\Rightarrow 0.10f = 1$ [Subtract 0.50 from both sides]
$\Rightarrow f = 10$ [Divide both sides by 0.10]
$\Rightarrow$ Therefore, 10 liters of the 15 percent solution must be added.

Method #2: $\Rightarrow w(D - W) = s(S - D)$
$\Rightarrow w(25 - 15) = 2(75 - 25)$ [Set up the equation]
$\Rightarrow w\ (10) = 2(50)$ [Solve within parentheses]
$\Rightarrow 10w = 100$ [Apply distributive property]
$\Rightarrow w = 10$ [Divide both sides by 10]

Question #6: How many liters of a solution that is 20 percent alcohol by volume must be added to 2 liters of a solution that is 75 percent alcohol by volume to create a solution that is 25 percent alcohol by volume?

Solution: **Method #1:** $\Rightarrow f$(First Solution%) + s(Second Solution%) = ($f + s$) (Desired Solution%)

$\Rightarrow f(20\%) + 2(75\%) = (f + 2)\ (25\%)$ [Set up the equation]
$\Rightarrow f(0.20) + 2(0.75) = (f + 2)\ (0.25)$ [Convert the percents into decimals]
$\Rightarrow 0.20f + 1.50 = 0.25f + 0.50$ [Apply distributive property]
$\Rightarrow 0.05f + 0.50 = 1.50$ [Subtract 0.20f from both sides]
$\Rightarrow 0.05f = 1$ [Subtract 0.50 from both sides]
$\Rightarrow f = 20$ [Divide both sides by 0.05]
$\Rightarrow$ Therefore, 20 liters of the 20 percent solution must be added.

Method #2: $\Rightarrow w(D - W) = s(S - D)$
$\Rightarrow w(25 - 20) = 2(75 - 25)$ [Set up the equation]
$\Rightarrow w\ (5) = 2(50)$ [Solve within parentheses]
$\Rightarrow 5w = 100$ [Apply distributive property]
$\Rightarrow w = 20$ [Divide both sides by 5]

Question #7: How many liters of a solution that is 10 percent alcohol by volume must be added to 2 liters of a solution that is 50 percent alcohol by volume to create a solution that is 15 percent alcohol by volume?

Solution: **Method #1:** $\Rightarrow f$(First Solution%) + s(Second Solution%) = ($f + s$) (Desired Solution%)

$\Rightarrow f(10\%) + 2(50\%) = (f + 2)\ (15\%)$ [Set up the equation]
$\Rightarrow f(0.10) + 2(0.50) = (f + 2)\ (0.15)$ [Convert the percents into decimals]
$\Rightarrow 0.10f + 1 = 0.15f + 0.30$ [Apply distributive property]
$\Rightarrow 0.05f + 0.30 = 1$ [Subtract 0.10f from both sides]
$\Rightarrow 0.05f = 0.70$ [Subtract 0.30 from both sides]
$\Rightarrow f = 14$ [Divide both sides by 0.05]
$\Rightarrow$ Therefore, 14 liters of the 10 percent solution must be added.

Method #2: $\Rightarrow w(D - W) = s(S - D)$
$\Rightarrow w(15 - 10) = 2(50 - 15)$ [Set up the equation]
$\Rightarrow w\ (5) = 2(35)$ [Solve within parentheses]
$\Rightarrow 5w = 70$ [Apply distributive property]
$\Rightarrow w = 14$ [Divide both sides by 5]

Question #8: How many liters of a solution that is 5 percent alcohol by volume must be added to 2 liters of a solution that is 50 percent alcohol by volume to create a solution that is 10 percent alcohol by volume?

Solution: **Method #1:** $\Rightarrow f$(First Solution%) + s(Second Solution%) = ($f + s$) (Desired Solution%)

$\Rightarrow f(5\%) + 2(50\%) = (f + 2)\ (10\%)$ [Set up the equation]

$\Rightarrow f(0.05) + 2(0.50) = (f + 2)(0.10)$ [Convert the percents into decimals]

$\Rightarrow 0.05f + 1 = 0.10f + 0.20$ [Apply distributive property]

$\Rightarrow 0.05f + 0.20 = 1$ [Subtract $0.05f$ from both sides]

$\Rightarrow 0.05f = 0.80$ [Subtract 0.20 from both sides]

$\Rightarrow f = 16$ [Divide both sides by 0.05]

$\Rightarrow$ Therefore, 16 liters of the 5 percent solution must be added.

Method #2: $\Rightarrow w(D - W) = s(S - D)$

$\Rightarrow w(10 - 5) = 2(50 - 10)$ [Set up the equation]

$\Rightarrow w(5) = 2(40)$ [Solve within parentheses]

$\Rightarrow 5w = 80$ [Apply distributive property]

$\Rightarrow w = 16$ [Divide both sides by 5]

Question #9: There are 10 liters of a solution that is 10 percent alcohol by volume. If we want to dilute the solution to 2 percent strength by adding water, how many liters of water must be added?

Solution: Amount of Alcohol in original solution $\Rightarrow$ (10 liters) (10% alcohol)   [Given]

$\Rightarrow$ (10) (0.10)   [Convert the percent to decimal]

$\Rightarrow$ 1 liter   [Simplify the expression]

The amount of alcohol is fixed and will remain the same before and after additional water is added. Since the solution is made by adding water, the new 2 percent alcohol solution will contain more water than the old solution, but will still contain the same 1 liter of alcohol.

Let the No. of liters of water added $\Rightarrow x$

Total Volume of new solution $\Rightarrow (10 + x)$ liters.

EZ Problem Set-Up $\Rightarrow$ In the new solution, 1 liter of alcohol will be 2 percent of the solution.

$\Rightarrow \dfrac{1}{10 + x} = 0.02$ [Set up the equation]

$\Rightarrow 1 = 0.02(10 + x)$ [Cross multiply]

$\Rightarrow 1 = 0.2 + 0.02x$ [Apply distributive property]

$\Rightarrow 0.8 = 0.02x$ [Subtract 0.2 from both sides]

$\Rightarrow x = 0.8 \div 0.02 = 40$ [Divide both sides by 0.8]

Therefore, 40 liters of water must be added to dilute the solution to 2 percent strength.

Question #10: Ten pounds of fruit salad contains 70 percent strawberries. How many pounds of strawberries must be added so that the final mixture has 80 percent strawberries?

Solution: Original: Amount of Total Mixture $\Rightarrow$ 10 pounds

Percent of Strawberries $\Rightarrow$ 70%

Amount of Strawberries $\Rightarrow$ 70% of 10 pounds = 7 pounds

Let the amount of Strawberries Added $\Rightarrow x$ pounds

New: Amount of Total Mixture $\Rightarrow (10 + x)$ pounds

Percent of Strawberries $\Rightarrow$ 80%

Amount of Strawberries $\Rightarrow (7 + x)$ pounds OR 80% of $(10 + x)$ pounds

EZ Problem set-Up $\Rightarrow$ 80% of the Total Mixture = $(7 + x)$ pounds of Strawberries:

$\Rightarrow$ 80% of $(10 + x) = 7 + x$ [Set up the equation]

$\Rightarrow 0.80(10 + x) = 7 + x$ [Write the percent as a decimal]

$\Rightarrow 8 + 0.80x = 7 + x$ [Apply distributive property]

$\Rightarrow 8 = 7 + 0.20x$ [Subtract $0.80x$ from both sides]

$\Rightarrow 0.20x = 1$ [Subtract 7 from both sides]

$\Rightarrow x = 5$ [Divide both sides by 0.20]

PART 9.0: MEASUREMENTS:

TABLE OF CONTENTS:

PART 9.0: MEASUREMENTS:...139
    9.1: Unit of Measure:...140
        9.1.1: Basics About Unit of Measure:..140
        9.1.2: U.S. Customary System:...140
            9.1.2.1: Different Units of Measure in U.S. Customary System: 140
            9.1.2.2: Methods for Measurement Conversions: 141
            9.1.2.3: Arithmetic Operations in US Customary Unit of Measurement: 142
        9.1.3: Metric System: 144
            9.1.3.1: Method for Measurement Conversions in Metric System: 144
            9.1.3.2: Different Units of Measure in Metric System:..145
            9.1.3.3: Arithmetic Operations in Metric System of Measurement:..146
        9.1.4: Conversions between U.S. Customary System and Metric System:...147
    9.2: Time Measures: 148
    9.3: Currency Exchange:..150
    9.4: Temperature Measures:..151
    9.5: Calibrated Scales:..152
    Practice Exercise – Questions and Answers With Explanations: Measurement Conversions: 153

9.1: UNIT OF MEASURE:

9.1.1: BASICS ABOUT UNIT OF MEASURE:
Measurements are used to express an object's length, weight, area, or volume. We also use measurements to express the time and temperatures.

Attributes of Measurement: "Unit of Measure" can measure length, weight, area, volume, time, temperature, etc. To measure any type of object means to compare an attribute of that object (such as length or weight) to a standard unit of measurement (such as an inch or a gallon).

PARTS OF MEASUREMENT: The Measurement of any object is expressed in the following two parts:
(A) The first part is a numerical value (such as length or weight) and
(B) The second part is the unit of measure (such as inch or meter)
For instance: 7 feet $\Rightarrow$ where 7 is the numerical value and feet is the standard unit of measurement.

A *"denominate number"* is a number that specifies a given measurement. The unit of measure is called the *"denomination"*. For instance: 9 miles, 7 pounds, 5 grams, and 2 liters are all denominate numbers.

OPERATION AND CONVERSION: Unit of Measure is important in many types of word problems that involve measurements.
- **Operations in Measurements:** You should be able to add, subtract, multiply, divide measurement units, and even raise them to higher powers.
- **Measurement Conversions:** You must also be able to convert measurements from one unit to another, such as from feet to inches, or pounds to ounces, etc.

EZ NOTE: If your test questions already provide you with the measurement conversions, then you don't have to worry about memorizing any of the more difficult conversion factors, like feet to miles, or liters to gallons, etc. However, there are some exceptions to this. Firstly, some questions won't give you the measurement conversions. Moreover, you are expected to know the basic conversions, such as, division of time – seconds in a minute, minutes in an hour, hours in a day, days in a week, months in a year, etc. Therefore, it would be a good idea to know some of the basic measurement conversions, something that will be useful while taking your test, and will come handy even in your daily life.

TYPES OF UNITS OF MEASURE:
Unit of Measure can be in one of the following two common systems of measurement:
(A) U.S. Customary System, also known as Standard Units of Measure, or English Units
(B) Metric System, also known as Metric Units of Measure, or SI System

9.1.2: U.S. CUSTOMARY SYSTEM:
The standard units of measure used in the United States are called the U.S. Customary System, also known as Standard Units of Measure, or English Units.

9.1.2.1: DIFFERENT UNITS OF MEASURE IN U.S. CUSTOMARY SYSTEM:

U.S. CUSTOMARY UNIT OF LENGTH MEASURE CONVERSION TABLE:

Mile (mi)	$\Rightarrow$ Yard (yd)	$\Rightarrow$ Feet (ft)	$\Rightarrow$ Inches (in)
1 mi	= 1,760 yd	= 5,280 ft	= 63,360 in
	$\Rightarrow$ 1 yd	= 3 ft	= 36 in
		$\Rightarrow$ 1 ft	= 12 in
			$\Rightarrow$ 1 in

U.S. CUSTOMARY UNIT OF MASS (WEIGHT) MEASURE CONVERSION TABLE:

Ton (t)	$\Rightarrow$ Pound (lbs)	$\Rightarrow$ Ounce (oz)
1 t	= 2,000 lbs	= 32,000 oz
	$\Rightarrow$ 1 lb	= 16 z
		$\Rightarrow$ 1 oz

U.S. CUSTOMARY UNIT OF VOLUME (LIQUID CAPACITY) MEASURE CONVERSION TABLE:

Gallon (gal)	⇒ Quart (qt)	⇒ Pint (pt)	⇒ Cup (c)	⇒ Fluid Ounce z(fl oz)	⇒ Table Spoon (tbsp)
1 gal	= 4 qt	= 8 pt	= 16 c	= 128 fl oz	= 256 tbsp
	⇒ 1 qt	= 2 pt	= 4 c	= 32 fl oz	= 64 tbsp
		⇒ 1 pt	= 2 c	= 16 fl oz	= 32 tbsp
			⇒ 1 c	= 8 fl oz	= 16 tbsp
				⇒ 1 fl oz	= 2 tbsp
					⇒ 1 tbsp

U.S. CUSTOMARY UNIT OF AREA MEASURE CONVERSION TABLE:

Square Yard (sq yd)	⇒ Square Feet (sq ft)	⇒ Square Inches (sq in)
⇒ 1 sq yd	= 9 sq ft	= 1296 sq in
	⇒ 1 sq ft	= 144 sq in
		⇒ 1 sq in

9.1.2.2: METHODS FOR MEASUREMENT CONVERSIONS:

The U.S. Customary System does not use a common factor to convert from one unit to another, so it is important to know the relationships between the units of measure. To convert from one unit of measure to another unit of measure, find in the Table of Measure how many units of the smaller denomination equal one unit of the larger denomination. This number is called the conversion factor. Next, either multiply or divide by the conversion number, depending on whether you are converting from larger units to smaller units or smaller units to larger units.

MEASUREMENT CONVERSION: TO CONVERT FROM LARGER UNITS TO SMALLER UNITS:

EZ RULE: To convert from a larger unit of measure to smaller units, we need a greater number of smaller units:
⇒ hence, multiply the given number of units by conversion factor, i.e., the appropriate measurement equivalence.

Example #1: A painting is 5 feet 6 inches long, what is the length of the painting in inches?
Solution:
⇒ 5 feet = 12 × 5 = 60 in   [Convert the feet into inches by multiplying: 1 ft = 12 in]
⇒ 5 feet & 6 inches = 60 + 6 = 66 in   [Add the remaining 6 inches]

Example #2: A box weighs 5 pounds and 8 ounces, what is the weight of the box in ounces?
Solution:
⇒ 5 lb = 16 × 5 = 80 oz   [Convert the pounds into ounces by multiplying: 1 lb = 16 oz]
⇒ 5 lb & 8 oz = 80 + 8 = 88 oz   [Add the remaining 8 ounces]

Example #3: A pitcher contains 5 gallons 2 quarts of milk, how much milk does the pitcher have in quarts?
Solution:
⇒ 5 gal = 4 × 5 = 20 qt   [Convert the gallons into quarts by multiplying: 1 gal = 4 qt]
⇒ 5 gal & 2 qt = 20 + 2 = 22 qt   [Add the remaining 2 quarts]

Example #4: A playground is 8 square yards and 5 square feet in area, what is the area of the playground in square feet?
Solution:
⇒ 8 sq yd = 9 × 8 = 72 sq ft   [Convert the sq yd into sq in by multiplying: 1 sq yd = 9 sq ft]
⇒ 8 sq yd & 5 sq ft = 72 + 5 = 77 sq ft [Add the remaining 5 sq ft]

MEASUREMENT CONVERSION: FROM SMALLER UNITS TO LARGER UNITS:

EZ RULE: To convert from a smaller unit of measure to larger units, we need a smaller number of larger units:
⇒ hence, divide the given number of units by the conversion factor, i.e., the appropriate measurement equivalence.

Example #1: A painting is 66 inches long, what is the length of the painting in feet?
Solution:
⇒ 66 inches = 66 ÷ 12 = 5.5 feet   [Convert the inches into feet by dividing: 12 in = 1 ft]
⇒ 66 inches = 5 feet and 6 inches   [Quotient is in feet and the remainder in inches]

Example #2: A box weighs 88 ounces, what is the weight of the box in pounds?
Solution:
⇒ 88 oz = 88 ÷ 16 = 5.5 lb   [Convert the ounces into pounds by dividing: 16 oz = 1 lb]

$\Rightarrow$ 88 oz = 5 lb and 8 oz   [Quotient is in pounds and remainder in ounces]

Example #3: A pitcher contains 22 quarts of milk, how much milk does the pitcher have in gallons?
Solution: $\Rightarrow$ 22 qt = 22 ÷ 4 = 5.5 qt   [Convert the quarts into gallons by dividing: 4 qt = 1 gal]
$\Rightarrow$ 22 qt = 5 gal and 2 qt   [Quotient is in gallons and the remainder in quarts]

Example #4: A playground is 77 square feet in area, what is the area of the playground in square yards?
Solution: $\Rightarrow$ 77 sq ft = 77 ÷ 9 = 8 and 5/9   [Convert the sq ft into sq yd by dividing: 9 sq ft = 1 sq yd]
$\Rightarrow$ 77 sq ft = 8 sq yd and 5 sq ft   [Quotient is in sq yd and the remainder in sq ft]

ALTERNATE METHOD FOR MEASUREMENT CONVERSION:

Units Cancellation Method (UCM): The Units Cancellation Method (UCM) is a useful method of converting measurements in different units, and also for keeping track of the units. Although, you still have to know the conversion factor. When multiplying or dividing by a conversion factor, the units cancel in the same way as numbers or variables.

For instance, if you want to convert inches into feet, simply multiply the inches times the equivalence of feet and inches, which is 1 foot over 12 inches, such that, the inches cancels out, and you are left only with the number of feet. So, the inches in a numerator cancel out with inches in a denominator. If you are unsure whether to multiply or divide by a conversion factor, check to see which will leave you with only the desired units.

Example #1: Change 108 inches to feet.
Solution: We want to cancel out the inches, so we have to multiply 108 inches by a fraction that is equal to 1, with feet in the numerator and inches in the denominator: $\Rightarrow$ 108 in = $108\,inches \times \dfrac{1\,foot}{12\,inches}$ = 9 feet

Example #2: Change 120 minutes to hours.
Solution: We want to cancel out the minutes, so we have to multiply 120 minutes by a fraction (equal to 1) with hours in the numerator and minutes in the denominator: $\Rightarrow$ 120 minutes = $120\,min \times \dfrac{1\,hour}{60\,min}$ = 2 hours

Example #3: Convert 10 inches per second to feet per minute. (1 foot = 12 inches)
Solution: Use the UCM successively twice to eliminate the unwanted units.

$$\Rightarrow \frac{10\,inches}{sec} = 10\,\frac{inches}{sec} \times \frac{1\,foot}{12\,inches} \times 60\,\frac{sec}{min} \quad \Rightarrow \frac{10 \times 60}{12} \times \frac{feet}{min} \quad \Rightarrow 50 \text{ feet per minute}$$

9.1.2.3: ARITHMETIC OPERATIONS IN US CUSTOMARY UNIT OF MEASUREMENT:

In a measurement problem, you may need to add, subtract, multiply or divide measurements.

ADDITION OR SUM:

EZ STEP-BY-STEP METHOD: Apply the following step(s) to add or find a sum of two or more measurements:

STEP 1: First, arrange the measurements in a column form, aligning like units.

STEP 2: Next, add like units in each column.

STEP 3: Finally, simplify the answer, starting with the smallest unit.

EZ TIP: When finding a sum or a difference, remember that you can only add or subtract like measurement units.

For Example: A yard needs two pieces of fencing that are 7 feet 11 inches and 9 feet 10 inches, what is the total length of fencing needed?
Solution: First arrange the measurements in a column form, aligning like units, and then add:

7 ft	11 in	[First, align the values in a column]
9 ft	10 in	[Next, add both the columns]
16 ft	21 in	

Since the inches are greater than 12, change the inches into feet $\Rightarrow$ 21 in = 1 ft 9 in
Next, add it to the feet $\Rightarrow$ 16 ft + (1 ft 9 in) = 17 ft 9 in
Therefore, the yard requires 17 feet 9 inches of fencing.

SUBTRACTION OR DIFFERENCE:

EZ STEP-BY-STEP METHOD: Apply the following step(s) to subtract or find a difference of two measurements:

STEP 1: First, arrange the measurements in a column form, aligning like units.

STEP 2: Next, subtract like units in each column, starting with the smallest unit.

STEP 3: Finally, simplify the answer.

EZ NOTE: When you subtract, you may need to regroup, or borrow to increase the number of a particular unit.

EZ TIP: When finding a sum or a difference, remember that you can only add or subtract like measurement units.

For Example: A yard which is 17 feet 9 inches wide needs to be reduced to 7 feet 11 inches, what is the length of fencing that needs to be taken off?

Solution: First arrange the measurements in a column form, aligning like units, and then subtract.

$$^{16}\cancel{17}\ ft \qquad ^{21}9\ in \qquad \text{[First, align the values in a column]}$$
$$\underline{\quad 7\ ft \qquad\quad 11\ in} \qquad \text{[Next, subtract the columns]}$$
$$\quad 9\ ft \qquad\quad 10\ in$$

Since we can't subtract 11 inches from 9 inches, borrow 1 foot from the feet column, and add it to the inches column as 12 inches, which will make it 21 inches.

Therefore, the yard requires 9 feet 10 inches of fencing to be taken off.

MULTIPLICATION OR PRODUCT:

EZ STEP-BY-STEP METHOD: Apply the following step(s) to multiply a measurement by a whole number:

STEP 1: First, write the measurements in a column form.

STEP 2: Next, multiply the number of each unit of measure separately by the given number.

STEP 3: Finally, simplify the answer.

For Example: A yard needs two pieces of 7 feet 9 inches fencing, what is the total length of the fencing needed?

Solution: First, arrange the measurements in a column form, aligning like units, and then multiply.

$$7\ ft \qquad 9\ in \qquad\quad \text{[First, align the values in a column]}$$
$$\underline{\times \qquad 2} \qquad\qquad\quad \text{[Next, subtract the columns]}$$
$$14\ ft \qquad 18\ in$$

Since the inches are greater than 12, change the inches into feet $\Rightarrow$ 18 in = 1 ft 6 in

Next, add it to the feet $\Rightarrow$ 14 ft + 1 ft 6 in = 15 ft 6 in

Therefore, the yard requires 15 feet 6 inches of fencing.

DIVISION OR QUOTIENT:

EZ STEP-BY-STEP METHOD: Apply the following step(s) to divide a measurement:

STEP 1: First, write the measurements in a column form.

STEP 2: Next, divide the units of measure separately by the given number in the following way:
  - $\Rightarrow$ Divide the number of the largest unit by the given number.
  - $\Rightarrow$ Convert any remainder to the next largest unit.
  - $\Rightarrow$ Divide the total number of that unit by the given number.
  - $\Rightarrow$ Again, convert any remainder to the next unit and divide.
  - $\Rightarrow$ Repeat this process until no units remain.

STEP 3: Finally, simplify the answer.

EZ ALTERNATE METHOD: It is often easier and faster to apply the following alternate method:

STEP 1: First, convert and rewrite all the measurements in terms of the smallest unit of measure.

STEP 2: Next, divide as usual.

STEP 3: Finally, simplify the answer.

For Example: A 15 feet 6 inches of yard fencing needs to be divided into two equal pieces, what is the length of each piece?

Solution: 15 feet = 180 inches   [Convert the feet into inches]
15 feet 6 inches = 180 + 6 = 186 inches   [Add it to the remaining inches]

186 ÷ 2 = 93 inches   [Divide by 2]
93 inches = 7 ft 9 in   [Convert the inches into feet and inches]
Therefore, the length of each piece is 7 feet 9 inches.

MULTIPLE OPERATIONS:

For Example: Starting at noon on a certain day, snow began to fall at a rate of 1¼ inches every two hours until 10 P.M. If there were already 2 ¼ inches of snow on the ground at noon, how many inches of snow were on the ground at 10 P.M. that day?

Solution: Snow already on the ground at noon   ⇒ 2¼ inches
Fresh snowfall started at noon until 10 P.M.   ⇒ 1¼ inches every 2 hours for 8 hrs
Total snowfall during those 5 two-hour periods ⇒ 1¼ × 5 = 6¼
Total snow on the ground at 10 P.M.   ⇒ 2¼ inches + 6¼ inches = 8½ inches

ALTERNATE METHOD TO ADD, SUBTRACT, MULTIPLY, DIVIDE MEASUREMENTS:

Alternately, Before adding, subtracting, multiplying, or dividing measurements, you can always convert all the measurements into one common unit of measure and then simply apply the operation.

EZ STEP-BY-STEP METHOD: Apply the following step(s) to add, subtract, multiply, or divide measurements:

STEP 1: First, convert all the measurements in terms of one common (smallest) unit of measure.

STEP 2: Next, perform the required mathematical operation, i.e. add, subtract, multiply or divide.

STEP 3: Finally, convert your answer in the unit of measure asked in the question.

9.1.3: METRIC SYSTEM:

The standard unit of measure or measurement system used outside of United States in most countries, or for all scientific measurements, is called the Metric System, also known as Metric Units of Measure, or SI System. These days, many measurements, even in the U.S., are given in the metric system, and it is important that you should know the basic units, together with common measures that are derived from the basic units. In all scientific measurement, all units of measure are related to each other by power (denomination) of 10. This makes it fairly easy to convert between different units of measure.

COMMON PREFIXES IN THE METRIC SYSTEM:

The units of measurement in the metric system are named by using some common prefixes to the basic units. The prefixes have the following specific meanings:

- milli-   ⇒ means one-thousandths, or 0.001
- centi-   ⇒ means one-hundredths, or 0.01
- deci-   ⇒ means one-tenths, or 0.1
- Basic Standard Unit   ⇒ means ones, or 1
- deka- or deca-   ⇒ means tens, or 10
- hecto-   ⇒ means hundreds, 100
- kilo-   ⇒ means one thousands, or 1,000

HOW METRIC SYSTEM WORKS:

Metric measurement works on the same principles as the decimal place-value system; both are written in the same way, just like in the decimal place-value system:
⇒ Each column in the chart below is ten times the column to its right and
⇒ Each column in the chart below is one-tenth the column to its left.

kilo- (km)	hecto- (hm)	deka- (dam)	**meter (m)**	deci- (dm)	centi- (cm)	milli- (mm)
1,000	100	10	**1**	0.1	0.01	0.001

Note: Although the table above uses meter as the basic unit, the table can also be used with liters and grams.

9.1.3.1: METHOD FOR MEASUREMENT CONVERSIONS IN METRIC SYSTEM:

STEP 1: First, count the number of times (column) that you must move to the right or left from the unit you are converting from to the unit you are converting to.

STEP 2: Next, move the decimal point that many number of place values in the same direction.

Example #1:   5 meters is equal to how many millimeters?
Solution: 5 meter = 5,000 millimeter $\Rightarrow$ since we have to move 3 columns to the right, move the decimal point 3 places to the right by adding zeros.
                  Alternately: 1 meter = 1000 millimeter $\Rightarrow$ 5 meter = 5 × 1,000 = 5,000 millimeter
Example #2:   5,000 millimeters is equal to how many meters?
Solution: 5,000 millimeter = 5 meter $\Rightarrow$ since we have to move 3 columns to the left, move the decimal point 3 places to the left.
                  Alternately: 1,000 mm = 1 meter $\Rightarrow$ 5,000 mm = 5,000 ÷ 1,000 = 5 meter

9.1.3.2: DIFFERENT UNITS OF MEASURE IN METRIC SYSTEM:

METRIC UNITS OF LENGTH MEASURE CONVERSION TABLE:

Kilometer	$\Rightarrow$ Hectometer	$\Rightarrow$ Decameter	$\Rightarrow$ Meter	$\Rightarrow$ Decimeter	$\Rightarrow$ Centimeter	$\Rightarrow$ Millimeter
1 km	= 10 hm	= 100 dam	= 1,000 m	= 10,000 dm	= 100,000 cm	= 1,000,000 mm
	$\Rightarrow$1 hm	= 10 dam	= 100 m	= 1,000 dm	= 10,000 cm	= 100,000 mm
		$\Rightarrow$1 dam	= 10 m	= 100 dm	= 1,000 cm	= 10,000 mm
			$\Rightarrow$1m	= 10 dm	= 100 cm	= 1,000 mm
				$\Rightarrow$1 dm	= 10 cm	= 100 mm
					$\Rightarrow$1 cm	= 10 mm
						$\Rightarrow$ 1 mm

Note: The basic standard unit of length measure in metric system is **meter (m)**.

METRIC UNITS OF MASS (WEIGHT) MEASURE CONVERSION TABLE:

Kilogram	$\Rightarrow$ Hectogram	$\Rightarrow$ Decagram	$\Rightarrow$ Gram	$\Rightarrow$ Decigram	$\Rightarrow$ Centigram	$\Rightarrow$ Milligram
1 kg	= 10 hg	= 100 dag	= 1,000 g	= 10,000 dg	= 100,000 cg	= 1,000,000 mg
	$\Rightarrow$1 hg	= 10 dag	= 100 g	= 1,000 dg	= 10,000 cg	= 100,000 mg
		$\Rightarrow$1 dag	= 10 g	= 100 dg	= 1,000 cg	= 10,000 mg
			$\Rightarrow$1g	= 10 dg	= 100 cg	= 1,000 mg
				$\Rightarrow$1 dg	= 10 cg	= 100 mg
					$\Rightarrow$1 cg	= 10 mg
						$\Rightarrow$ 1 mg

Note: The basic standard unit of mass measure in metric system is **gram (g)**.

METRIC UNITS OF AREA MEASURE CONVERSION TABLE:

Kilometer	$\Rightarrow$ Hectometer	$\Rightarrow$ Decameter	$\Rightarrow$ Meter	$\Rightarrow$ Decimeter	$\Rightarrow$ Centimeter	$\Rightarrow$ Millimeter
1 km	= 10 hm	= 100 dam	= 1,000 m	= 10,000 dm	= 100,000 cm	= 1,000,000 mm
	$\Rightarrow$1 hm	= 10 dam	= 100 m	= 1,000 dm	= 10,000 cm	= 100,000 mm
		$\Rightarrow$1 dam	= 10 m	= 100 dm	= 1,000 cm	= 10,000 mm
			$\Rightarrow$1m	= 10 dm	= 100 cm	= 1,000 mm
				$\Rightarrow$1 dm	= 10 cm	= 100 mm
					$\Rightarrow$1 cm	= 10 mm
						$\Rightarrow$ 1 mm

Note: The basic standard unit of area measure in metric system is **square meter (sq m)**.

METRIC UNITS OF VOLUME (LIQUID CAPACITY) MEASURE CONVERSION TABLE:

Kiloliter	$\Rightarrow$ Hectoliter	$\Rightarrow$ Dekaliter	$\Rightarrow$ Liter	$\Rightarrow$ Deciliter	$\Rightarrow$ Centiliter	$\Rightarrow$ Milliliter
1 kl	= 10 hl	= 100 dal	= 1,000 l	= 10,000 dl	= 100,000 cl	= 1,000,000 ml
	$\Rightarrow$1 hl	= 10 dal	= 100 l	= 1,000 dl	= 10,000 cl	= 100,000 ml
		$\Rightarrow$ 1 dal	= 10 l	= 100 dl	= 1,000 cl	= 10,000 ml
			$\Rightarrow$ 1 l	= 10 dl	= 100 cl	= 1,000 ml
				$\Rightarrow$ 1 dl	= 10 cl	= 100 ml
					$\Rightarrow$1 cl	= 10 ml
						$\Rightarrow$ 1 ml

Note: The basic standard unit of volume measure in metric system is **liter (l)**.

9.1.3.3: ARITHMETIC OPERATIONS IN METRIC SYSTEM OF MEASUREMENT:

Since metric measurements are written as decimal numbers, you can perform mathematical operations with metric system using the same rules for adding, subtracting, multiplying, and dividing decimals. First convert all units to the same unit and then perform the desired operation.

ADDITION OR SUM:

EZ RULE: First, convert all units to the same unit and then add, applying the same rules for adding decimals.

For Example: A yard needs two pieces of fencing that are 2.5 meters and 710 centimeters, what is the total length of fencing needed in meters?

Solution:
2.5	[Already in meters]
+7.1	[Convert: 710 centimeter = 7.1 meters]
9.6	[Add the columns from top to bottom]

Therefore, the total length of fencing need in meters is 9.6 meters.

SUBTRACTION OR DIFFERENCE:

EZ RULE: First, convert all units to the same unit and then subtract, applying the same rules for subtracting decimals.

For Example: A yard which is 9.6 meters wide needs to be reduced to 250 centimeters, what is the length of fencing that needs to be taken off in meters?

Solution:
9.6	[Already in meters]
−2.5	[Convert: 250 centimeter = 2.5 meters]
7.1	[Subtract the columns from top to bottom]

Therefore, the total length of fencing the needs to be taken off in meters is 7.1 meters.

MULTIPLICATION OR PRODUCT:

EZ RULE: First, convert all units to the same unit and then multiply, applying the same rules for multiplying decimals.

For Example: A yard needs nine pieces of 7.5 meters fencing, what is the total length of the fencing needed?

Solution:
7.5
× 9
67.5

DIVISION OR QUOTIENT:

EZ RULE: First, convert all units to the same unit and then divide, applying the same rules for dividing decimals.

For Example: A 67.5 meters of yard fencing needs to be divided into nine equal pieces, what is the length of each piece in meters?

Solution: $67.5 \div 9 = 7.5$ meters

MULTIPLE OPERATIONS:

For Example: Starting at noon on a certain day, snow began to fall at a rate of 1.25 centimeters every two hours until 10 P.M. If there were already 2.25 centimeters of snow on the ground at noon, how many centimeters of snow were on the ground at 10 P.M. that day?

Solution:
Snow already on the ground at noon	⇒ 2.25 cm
Fresh snowfall started at noon until 10 P.M.	⇒ 1.25 cm every 2 hours for 8 hrs
Total snowfall during those 5 two-hour periods	⇒ 1.25 × 5 = 6.25
Total snow on the ground at 10 P.M.	⇒ 2.25 cm + 6.25 cm = 8.5 cm

9.1.4: CONVERSIONS BETWEEN U.S. CUSTOMARY SYSTEM AND METRIC SYSTEM:

When changing from one system of measurement to another, that is, from U.S. Customary Units of Measure to Metric Units of Measure or vice versa, one needs to either use a conversion table or perform a mathematical operation, that is, multiplying or dividing by a constant.

BASIC CONVERSIONS TABLE BETWEEN U.S. CUSTOMARY SYSTEM AND METRIC SYSTEM:

LENGTH MEASURE:

US Units	to	Metric Units	Metric Units	to	US Units
⇒ 1 inch (in)		= 2.54 centimeters (cm)	⇒ 1 centimeter (cm)		= 0.39 inches (in)
⇒ 1 yard (yd)		= 0.9144 meters (m)	⇒ 1 meter (m)		= 1.1 yards (yd)
⇒ 1 mile (mi)		= 1.6 kilometers (km)	⇒ 1 Kilometer (km)		= 0.6 miles (mi)

MASS MEASURE:

US Units	to	Metric Units	Metric Units	to	US Units
⇒ 1 pound (lb)		= 0.4545 kilograms (kg)	⇒ 1 kilogram (kg)		= 2.2 pounds (lbs)
⇒ 1 pound (lb)		= 454 grams (gm)			
⇒ 1 ounce (oz)		= 28 grams (gm)			
⇒ 1 metric ton (MT)		= 1.1 ton (t)			

FLUID MEASURE:

US Units	to	Metric Units	Metric Units	to	US Units
⇒ 1 fluid ounce (fl oz)		= 29.574 milliliters (ml)			
⇒ 1 fluid quart (qt)		= 0.9464 liter (ltr)	⇒ 1 liter (ltr)		= 1.056 fluid quart (qt)
⇒ 1 gallon (gal)		= 3.785 liters (ltr)			

9.2: TIME MEASURES:

TIME CONVERSIONS:

Century	Decade	Years
1 Millennium/Century	= 10 Decades	= 100 Years
	⇒ 1 Decade	= 10 Years
		⇒ 1 Year

Year	⇒ Month	⇒ Week	⇒ Day	⇒ Hour	⇒ Minutes	⇒ Seconds
1 Year	= 12 Months	= 52 Weeks	= 365 Days	= 8760 Hours	= 525600 Min	= 31536000 Seconds
	⇒ 1 Month	= 4 Weeks	= 30 Days	= 720 Hours	= 43200 Min	= 2592000 Seconds
		⇒ 1 Week	= 7 Days	= 168 Hours	= 10080 Min	= 604800 Seconds
			⇒ 1 Day	= 24 Hours	= 1440Min	= 86400 Seconds
				⇒ 1 Hour	= 60 Min	= 360 Seconds
					⇒ 1 Minute	= 60 Seconds
						⇒ 1 Second

Leap Year (a year that is divisible by 4) = 366 days (once every four years)

24 HOURS IN A DAY IS DIVIDED EQUALLY INTO A.M. AND P.M.:
A.M.   Stands for the Latin phrase Ante Meridiem, which means "before noon" ⇒ the time between midnight and noon
P.M.   Stands for the Latin phrase Post Meridiem, which means "after noon" ⇒ the time between noon and midnight

TIME ZONES ⇒ Total Number of Time Zones in the World = 24 Time Zones
⇒ Total Number of Time Zones in the United States = 4 Time Zones

TIME VARIATIONS IN DIFFERENT PARTS OF THE WORLD:
As we travel east   ⇒ the sun rises earlier   ⇒ and therefore the clock is ahead.
As we travel west   ⇒ the sun rises later   ⇒ and therefore the clock is behind.

U.S. TIME ZONES:

Time Zone:	U.S. States:
Eastern Standard Time Zone (EST)	ME, NH, VT, MA, CT, RI, NY, NJ, MI, IN, OH, PA, MD, DC, VA, WV, KY, NC, SC, GA, FL
Central Standard Time Zone (CST)	WI, IL, MN, IA, ND, SD, NE, KS, MO, OK, AR, TN, MS, AL, TX, LA
Mountain Standard Time Zone (MST)	MT, ID, WY, UT, CO, AZ, NM
Pacific Standard Time Zone (PST)	WA, OR, CA, NV

TIME CONVERSIONS AMONG DIFFERENT U.S. TIME ZONES:
From East To West:

EST	CST	MST	PST
EST	⇒ 1 Hour ahead of CST	⇒ 2 Hours ahead of MST	⇒ 3 Hours ahead of PST
	⇒ CST	⇒ 1 Hour ahead of MST	⇒ 2 Hours ahead of PST
		⇒ MST	⇒ 1 Hour ahead of PST
			⇒ PST

From West To East:

PST	MST	CST	EST
PST	⇒ 1 Hour behind MST	⇒ 2 Hours behind CST	⇒ 3 Hours behind EST
	⇒ MST	⇒ 1 Hour behind CST	⇒ 2 Hours behind EST
		⇒ CST	⇒ 1 Hour behind EST
			⇒ EST

For Instance: 7 A.M. in PST = 8 A.M. in MST = 9 A.M. in CST = 10 A.M. in EST.
7 A.M. in Los Angeles, CA = 8 A.M. in Arizona = 9 A.M. in Chicago, IL = 10 A.M. in New York

Example #1:   A 10-year-old child is approximately how many minutes old?
Solution: Age in Years   ⇒ 10
Age in Days   ⇒ 10 × 365

Age in Hours   ⇒ 10 × 365 × 24
Age in Minutes ⇒ 10 × 365 × 24 × 60 = 5,256,000 minutes

Example #2: On a certain day, high tide occurred at 6:55 A.M. and again at 7.12 P.M. What was the length of time between the two high tides?

Solution: Two times within a 24-hour period in the same time zone are given, and you are asked to find the number of hours and minutes between the two times. This can be done in the following two ways:

    Method #1:   By using noon as the dividing point:
                   (Find the time elapsed on either side of noon, and add them)

From 6:55 A.M. to Noon	⇒ 05 hours and 05 minutes
From Noon to 7:12 P.M.	⇒ 07 hours and 12 minutes
From 6:55 A.M to 7:12 P.M.	⇒ 12 hours and 17 minutes

    Method #2:   By simple subtraction of two units:
                  ⇒ We can write 7:12 P.M. as 19:12 hours, and then subtract 6:55 hours from it:

Hours	Minutes
18	
~~19~~	12 + 60
−6	−55
12	17

Note: Since it is not possible to subtract 55 minutes from 12 minutes, we have to borrow 1 hour or 60 minutes from the "hours" and add it to the "minutes".

Example #3: According to a painting expert, a coat of paint is supposed to dry for 25 hours and 25 minutes. If the painter finished painting at 7:25 P.M., at what time will the paint be dry?

Solution: Current time: 7:25 P.M.
Let's break 25 hours & 25 minutes into 2 pieces: 24 hrs + 1 hrs & 25 min
Add first part: After 24 hours, time   ⇒ 7:25 P.M.
Add second part: After 1 hr & 25 min, time ⇒ 8:50 P.M.
Therefore, the paint will dry at 8:50 P.M., the next evening.

Example #4: If it is 6 A.M. in Los Angeles, CA, what time is it in New York, NY?
Solution: 6 A.M. in Los Angeles, CA (PST) = 9 A.M. in New York, NY (EST)
EST is three hours ahead of PST

Example #5: If it is 8 P.M. in Washington D.C., what time is it in Las Vegas, NV?
Solution: 8 P.M. in Washington D.C. (EST) = 5 P.M. in Las Vegas, NV (PST)
PST is three hours behind EST

Example #6: If a plane leaves from Washington State at 2:15 P.M. (local time) and reaches Maine at 11:45 P.M. (local time), what is the travel time?
Solution: 2:15 P.M. in Washington State = 5:15 P.M. in Maine
5:15 P.M. to 11:45 P.M. = 6.5 Hours

Example #7: If a plane leaves Washington D.C. at 8:15 A.M. (local time) and reaches Las Vegas, NV at 10:45 A.M. (local time), what is the travel time?
Solution: 8:15 A.M. in Washington DC = 5:15 A.M. in Las Vegas, NV
5:15 A.M. to 10:45 A.M. = 5.5 Hours.

Example #8: How many hours are there in the month of February in a leap year?
Solution: ⇒ February in a Leap Year = 29 Days × 24 Hours = 696 Hours

9.3: CURRENCY EXCHANGE:

Questions related to currency exchange will always provide you with the exchange rate and ask you the conversion from one currency into another. Simply apply the conversion rate and get the answer.

US CURRENCY EXCHANGES:

Dollar	⇒ Quarter	⇒ Dime	⇒ Nickel	⇒ Cent
1 Dollar	= 4 Quarters	= 10 Dimes	= 20 Nickels	= 100 Cents
	⇒ 1 Quarter	= 2.5 Dimes	= 5 Nickels	= 25 cents
		⇒ 1 Dime	= 2 Nickels	= 10 Cents
			⇒ 1 Nickel	= 5 Cents
				⇒ 1 Cent

Note: You must know the above US currency conversions. You are not likely to get any questions on your test that ask for the conversion from US dollars to cents, however, a question may require you to know this information. You don't have to know or memorize any foreign currency exchange rates. These will be provided in the question.

Example #1: If 1 US dollar equals 1.6 Pound Sterling, 50 US dollars equals how many pound sterling?
Solution: 1 US Dollar = 1.6 Pound Sterling
50 US Dollars = 50 × 1.6 = 80 Pound Sterling

Example #2: If 1 Pound Sterling equals 0.625 US dollars, 80 Pound Sterling equals how many US dollars?
Solution: 1 Pound Sterling = 0.625 US Dollars
80 Pound Sterling = 80 × 0.625 = 50 US Dollars

9.4: TEMPERATURE MEASURES:

Temperature is the measure of degree of warmth or cold, and thermometer is a device used to measure the degree of temperatures.

UNIT OF MEASURE OF TEMPERATURE:
Temperature can be measured in the following two different units:
- Degree Fahrenheit ($F°$) ⇒ Temperature measurement is US System
- Degree Celsius ($C°$) ⇒ Temperature measurement in Metric System

Fahrenheit = $F°$ Freezing Point = $32°F$ Boiling Point = $212°F$ Normal Body Temp = $98.6°F$
Celsius = $C°$ Freezing Point = $0°C$ Boiling Point = $100°C$ Normal Body Temp = $37°C$

TEMPERATURE CONVERSION FORMULA: To convert temperatures between Fahrenheit and Celsius.

$$\Rightarrow C = \frac{5}{9}(F - 32) \qquad \text{or} \qquad \Rightarrow F = \frac{9}{5}C + 32$$
$$\Rightarrow 9C = 5(F - 32) \qquad \text{or} \qquad \Rightarrow 5F = 9C + 32 \times 5$$
$$\Rightarrow 9C = 5F - 160 \qquad \text{or} \qquad \Rightarrow 5F = 9C + 160$$

Where, C = Celsius and F = Fahrenheit.
Note: Any one of the above formulas can be applied

Example #1:   100° Celsius is approximately how many degrees in Fahrenheit?
Solution: $\Rightarrow 9C = 5F - 160$
  $\Rightarrow 9 \times 100 = 5F - 160$
  $\Rightarrow 900 = 5F - 160$
  $\Rightarrow 1060 = 5F$
  $\Rightarrow F = 212$
  Therefore, $100°C = 212°F$ (This is also the boiling point)

Example #2:   32° Fahrenheit is approximately how many degrees in Celsius?
Solution: $\Rightarrow 9C = 5F - 160$
  $\Rightarrow 9C = 5 \times 32 - 160$
  $\Rightarrow 9C = 160 - 160$
  $\Rightarrow 9C = 0$
  $\Rightarrow C = 0$
  Therefore, $32°F = 0°C$ (This is also the freezing point)

9.5: CALIBRATED SCALES:

STANDARDIZED OR CALIBRATED SCALE & GAUGES:

Some type of questions require you to read standardized or calibrated scales and gauges, such as, a car's speedometer or odometer, thermometer, weighing scale, or any other type of scale. Such type of problems can usually be solved by careful observation and eliminating out of range answer choices.

Example #1:   On the gauge below, the arrow is pointing towards what number?

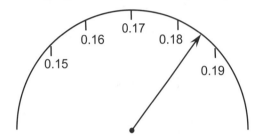

Solution: If you carefully observe the scale, you'll realize that the correct answer must be in between 0.18 & 0.19; in fact, it must right in the middle of 0.18 and 0.19. To find the midpoint of 0.18 and 0.19, find their average.
Average of 0.18 and 0.19 $\Rightarrow$ (0.18 + 0.19) ÷ 2 = 0.185.
Therefore, in the gauge above, the arrow is pointing at 0.185.

Example #2:   On the thermometer below, what is the temperature?

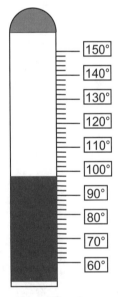

Solution: If you carefully observe the scale, you'll realize that the correct answer must be in between 90 & 100, and it has to be closer to 100 than 90.
Each of the bigger mark is at an interval of 10 units, i.e., 60, 70, 80, 100.......
Each of the smaller mark is at an interval of 2 units, i.e., 92, 94, 96, 98.......
Therefore, if we count the level of the thermometer, it is at 98°F.

PRACTICE EXERCISE – QUESTIONS AND ANSWERS WITH EXPLANATIONS: MEASUREMENT CONVERSIONS:

Question #1: A yard needs two pieces of fencing that are 6 feet 11 inches and 8 feet 10 inches, what is the total length of fencing needed?

Solution: First arrange the measurements in a column form, aligning like units, and then add:

```
6 ft      11 in          [First, align the values in a column]
8 ft      10 in          [Next, add both the columns]
14 ft     21 in
```

Since the inches are greater than 12, change the inches into feet $\Rightarrow$ 21 in = 1 ft 9 in
Next, add it to the feet $\Rightarrow$ 14ft + (1 ft 9 in) = 15 ft 9 in
Therefore, the yard requires 15 feet 9 inches of fencing.

Question #2: A yard which is 15 feet 9 inches wide needs to be reduced to 6 feet 11 inches, what is the length of fencing that needs to be taken off?

Solution: First arrange the measurements in a column form, aligning like units, and then subtract.

```
14 15 ft     21 9 in       [First, align the values in a column]
   6 ft        11 in       [Next, subtract the columns]
   8 ft        10 in
```

Since we can't subtract 11 inches from 9 inches, borrow 1 foot from the feet column, and add it to the inches column as 12 inches, which will make it 21 inches.
Therefore, the yard requires 8 feet 10 inches of fencing to be taken off.

Question #3: A yard needs nine pieces of 6 feet 2 inches fencing, what is the total length of the fencing needed?
Solution: First arrange the measurements in a column form, aligning like units, and then multiply.

```
6 ft       2 in
×          9
54 ft     18 in
```

Since the inches are greater than 12, change the inches into feet $\Rightarrow$ 18 in = 1 ft 6 in
Next, add it to the feet $\Rightarrow$ 54 ft + 1 ft 6 in = 55 ft 6 in
Therefore, the yard requires 55 feet 6 inches of fencing.

Question #4: A 55 feet 6 inches of yard fencing needs to be divided into nine equal pieces, what is the length of each piece?

Solution:
55 feet = 660 inches	[Convert the feet into inches]
55 feet 6 inches = 660 + 6 = 666 inches	[Add it to the remaining inches]
666 ÷ 9 = 74 inches	[Divide by 9]
74 inches = 6 ft 2 in	[Convert the inches into feet and inches]

Therefore, the length of each piece is 6 feet 2 inches.

Question #5: Starting at noon on a certain day, snow began to fall at a rate of 2¼ inches every two hours until 8 P.M. If there were already 1¼ inches of snow on the ground at noon, how many inches of snow were on the ground at 10 P.M. that day?

Solution:
Snow already on the ground at noon	$\Rightarrow$ 1¼ inches
Fresh snowfall started at noon until 8 P.M.	$\Rightarrow$ 2¼ inches every 2 hours for 8 hrs
Total snowfall during those 5 two-hour periods	$\Rightarrow$ 2¼ × 5 = 11¼
Total snow on the ground at 10 P.M.	$\Rightarrow$ 1¼ inches + 11¼ inches = 12½ inches

Question #6: A yard needs two pieces of fencing that are 2.6 meters and 610 centimeters, what is the total length of fencing needed in meters?

Solution: Simply add both the lengths as usual:

```
 2.6           [Already in meters]
+6.1           [Convert: 610 centiliter = 6.1 meters]
 8.7           [Add the columns from top to bottom]
```

Therefore, the total length of fencing need in meters is 8.7 meters.

Question #7:   A yard which is 8.7 meters wide needs to be reduced to 260 centimeters, what is the length of fencing that needs to be taken off in meters?

Solution: Simply subtract the lengths as usual:

    8.7   [Already in meters]
    −2.6   [Convert: 260 centimeter = 2.6 meters]
    6.1   [Subtract the columns from top to bottom]

Therefore, the total length of fencing the needs to be taken off in meters is 6.1 meters.

Question #8:   A yard needs nine pieces of 8.5 meters fencing, what is the total length of the fencing needed?

Solution: Simply multiply the lengths as usual:

    8.5
    × 9
    76.5

Question #9:   A 76.5 meters of yard fencing needs to be divided into nine equal pieces, what is the length of each piece in meters?

Solution: Simply divide the lengths as usual $\Rightarrow 76.5 \div 9 = 8.5$ meters

Question #10:   Starting at noon on a certain day, snow began to fall at a rate of 2.25 centimeters every two hours until 10 P.M. If there were already 1.25 centimeters of snow on the ground at noon, how many centimeters of snow were on the ground at 10 P.M. that day?

Solution:

Snow already on the ground at noon $\Rightarrow$ 1.25 cm
Fresh snowfall started at noon until 10 P.M. $\Rightarrow$ 2.25 cm every 2 hours for 8 hrs
Total snowfall during those 5 two-hour periods $\Rightarrow 2.25 \times 5 = 11.25$
Total snow on the ground at 10 P.M. $\Rightarrow$ 1.25 cm + 11.25 cm = 12.5 cm

Question #11:   If 1 US dollar equals 1.6 Pound Sterling, 500 US dollars equals how many pound sterling?

Solution: 1 US Dollar $\Rightarrow$ 1.6 Pound Sterling
500 US Dollars $\Rightarrow 500 \times 1.6 = 800$ Pound Sterling

Question #12:   If 1 US dollar equals 1.6 Pound Sterling, 120 US dollars equals how many pound sterling?

Solution: 1 US Dollar $\Rightarrow$ 1.6 Pound Sterling
120 US Dollars $\Rightarrow 120 \times 1.6 = 192$ Pound Sterling

Question #13:   If 1 Pound Sterling equals 0.625 US dollars, 800 Pound Sterling equals how many US dollars?

Solution: 1 Pound Sterling $\Rightarrow$ 0.625 US Dollars
800 Pound Sterling $\Rightarrow 800 \times 0.625 = 500$ US Dollars

Question #14:   If 1 Pound Sterling equals 0.625 US dollars, 192 Pound Sterling equals how many US dollars?

Solution: 1 Pound Sterling $\Rightarrow$ 0.625 US Dollars
192 Pound Sterling $\Rightarrow 192 \times 0.625 = 120$ US Dollars

Question #15:   A 20 year old person is approximately how many minutes old?

Solution: Age in Years $\Rightarrow$ 20
Age in Days $\Rightarrow 20 \times 365$
Age in Hours $\Rightarrow 20 \times 365 \times 24$
Age in Minutes $\Rightarrow 20 \times 365 \times 24 \times 60 = 10{,}512{,}000$ minutes

Question #16:   John programmed his VCR to record for exactly 125 minutes. If it began recording at 10:20 AM, at what time did it stop recording?

Solution: Recording Time $\Rightarrow$ 125 Minutes $\Rightarrow$ 120 Minutes + 5 Minute
                              $\Rightarrow$ 2 Hours + 5 Minutes

    Start Time $\Rightarrow$ 10:20 AM + 2 Hours and 5 Minutes $\Rightarrow$ End Time
                    $\Rightarrow$ 12:25 PM

Question #17:   According to a painting expert, a coat of paint is supposed to dry for 26 hours and 25 minutes. If the painter finished painting at 7:25 P.M., at what time will the paint be dry?

Solution: Starting time: 7:25 P.M.
Let's break 26 hours & 15 minutes into 2 pieces: 24 hrs + 2 hrs & 25 min
Add first part: After 24 hours, time $\Rightarrow$ 7:25 P.M. (next day)
Add second part: After 2 hrs & 25 min, time $\Rightarrow$ 9:50 P.M.
Therefore, the paint will dry at 9:50 P.M., the next evening.

Question #18: At 6:00 A.M. the temperature was 18° below zero, and by noon it had risen to 24°, What was the average hourly increase in temperature?

Solution: Time Period = 6:00 A.M. to Noon $\Rightarrow$ 6 hours
Temperature Increase $\Rightarrow$ 24 – (–18) = 42°
Average Hourly Increase $\Rightarrow$ 42° ÷ 6 = 7°

Question #19: Nine temperature readings are taken, one reading every two hours, with the first reading taken at 7:00 P.M. What will be the time at which the final reading is taken?

Solution: The easiest way to solve this problem is to count in increments of two hours until the ninth reading:
1st Reading: 7:00 P.M.
2nd Reading: 9:00 P.M.
3rd Reading: 11:00 P.M.
4th Reading: 1:00 A.M.
5th Reading: 3:00 A.M.
6th Reading: 5:00 A.M.
7th Reading: 7:00 A.M.
8th Reading: 9:00 A.M.
9th Reading: 11:00 A.M.
Alternately: We can also start with the first reading taken at 7:00 P.M., after which 8 more readings are taken at an interval of every 2 hours, that means 8 × 2 = 16 must have elapsed after all 9 readings are taken $\Rightarrow$ 7:00 P.M. + 16 hours = 11:00 AM.

Question #20: On a certain day, high tide occurred at 5:59 A.M. and again at 6.08 P.M. What was the length of time between the two high tides?

Solution: Two times within a 24-hour period in the same time zone are given, and you are asked to find the number of hours and minutes between the two times. This can be done in the following two ways:

Method #1: By using noon as the dividing point:
(Find the time elapsed on either side of noon, and add them)
From 5:59 A.M. to Noon $\Rightarrow$ 06 hours and 01 minutes
From Noon to 6:08 P.M. $\Rightarrow$ 06 hours and 08 minutes
From 6:55 A.M. to 7:12 P.M. $\Rightarrow$ 12 hours and 09 minutes

Method #2: By simple subtraction of two units:
$\Rightarrow$ We can write 6:08 P.M. as 18:08, and then subtract 5:59 from it:

Hours	**Minutes**
17	
~~18~~	08 + 60
–5	–59
12	09

Note: Since it is not possible to subtract 59 minutes from 08 minutes, we have to borrow 1 hour or 60 minutes from the "hours" and add it to the "minutes"

Question #21: If it is 6 A.M. in Los Angeles, CA, what time is it in New York, NY?
Solution: $\Rightarrow$ 6 A.M. in Los Angeles, CA (PST) = 9 A.M. in New York, NY (EST)
EST is three hours ahead of PST.

Question #22: If it is 8 P.M. in Washington D.C., what time is it in Las Vegas, NV?
Solution: $\Rightarrow$ 8 P.M. in Washington D.C. (EST) = 5 P.M. in Las Vegas, NV (PST)
PST is three hours behind EST.

Question #23: If a plane leaves from Washington State at 2:15 P.M. (local time) and reaches Maine at 11:45 P.M. (local time), what is the travel time?
Solution: $\Rightarrow$ 2:15 P.M. in Washington State = 5:15 P.M. in Maine

         5:15 P.M. to 11:45 P.M. = 6.5 Hours

Question #24: If a plane leaves Washington D.C. at 8:15 A.M. (local time) and reaches Las Vegas, NV at 10:45 A.M. (local time), what is the travel time?

Solution: $\Rightarrow$ 8:15 A.M. in Washington DC = 5:15 A.M. in Las Vegas, NV
5:15 A.M. to 10:45 A.M. = 5.5 Hours.

Question #25: 50° Fahrenheit is approximately how many degrees in Celsius?

Solution: $\Rightarrow 9C = 5F - 160$
$\Rightarrow 9C = 5 \times 50 - 160$
$\Rightarrow 9C = 250 - 160$
$\Rightarrow 9C = 90$
$\Rightarrow C = 10$
Therefore, 50° Fahrenheit = 10° Celsius

Question #26: 15° Celsius is approximately how many degrees in Fahrenheit?

Solution: $\Rightarrow 9C = 5F - 160$
$\Rightarrow 9 \times 15 = 5F - 160$
$\Rightarrow 135 = 5F - 160$
$\Rightarrow 295 = 5F$
$\Rightarrow F = 59$
$\Rightarrow 15°C = 59°F$

Question #27: On the gauge below, the arrow is pointing towards what number?

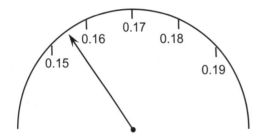

Solution: If you carefully observe the scale, you'll realize that the correct answer must be in between 0.15 & 0.16; in fact, it must right in the middle of 0.15 and 0.16. To find the midpoint of 0.15 and 0.16, find their average
Average of 0.15 and 0.16 $\Rightarrow$ (0.15 + 0.16) ÷ 2 = 0.155.
Therefore, in the gauge above, the arrow is pointing at 0.155.

Question #28: On the thermometer below, what is the temperature?

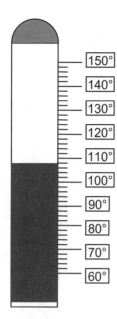

Solution: If you carefully observe the scale, you'll realize that the correct answer must be in between 100 and 110, and it has to be closer to 100 than 90.

Each of the bigger mark is at an interval of 10 units, i.e., 60, 70, 80, 100.......

Each of the smaller mark is at an interval of 2 units, i.e., 102, 104, 106, 108.......

Therefore, if we count the level of the thermometer, it is at 108°F.

THIS PAGE HAS BEEN INTENTIONALLY LEFT BLANK

EZ BOOK STORE: ORDERS & SALES:

ORDERS & SALES INFORMATION: EZ Solutions books can be ordered via one of the following methods:

🖥 ON-LINE ORDERS:

On-line Orders can be placed 24/7 via internet by going to: www.EZmethods.com

✉ E-MAIL ORDERS:

E-Mail Orders can be placed 24/7 via internet by emailing: orders@EZmethods.com

☎ PHONE ORDERS:

Phone Orders can be placed via telephone by calling: ++301.622.9597

📠 FAX ORDERS:

Fax Orders can be placed via fax by faxing: ++301.622.9597

📧 MAIL ORDERS:

Mail Orders can be placed via regular mail by mailing to the address given below:
EZ Solutions
Orders Department
P.O. Box 10755
Silver Spring, MD 20914
USA

OTHER OPTIONS: EZ Solutions books are also available at most major bookstores.

Institutional Sales: For volume/bulk sales to bookstores, libraries, schools, colleges, universities, organization, and institutions, please contact us. Quantity discount and special pricing is available.

EZ BOOK LIST:

LIST OF EZ TEST PREP SERIES OF BOOKS:

EZ Test Prep Series books are available for the following sections:
- EZ Solutions – Test Prep Series – General Test Taking Strategies
- EZ Solutions – Test Prep Series – Math Strategies
- EZ Solutions – Test Prep Series – Math Review – Arithmetic
- EZ Solutions – Test Prep Series – Math Review – Algebra
- EZ Solutions – Test Prep Series – Math Review – Applications
- EZ Solutions – Test Prep Series – Math Review – Geometry
- EZ Solutions – Test Prep Series – Math Review – Word Problems
- EZ Solutions – Test Prep Series – Math Review – Logic & Stats
- EZ Solutions – Test Prep Series – Math Practice – Basic Workbook
- EZ Solutions – Test Prep Series – Math Practice – Advanced Workbook
- EZ Solutions – Test Prep Series – Verbal Section – Reading Comprehension
- EZ Solutions – Test Prep Series – Verbal Section – Sentence Correction/Completion
- EZ Solutions – Test Prep Series – Verbal Section – Critical Reasoning
- EZ Solutions – Test Prep Series – Verbal Section – Vocabulary
- EZ Solutions – Test Prep Series – Verbal Section – Grammar
- EZ Solutions – Test Prep Series – Verbal Section – Writing Skills

Note: Some of these books have already been published and others will be released shortly.

EZ Test Prep Series books are available for the following standardized tests:
- EZ Solutions GMAT Test Prep Series of Books
- EZ Solutions GRE Test Prep Series of Books
- EZ Solutions SAT Test Prep Series of Books
- EZ Solutions ACT Test Prep Series of Books
- EZ Solutions PRAXIS Test Prep Series of Books
- EZ Solutions POWER MATH Test Prep Series of Books